The Teaching Assistant Key

The Teaching Assistant Key: Scalable Instructional Support for Student Engagement and Faculty Alignment

Dave Schippers, Sc.D.

Iron Dog LLC

Grand Rapids

Published in the United States by Iron Dog LLC

David Schippers.

the teaching assistant key: scalable instructional support for student engagement and faculty alignment

Includes bibliographical references and index.

ISBN 979-8-9922934-7-0

1. Teaching assistants in higher education, 2. Graduate teaching assistant training and development, 3. College pedagogy and andragogy, 4. Instructional support and faculty alignment, 5. Assessment, grading, and feedback practices, 6. Academic integrity and ethical conduct, 7. Teaching assistant professionalism and role clarity, 8. Inclusive and student-centered teaching, 9. Educational psychology for teaching assistants, 10. Technology and artificial intelligence in teaching and assessment, 11. Learning management systems and digital pedagogy, 12. Teaching assistant mentorship and academic guidance, 13. Academic career preparation for graduate students, 14. Teaching assistant well-being and resilience.

Table of Contents

Chapter 1: Foundations of Teaching Assistance

Figure 1.1. Teaching and Learning [113].

Teaching Assistants (TAs) are the backbone of instructional support in higher education, playing a crucial role in bridging the gap between students and faculty [1]. More than just graders or administrative aides, TAs serve as mentors, facilitators, and guides who enhance the learning experience by providing individualized support, clarifying complex concepts, and fostering academic engagement. Their contributions extend beyond the classroom, influencing student success through mentorship, structured learning environments, and the strategic use of technology to enhance accessibility [2].

This chapter lays the foundation for understanding the multifaceted role of a Teaching Assistant. It explores the expectations, responsibilities, and impact of TAs in higher education, emphasizing the significance of instructional support, grading and assessment, student mentorship, classroom management, and technological integration. Additionally, it highlights the balance between maintaining academic integrity and fostering an inclusive learning environment that meets diverse student needs.

As institutions continue to evolve with digital transformation and innovative teaching methodologies, the role of a TA has never been more dynamic. By mastering essential skills such as effective communication, critical thinking, and adaptive teaching strategies, TAs can cultivate a positive academic environment that empowers students and enhances the overall educational experience. This chapter provides the foundational knowledge and practical insights necessary for TAs to excel in their roles and contribute meaningfully to student learning and institutional success.

Understanding the Role of a Teaching Assistant (TA) in Higher Education

Teaching Assistants (TAs) serve as an essential pillar in the structure of higher education, acting as both instructional supporters and academic mentors. They provide critical assistance to faculty, ensuring that students receive the guidance, feedback, and resources necessary to excel in their coursework. The responsibilities of a TA are diverse and multifaceted, ranging from administrative support and classroom facilitation to mentorship and assessment. However, beyond these functional duties, TAs also contribute significantly to fostering an inclusive and engaging learning environment, helping bridge the gap between students and professors.

In many institutions, the role of a TA is structured to provide graduate students—and in some cases, advanced undergraduates—with an opportunity to gain practical teaching experience while deepening their expertise in their respective disciplines [3]. This dual benefit positions TAs as both learners and educators, offering them an opportunity to refine their instructional strategies while supporting students in their academic journey.

The Multifaceted Responsibilities of a Teaching Assistant

While the specific expectations of a TA may vary based on the course, department, and institution, their responsibilities can generally be categorized into several key areas:

1. Instructional Support

TAs play a vital role in the instructional process by assisting faculty in various aspects of course delivery [4]. Their instructional responsibilities may include:

- **Leading Discussion Sections:** Many large lecture courses include smaller discussion groups, which TAs facilitate to encourage deeper engagement with the material. These sessions allow students to ask questions, explore topics in greater detail, and apply concepts in interactive settings.

- **Conducting Review Sessions:** TAs often hold additional review sessions before exams or major assessments, helping students reinforce their understanding of key concepts. These sessions may include problem-solving exercises, Q&A discussions, and guided practice.

- **Assisting with Lecture Preparation:** Some TAs work closely with professors to prepare instructional materials, such as PowerPoint presentations, case studies, problem sets, and reading guides. In some cases, TAs may even have the opportunity to deliver guest lectures.

- **Facilitating Lab Sessions:** For science, engineering, and technology courses, TAs are often responsible for supervising laboratory activities, ensuring that students properly conduct experiments, adhere to safety protocols, and accurately analyze results.

- **Supporting Active Learning Strategies:** TAs may help implement pedagogical strategies such as flipped classrooms, collaborative learning activities, role-playing exercises, and case studies to foster student engagement and critical thinking.

2. Grading and Assessment

Evaluating student work is one of the most time-consuming aspects of teaching, and TAs play a crucial role in ensuring timely and fair grading [5]. Their responsibilities in this area include:

- **Grading Assignments, Exams, and Projects:** TAs assess student work based on predetermined rubrics, ensuring consistency and fairness in evaluations.

- **Providing Constructive Feedback:** Effective feedback is essential for student growth. TAs must provide detailed, constructive, and timely feedback that helps students understand their strengths and areas for improvement.

- **Managing Grade Records:** Many TAs use Learning Management Systems (LMS) such as Canvas, Blackboard, or Moodle to record grades, track student performance, and communicate assessment results.

- **Ensuring Academic Integrity:** TAs help maintain academic standards by identifying and reporting cases of plagiarism or cheating. They may also use plagiarism detection tools such as Turnitin or Grammarly to verify the originality of student submissions.

3. Student Mentorship and Support

As individuals who are often closer in academic experience to students than faculty members, TAs play a valuable mentorship role by:

- **Providing One-on-One Assistance:** Students may feel more comfortable seeking help from a TA than from a professor, making TAs a critical support system for students struggling with coursework.

- **Offering Study Strategies and Academic Guidance:** TAs can guide students on effective study habits, time management, and exam preparation techniques.

- **Acting as a Liaison Between Faculty and Students:** Because they interact closely with students, TAs can provide faculty with insights into student challenges, misunderstandings, and common areas of confusion.

4. Classroom and Learning Environment Management

Beyond delivering content, TAs contribute to shaping the classroom atmosphere. Responsibilities in this domain include:

- **Encouraging Student Engagement:** TAs help create a welcoming and inclusive classroom culture, encouraging students to participate in discussions, group activities, and collaborative projects.

- **Handling Student Conflicts:** Whether managing group dynamics or addressing disruptive behavior, TAs must navigate conflicts professionally and ensure a respectful learning environment.

- **Assisting with Course Logistics:** TAs often help with administrative tasks such as taking attendance, organizing course materials, and coordinating communication between students and faculty [6].

5. Utilizing Technology to Enhance Learning

Modern education relies heavily on technology, and TAs play an instrumental role in its effective use by [6]:

- **Managing Online Learning Platforms:** Many TAs assist in maintaining course materials on LMS platforms, responding to student inquiries, and ensuring that online assignments and discussions run smoothly.

- **Utilizing Educational Tools:** TAs may leverage tools like Zoom for virtual office hours, Poll Everywhere for in-class engagement, or AI-driven platforms for personalized learning experiences.

- **Ensuring Digital Accessibility:** TAs help ensure that course materials are accessible to all students, including those with disabilities, by adhering to Universal Design for Learning (UDL) principles.

TAs as a Bridge Between Faculty and Students

One of the most significant contributions of a TA is their role as an intermediary between students and faculty. Professors often have limited time to address every student's concerns individually, especially in large courses. TAs help bridge this gap by:

- **Offering Personalized Academic Support:** Students may feel more comfortable seeking clarification from a TA before approaching the professor.

- **Relaying Student Concerns to Faculty:** TAs provide faculty with valuable insights regarding common student struggles, allowing instructors to adjust teaching approaches accordingly.

- **Providing Additional Learning Resources:** When students need supplementary materials, TAs can recommend textbooks, online resources, or alternative explanations to help reinforce learning.

The Teaching Assistant Experience: A Professional and Academic Growth Opportunity

Beyond supporting students and faculty, serving as a TA is an invaluable opportunity for personal and professional development. Benefits include:

1. Gaining Teaching Experience

- TAs develop essential teaching skills, such as public speaking, lesson planning, and classroom management.

- They gain first-hand experience in assessing student learning and modifying instructional strategies.

2. Enhancing Communication and Leadership Skills

- TAs refine their ability to explain complex concepts in accessible ways.

- They develop leadership skills by guiding students, facilitating discussions, and resolving conflicts.

3. Strengthening Research and Academic Skills

- Many TAs assist with research-related courses, deepening their expertise in their field.

- They develop skills in academic writing, citation practices, and scholarly communication.

4. Building a Professional Network

- Serving as a TA allows students to develop relationships with faculty, peers, and academic mentors, which can lead to research collaborations and future job opportunities [7].

Conclusion

The role of a Teaching Assistant is far more than a support position—it is an integral component of higher education that enhances the learning experience for students while providing valuable teaching and professional development opportunities for the TA. By assisting faculty, engaging with students, and fostering a positive learning environment, TAs contribute significantly to academic success and institutional excellence. Whether through direct instruction, mentorship, assessment, or the integration of technology, their influence extends well beyond the classroom, shaping the future of both students and educators.

For those pursuing careers in education, instructional design, or academic leadership, serving as a TA is a transformative experience that builds foundational skills for future success. The knowledge gained through this role not only strengthens teaching abilities but also fosters a deeper appreciation for the complexities of higher education and the vital role of educators in shaping lifelong learners.

Responsibilities and Expectations of Teaching Assistants (TAs)

Teaching Assistants (TAs) play a vital role in higher education by providing instructional, administrative, and mentoring support to faculty and students [8]. They serve as a bridge between professors and learners, facilitating course delivery, assessment, and student engagement. While TAs may not bear full responsibility for a course, their contributions significantly impact student learning outcomes and the overall efficiency of academic programs.

The role of a TA is diverse and multifaceted, requiring strong subject-matter expertise, excellent communication skills, and a commitment to supporting student success [9]. Institutions and faculty rely on TAs to uphold academic standards, model professional behavior, and enhance the learning environment. This chapter outlines the core responsibilities and expectations of TAs, providing insight into how they contribute to higher education.

Key Responsibilities of a Teaching Assistant

Although specific TA duties may vary based on the institution, department, and course structure, there are common responsibilities that most TAs are expected to fulfill. These responsibilities can be broadly categorized into instructional support, grading and assessment, student mentorship, classroom management, administrative duties, and technology integration.

1. Instructional Support

TAs assist faculty in various aspects of teaching, often serving as facilitators in smaller groups where students can engage more actively with course content [10]. Their instructional responsibilities include:

Leading Discussion Sections or Labs

- Many large lecture-based courses include smaller discussion groups or lab sessions led by TAs. These sessions allow students to delve deeper into course material, ask questions, and participate in problem-solving exercises.

- TAs facilitate structured discussions, encourage student participation, and help students apply theoretical concepts through hands-on learning.

- In lab-based courses, TAs ensure students follow proper protocols, use equipment safely, and analyze data correctly.

Conducting Review Sessions

- TAs often organize and lead review sessions before exams, quizzes, or major assignments.

- They help students clarify difficult concepts, review key topics, and practice applying knowledge through problem-solving exercises.

- Review sessions provide an opportunity for students to ask questions in a less formal setting, reinforcing learning outside of lecture hours.

Delivering Guest Lectures or Presentations

- Some TAs may be assigned short lectures or presentations by faculty as a means of developing their teaching skills.

- Guest lectures allow TAs to practice explaining complex topics, develop their own instructional style, and receive feedback from both students and faculty.

Providing Supplemental Instruction

- TAs often provide additional explanations and examples that reinforce faculty lectures.

- They help students connect theoretical concepts with real-world applications, making learning more meaningful and relevant.

2. Grading and Assessment

One of the most time-intensive duties of a TA is evaluating student work. TAs are responsible for ensuring fair, transparent, and consistent grading across assignments, quizzes, exams, and projects [11]. Their grading responsibilities include:

Assessing Student Work

- TAs grade assignments, exams, and lab reports according to rubrics provided by faculty.
- They must ensure consistency and fairness when evaluating student work, applying the same criteria to all submissions.

Providing Constructive Feedback

- Effective feedback is more than just assigning a grade—it should help students understand their mistakes, recognize strengths, and improve their performance.
- TAs must develop feedback strategies that are clear, constructive, and encouraging, helping students learn from their work.

Maintaining Academic Integrity

- TAs are responsible for identifying and preventing academic misconduct, including plagiarism and cheating.
- They may use plagiarism detection tools like Turnitin or Grammarly to check for copied content.
- If they suspect academic dishonesty, TAs must follow institutional policies for reporting and handling such cases.

Managing Grade Records

- Many TAs enter and track student grades using Learning Management Systems (LMS) such as Canvas, Blackboard, or Moodle.
- They must ensure grades are recorded accurately and securely, avoiding errors that could impact student performance evaluations.

3. Student Mentorship and Support

TAs often serve as mentors and academic advisors, helping students navigate the challenges of higher education [12]. Their mentorship responsibilities include:

Holding Office Hours

- TAs are expected to set aside designated hours where students can seek assistance outside of class.
- These sessions provide opportunities for personalized guidance, clarification of concepts, and exam preparation.

Encouraging Student Success Strategies

- Many students struggle with time management, effective studying, and exam preparation.

- TAs can offer guidance on active learning techniques, note-taking strategies, and test-taking approaches.

Fostering a Growth Mindset

- TAs should encourage students to view challenges as opportunities for learning rather than obstacles.

- They can help students build resilience by emphasizing effort, persistence, and critical thinking.

Acting as a Liaison Between Faculty and Students

- Students may feel more comfortable discussing concerns with a TA than with a professor.

- TAs can relay student concerns to faculty while maintaining confidentiality and professionalism.

4. Classroom and Learning Environment Management

TAs contribute significantly to maintaining an inclusive and engaging classroom atmosphere [13]. Their responsibilities in this area include:

Encouraging Participation and Engagement

- TAs should create a welcoming and interactive classroom culture, ensuring that students feel comfortable contributing to discussions.

- They can implement collaborative learning activities, such as peer discussions, debates, and group projects, to enhance engagement.

Managing Classroom Conflicts

- TAs may need to mediate disputes among students, handle disruptions, and enforce class policies.

- They should practice diplomacy and conflict resolution to maintain a respectful learning environment.

5. Administrative and Logistical Support

Beyond direct teaching responsibilities, TAs help organize course materials, track attendance, and manage communication [14]. Their administrative duties include:

Organizing Course Content

- TAs assist in preparing handouts, managing course readings, and maintaining the LMS.

- They may help faculty update syllabi, distribute assignments, and post announcements.

Tracking Student Attendance and Participation

- Some courses require attendance monitoring, and TAs often keep attendance records or track participation.

Coordinating Communication

- TAs may respond to student emails, clarify assignment instructions, and provide reminders about due dates.

Professional Expectations of Teaching Assistants

Being a TA is not just about completing tasks—it's about demonstrating professionalism, academic integrity, and commitment to student success. Institutions and faculty expect TAs to:

1. Uphold Academic and Professional Integrity

- TAs must adhere to institutional policies regarding grading, confidentiality, and academic honesty [15].
- They should model ethical behavior and fairness in all interactions with students.

2. Communicate Clearly and Professionally

- TAs must articulate ideas effectively in both written and spoken communication.
- They should maintain professionalism when addressing student concerns, conflicts, and disciplinary matters.

3. Manage Time Effectively

- Balancing coursework, research, and TA duties requires strong time management and prioritization skills.
- TAs should meet grading deadlines, arrive on time for class, and be prepared for office hours.

4. Adapt and Solve Problems Proactively

- Classroom challenges require flexibility and problem-solving abilities—TAs should remain adaptable in their teaching approach.
- Whether handling technical issues, classroom disruptions, or difficult student questions, TAs should respond with professionalism and confidence.

Conclusion

The responsibilities and expectations of TAs extend far beyond grading assignments and assisting faculty. They are educators, mentors, facilitators, and role models who contribute to the academic success of students while gaining invaluable teaching experience.

By embracing their responsibilities with professionalism, integrity, and enthusiasm, TAs not only enhance student learning but also develop essential skills that will benefit their future academic and professional careers. Whether aspiring to become full-time educators, researchers, or industry leaders, the TA experience is an invaluable stepping stone toward mastering teaching, leadership, and communication skills.

Working with Professors and Faculty

Teaching Assistants (TAs) play an essential role in higher education, acting as a bridge between students and faculty while supporting course delivery, assessment, and student engagement. A critical aspect of this role is collaborating effectively with professors and faculty members to ensure that the course runs smoothly and that students receive the best possible learning experience.

Working with faculty requires more than simply following instructions—it demands clear communication, adaptability, professionalism, and a proactive approach to both teaching and administrative tasks. TAs must understand faculty expectations, establish productive relationships with instructors, and develop strategies for effective collaboration. This section explores the various dimensions of working with faculty, from understanding the instructor's teaching philosophy to managing responsibilities and maintaining a professional rapport.

Understanding Faculty Expectations

Professors and faculty members have distinct teaching styles, assessment strategies, and classroom management approaches. Some prefer a highly collaborative relationship with their TAs, involving them in decision-making and instructional design, while others assign more structured, task-based duties with minimal autonomy.

To work effectively with faculty, TAs should take the initiative to understand:

- **The professor's teaching philosophy** – Does the professor emphasize active learning, Socratic questioning, or traditional lectures?

- **Course objectives and learning outcomes** – What are the key learning goals for students, and how can the TA support them?

- **Expectations for classroom engagement** – Will the TA lead discussions, facilitate group work, or primarily provide logistical support?

- **Grading policies and assessment methods** – What grading rubric does the professor use, and what level of discretion does the TA have in grading?

- **Communication preferences** – Does the professor prefer email updates, in-person meetings, or informal check-ins before class?

By clarifying these expectations early in the semester, TAs can align their approach with the instructor's goals, minimizing confusion and ensuring smooth collaboration.

Establishing Effective Communication

A productive working relationship with faculty is built on clear, professional, and respectful communication. TAs should establish open lines of communication early in their role, ensuring that both they and the professor are aligned on responsibilities, deadlines, and expectations.

Best Practices for Communicating with Faculty

1. **Schedule an Initial Meeting**

   o Before the semester begins, set up a meeting to discuss responsibilities, teaching expectations, grading policies, and the overall structure of the course.

   o Ask about preferred methods of communication—some faculty members prefer formal emails, while others may favor quick check-ins before or after class.

2. **Provide Regular Updates**

   o Keep the professor informed about student progress, common concerns, and any academic challenges that arise.

   o If grading is part of the TA's responsibilities, provide summaries of student performance trends and highlight areas where students may need additional support.

3. **Seek Clarification When Necessary**

   o If unsure about an assignment, grading policy, or student concern, ask questions early rather than making assumptions.

   o Professors appreciate when TAs seek guidance rather than risk miscommunicating expectations to students.

4. **Be Respectful and Professional in Emails and Meetings**

   o When sending emails, use a clear subject line, maintain a professional tone, and avoid overly casual language.

   o If meeting in person, be punctual and prepared with any necessary materials or discussion points.

5. **Balance Independence with Faculty Guidance**

   o While many professors allow TAs some level of autonomy, it's important to consult with faculty before making major decisions about course content, grading adjustments, or academic accommodations.

   o If given the freedom to lead discussions or lectures, ensure that the material aligns with the course syllabus and faculty expectations.

Effective communication fosters trust and ensures that both faculty and TAs are working toward the same educational goals.

Supporting Faculty in Course Delivery

TAs play a crucial supporting role in course instruction, assisting with tasks such as lesson preparation, classroom activities, and student interactions. The extent of TA involvement depends on the professor's preferences, the complexity of the course, and the institutional policies.

Ways TAs Support Faculty in Course Instruction

- **Preparing Course Materials**

    - TAs may help organize lecture slides, distribute handouts, upload assignments to Learning Management Systems (LMS), or create supplementary study guides.

    - For lab-based courses, TAs may set up equipment, prepare experiments, and ensure that students have the necessary materials.

- **Assisting in Lectures and Discussions**

    - Some professors expect TAs to actively participate in class discussions, answer student questions, or facilitate small-group activities.

    - In large classes, TAs may walk around during exercises, providing guidance and clarification as students work through problems.

- **Leading Review Sessions**

    - Professors may assign TAs the task of conducting review sessions before exams, reinforcing key concepts, and helping students practice problem-solving techniques.

- **Classroom Management**

    - In cases where the professor is leading a large lecture, TAs help manage student participation, enforce classroom policies, and address disruptions.

    - TAs may also assist in tracking attendance and ensuring students adhere to academic policies.

By taking an active and engaged role in supporting faculty, TAs contribute to a more organized, effective, and student-centered learning environment.

Collaborating on Assessment and Grading

One of the most significant areas of faculty-TA collaboration involves grading, feedback, and student evaluation. Faculty members rely on TAs to ensure that assessments are graded consistently and fairly.

Best Practices for Collaborating on Grading

- **Understand the Grading Rubric**

    - Meet with the professor to discuss grading criteria and ensure alignment on how different types of work should be evaluated.

- **Maintain Consistency and Fairness**

    - If multiple TAs are grading, establish grading norms to avoid inconsistencies.

- o Avoid personal biases and grade based on the rubric rather than subjective interpretation.

- **Communicate Grading Concerns**

  - o If a student submits questionable work, or if grading criteria seem unclear, consult with faculty before making judgment calls.

- **Provide Meaningful Feedback**

  - o Professors often expect TAs to give constructive feedback that helps students improve.

  - o Feedback should be specific, actionable, and aligned with the professor's teaching philosophy.

By collaborating closely on assessment and grading, TAs ensure academic integrity and contribute to a fair, transparent evaluation process.

Handling Student Issues and Faculty Expectations

TAs often act as intermediaries between students and faculty, addressing student concerns while upholding institutional policies and course requirements.

Best Practices for Handling Student Issues

- **Know When to Refer Students to Faculty**

  - o While TAs can address routine questions about coursework, issues related to grade appeals, academic misconduct, or disability accommodations should be escalated to faculty.

- **Maintain Confidentiality and Professionalism**

  - o Student performance and personal concerns should be treated with discretion— TAs must respect FERPA (Family Educational Rights and Privacy Act) regulations regarding student privacy.

- **Follow Faculty Guidelines on Extensions and Exceptions**

  - o If students request deadline extensions or policy exceptions, TAs should defer to faculty guidelines rather than making independent decisions.

By handling student concerns professionally and consulting faculty when necessary, TAs reinforce institutional standards while fostering a positive learning environment.

Conclusion

A strong and collaborative relationship between TAs and faculty is essential for a successful academic experience. Professors depend on TAs to help facilitate instruction, manage student engagement, and uphold academic standards, while TAs rely on faculty for guidance, mentorship, and professional development.

By understanding faculty expectations, communicating effectively, supporting course delivery, maintaining professionalism, and handling student concerns appropriately, TAs can establish themselves as valuable members of the academic team.

Ultimately, the TA experience serves as an opportunity not only to support student learning but also to develop essential teaching, leadership, and organizational skills that will benefit future academic and professional endeavors.

Professionalism and Ethical Considerations for Teaching Assistants

Professionalism and ethical conduct are fundamental pillars of the Teaching Assistant (TA) role. As both an extension of faculty and a point of contact for students, a TA's behavior, communication, and decision-making profoundly impact the academic environment. A TA must balance their responsibilities with integrity, demonstrating respect, fairness, and accountability in every aspect of their role.

Professionalism in academia encompasses appropriate conduct, adherence to institutional policies, respect for students and faculty, and a commitment to fostering a positive learning environment. Ethical considerations, on the other hand, involve academic integrity, student confidentiality, fairness in grading, and the responsible use of authority.

This section explores the principles of professionalism and ethical considerations that every TA must uphold to maintain credibility, build trust, and contribute to a culture of academic excellence.

Professionalism in the TA Role

Professionalism for TAs extends beyond simply following rules—it reflects a dedication to teaching, a respect for academic integrity, and an awareness of the impact of one's actions on students and faculty. It includes elements such as reliability, effective communication, appropriate behavior, and maintaining professional boundaries.

1. Reliability and Accountability

TAs serve as an integral part of the instructional team and are expected to meet their commitments with diligence and consistency. This includes:

- **Punctuality** – Arriving on time for lectures, office hours, grading deadlines, and scheduled meetings with faculty.

- **Preparedness** – Completing assigned tasks in a timely manner, whether it be grading, lesson planning, or facilitating discussions.

- **Meeting Deadlines** – Submitting grades and student feedback within the timeframe specified by the professor to ensure a smooth academic process.

- **Following Through on Commitments** – If a TA commits to holding office hours, leading a review session, or responding to student inquiries, they must follow through and communicate any changes in advance.

A TA's reliability reflects their commitment to the academic community and directly impacts the experience of students and faculty.

2. Effective and Professional Communication

TAs regularly interact with faculty, students, and other university staff, making clear and respectful communication essential. Professional communication includes:

- **Using a respectful and professional tone** in emails, meetings, and classroom interactions.
- **Listening actively and responding thoughtfully** to student questions, concerns, and feedback.
- **Clarifying expectations and policies** to prevent misunderstandings.
- **Providing constructive and diplomatic responses** when handling student grievances or conflicts.

Email and Written Communication Best Practices:

- Use a clear and descriptive subject line (e.g., "Clarification on Grading Policy for Assignment 3").
- Address faculty and students formally unless a more casual tone is established.
- Be concise and professional while maintaining a helpful and approachable tone.
- Use correct grammar, spelling, and punctuation—errors can undermine credibility.

Example of an Unprofessional vs. Professional Email:

Unprofessional:

Hey Dr. Smith,
I don't really know how to grade the latest assignments. What should I do? Let me know ASAP.
Thanks,
Alex

Professional:

Subject: Clarification on Grading Rubric for Assignment 3

Dear Dr. Smith,

I hope you're doing well. As I begin grading Assignment 3, I wanted to confirm the expectations for the application of the rubric, particularly for the critical analysis section. Would you be available to provide some guidance on how to approach borderline cases?

Thank you for your time and assistance.

Best regards,
Alex Turner

Maintaining professional communication builds credibility and fosters productive relationships with both faculty and students.

3. Professional Boundaries and Role Awareness

A TA holds a position of authority, even if they are close in age or experience to the students they support. Maintaining clear professional boundaries is crucial for ensuring fairness, impartiality, and ethical conduct.

Establishing Professional Boundaries:

- Avoid personal relationships with students. While being approachable is important, socializing too closely with students outside of class may create conflicts of interest, favoritism, or ethical dilemmas.

- Maintain objectivity in grading and interactions. Ensure that personal biases, friendships, or outside influences do not affect academic evaluations.

- Refrain from discussing personal academic struggles or frustrations. While TAs are also students, they should project confidence and reliability to maintain their role as an authority figure.

- Follow faculty guidelines on handling sensitive student concerns. If a student discloses a serious personal issue (e.g., mental health concerns, financial struggles), refer them to university support services rather than offering personal advice.

By upholding professional boundaries, TAs reinforce their credibility and maintain a respectful and ethical academic environment.

Ethical Considerations for TAs

As representatives of an academic institution, TAs must uphold ethical principles that protect student rights, ensure academic integrity, and foster a fair learning environment. Ethical considerations include confidentiality, fairness in grading, preventing academic dishonesty, and upholding institutional policies.

1. Student Confidentiality and FERPA Compliance

Under the Family Educational Rights and Privacy Act (FERPA), TAs are legally required to protect student records, grades, and personal information. This means:

- Never discussing a student's grades or academic performance with other students or unauthorized individuals.

- Keeping grading records secure—avoid leaving grade sheets in open areas or discussing student performance in public spaces.

- Using official university email accounts for student-related communication to ensure compliance with institutional privacy policies.

Failure to adhere to FERPA regulations can result in disciplinary action and legal consequences, making student confidentiality a non-negotiable ethical responsibility.

2. Fair and Impartial Grading

Grading must be unbiased, transparent, and based solely on academic performance. Ethical grading practices include:

- **Following the professor's grading rubric rigorously** to ensure consistency across student submissions.

- **Avoiding favoritism or punitive grading.** TAs should never allow personal opinions, relationships, or external factors to influence a student's grade.

- **Providing objective and constructive feedback** rather than vague or overly critical remarks.

- **Addressing grade disputes professionally** by referring to the rubric and discussing concerns calmly and logically.

Example of Ethical vs. Unethical Grading:

Unethical: Lowering a student's grade due to personal dislike or giving an unfair advantage to a friend.
Ethical: Applying consistent evaluation criteria to all students, regardless of personal feelings or relationships.

3. Preventing and Addressing Academic Dishonesty

TAs play a role in maintaining academic integrity by identifying and addressing issues of plagiarism, cheating, or unauthorized collaboration. Best practices include:

- **Recognizing common signs of plagiarism** and using detection tools (e.g., Turnitin, Grammarly) when allowed.

- **Monitoring exams and quizzes to prevent cheating.**

- **Reporting suspected cases of academic dishonesty to faculty.** It is not the TA's role to determine disciplinary action, but rather to follow institutional policies for addressing misconduct.

4. Ethical Use of Authority

- TAs must never misuse their position to gain personal benefits, influence students unfairly, or impose personal beliefs.

- They should treat all students with respect and impartiality, ensuring that their role remains focused on education and mentorship rather than control or power dynamics.

Conclusion

Professionalism and ethical considerations are at the core of a Teaching Assistant's responsibilities. TAs must act with integrity, maintain confidentiality, communicate effectively, and apply fairness in grading and student interactions [16].

By upholding these principles, TAs not only contribute to a positive learning environment but also establish themselves as credible and trustworthy educators. Professionalism in the TA role is not just about following rules—it is about embodying the values of higher education and setting a strong example for students.

Through ethical decision-making, responsible conduct, and a commitment to fairness, TAs play a vital role in upholding academic excellence and institutional integrity, preparing themselves for future leadership roles in academia and beyond.

Chapter 2: Understanding Student Learning

Teaching Assistants (TAs) play a crucial role in facilitating student learning, bridging the gap between instructors and learners by offering personalized guidance and support. However, effective instructional support requires more than just familiarity with course content—it demands an understanding of how students learn, what motivates them, and how to adapt teaching strategies to meet diverse learning needs. Chapter 2 explores the fundamental principles of student learning, delving into key learning theories, cognitive processes, motivation strategies, and methods for identifying and addressing diverse student needs.

In higher education, students come from varied academic backgrounds, cultural experiences, and personal learning preferences. Some students thrive in structured lecture settings, while others excel in interactive and discussion-based environments. Some are independent learners who require minimal guidance, while others benefit from structured mentorship and continuous feedback. Understanding these variations is essential for TAs to create inclusive and effective learning experiences that empower all students.

Figure 2.1. Teaching and Learning [113].

This chapter provides an in-depth examination of learning theories that shape instructional strategies, such as behaviorism, cognitivism, constructivism, and humanism. It also introduces the concept of andragogy—the science of teaching adults—offering insights into how college and university students engage with academic content differently from younger learners [17]. Additionally, the chapter addresses key psychological and environmental factors that impact student learning, such as motivation, cognitive load, prior knowledge, and learning styles.

Beyond theory, this chapter provides practical techniques that TAs can use to enhance student learning. From active learning techniques and metacognitive strategies to fostering a growth mindset, these methods will equip TAs with the tools needed to guide students through academic challenges effectively. Furthermore, the chapter discusses ways to recognize and accommodate diverse student needs, ensuring that all students—regardless of background, ability, or preferred learning style—receive equitable opportunities for success.

By the end of this chapter, TAs will be able to:
- Identify key learning theories and their applications in higher education.
- Understand the role of motivation and cognitive factors in student learning.
- Recognize and adapt to different learning styles and needs.
- Implement strategies to foster student engagement and critical thinking.
- Support students in developing self-regulated learning skills.

Mastering the art of understanding student learning is not just about improving classroom dynamics—it is about fostering a culture of curiosity, resilience, and academic growth. Whether leading discussions, grading assignments, or mentoring students one-on-one, a well-informed TA can make a meaningful difference in shaping students' educational journeys.

Learning Theories and Adult Learning Principles

Understanding how students learn is essential for Teaching Assistants (TAs) who support instructors in higher education. Learning is not a one-size-fits-all process, and students enter the classroom with diverse backgrounds, experiences, and ways of absorbing and processing information. Effective TAs must be familiar with key learning theories and adult learning principles to adapt their teaching strategies, foster engagement, and facilitate meaningful learning experiences.

In higher education, many students are adult learners, meaning that traditional pedagogical methods (which often focus on teacher-directed instruction) may not be sufficient. Instead, andragogical approaches (methods tailored for adult learners) become more relevant, emphasizing autonomy, practical application, and self-directed learning.

This section explores foundational learning theories that shape teaching approaches, followed by principles of adult learning that guide how educators, including TAs, can support and engage university students effectively.

Key Learning Theories

Learning theories explain how individuals acquire, process, and retain knowledge. While numerous theories exist, the most influential in higher education include behaviorism, cognitivism, constructivism, and humanism [18]. Each theory offers a unique perspective on how students learn and how instructors can optimize teaching methods.

1. Behaviorism: Learning Through Reinforcement

Key Theorists: B.F. Skinner, Ivan Pavlov, John Watson

Behaviorism suggests that learning occurs through external stimuli, reinforcement, and conditioning. In this view, students learn best when they receive clear instructions, repetition, and immediate feedback on their performance [19].

Implications for TAs:

- **Use positive reinforcement** (e.g., praise, encouraging feedback) to motivate students.

- **Provide structured practice** through exercises, quizzes, and guided problem-solving.

- **Use clear grading rubrics** to ensure students understand expectations and consequences.

Example: If a student struggles with a mathematical concept, a TA using behaviorist techniques might provide step-by-step practice problems with immediate feedback, reinforcing correct responses.

2. Cognitivism: Learning Through Mental Processes

Key Theorists: Jean Piaget, Jerome Bruner, Robert Gagné

Cognitivism focuses on how learners process, store, and retrieve information. It views the brain as an information processor, emphasizing critical thinking, problem-solving, and the organization of knowledge [20].

Implications for TAs:

- **Break down complex information** into manageable steps (scaffolding).

- **Encourage active engagement** through questioning and discussion.

- **Help students develop metacognitive skills** (e.g., reflecting on their learning strategies) [21].

Example: A TA helping students analyze historical events might use concept maps or problem-based learning to help them organize relationships between key ideas.

3. Constructivism: Learning Through Experience

Key Theorists: Lev Vygotsky, John Dewey, Jean Piaget

Constructivism posits that learning is an active, social process where students construct their own understanding based on prior knowledge and real-world experiences. This theory promotes collaborative and experiential learning [22].

Implications for TAs:

- Encourage students to explore and ask questions rather than providing direct answers.

- Facilitate group discussions, projects, and problem-solving exercises.

- Use real-world examples to help students relate concepts to practical applications.

Example: A TA in an engineering course might encourage students to design and prototype a small project instead of just studying theoretical formulas.

4. Humanism: Learning Through Personal Growth

Key Theorists: Carl Rogers, Abraham Maslow

Humanistic learning theories focus on self-actualization, intrinsic motivation, and student-centered learning. This perspective emphasizes emotional well-being, creativity, and a supportive learning environment [23].

Implications for TAs:

- Create a respectful and encouraging classroom atmosphere.

- Recognize individual student strengths and learning preferences.

- Encourage self-directed learning and personal reflection.

Example: A TA working with a struggling student might take the time to understand their challenges and help them develop a personalized study plan that aligns with their goals.

Each of these learning theories offers different strategies for how students learn, and TAs can combine elements from multiple theories to create an inclusive and effective teaching approach.

Principles of Adult Learning (Andragogy)

Unlike children, adult learners have unique needs and characteristics that require a different instructional approach [24]. Malcolm Knowles, a key figure in adult education, proposed six principles of andragogy (the art and science of teaching adults) that help explain how university students—especially non-traditional learners—engage with new knowledge [25].

1. Adult Learners Are Self-Directed

Adults prefer to take responsibility for their own learning rather than passively receiving information. They benefit from autonomy, choice, and opportunities to direct their educational experiences [26].

How TAs Can Support Self-Directed Learning:

- Provide optional learning resources for further exploration.

- Encourage students to set personal learning goals and track their progress.

- Offer flexible learning pathways (e.g., allowing students to choose essay topics or project formats).

Example: Instead of giving students a rigid reading assignment, a TA might provide a selection of relevant articles and let students choose the one most applicable to their interests.

2. Adults Bring Prior Experience

Unlike younger students, adults come with a wealth of prior knowledge, professional experience, and personal perspectives that shape how they learn [27].

How TAs Can Integrate Prior Knowledge:

- Encourage students to connect new concepts to real-life experiences.

- Use case studies and examples relevant to students' backgrounds.

- Acknowledge diverse perspectives and learning histories in classroom discussions.

Example: In a business ethics course, a TA might ask students to share workplace dilemmas they've encountered and analyze them through the lens of ethical theories.

3. Learning Must Be Relevant

Adult learners need to see how information applies to their personal, academic, or professional lives. They are less likely to engage with abstract concepts that lack practical application [28].

How TAs Can Make Learning Relevant:

- Show real-world applications of academic content.

- Frame assignments around practical problems or case studies.

- Discuss how the material connects to career paths and industry demands.

Example: In a cybersecurity class, a TA might introduce real-world hacking case studies to demonstrate security vulnerabilities rather than just explaining encryption algorithms in theory.

4. Adults Are Internally Motivated

Adult learners are often driven by personal and professional goals rather than external rewards (e.g., grades). They want to gain useful knowledge that enhances their competence.

How TAs Can Encourage Motivation:

- Highlight how course content relates to students' personal aspirations.

- Encourage students to set learning goals beyond the classroom.

- Provide positive reinforcement and constructive feedback to support long-term growth.

Example: A TA might ask students, "How do you see this skill being useful in your future career?" to reinforce its long-term relevance.

Conclusion

By understanding learning theories and adult learning principles, TAs can adapt their teaching strategies to meet the diverse needs of students in higher education.

- Behaviorism helps with structured learning and reinforcement.

- Cognitivism emphasizes mental processing and critical thinking.

- Constructivism encourages active, experience-based learning.

- Humanism focuses on student well-being and self-actualization.

Meanwhile, adult learning principles stress the importance of self-direction, prior experience, relevance, and motivation—key factors that differentiate adult learners from younger students.

A successful TA doesn't just deliver information—they facilitate deep learning by integrating these theories and principles into their teaching approach, making learning more engaging, personalized, and effective for students.

Differences Between Undergraduate and Graduate-Level Students

Understanding the differences between undergraduate and graduate students is essential for Teaching Assistants (TAs) who work across various academic levels. While both groups share fundamental learning goals, they differ significantly in motivation, academic maturity, cognitive engagement, and expectations for faculty interaction. These distinctions shape the way TAs must approach instruction, mentorship, assessment, and classroom management to best support student success at each level.

This section explores the key differences in learning styles, expectations, and engagement between undergraduate and graduate students, helping TAs adapt their instructional strategies accordingly.

1. Academic Maturity and Cognitive Development

Undergraduate Students: Learning Foundations and Guided Instruction

Undergraduate students are in the early stages of academic development, often transitioning from the structured learning environment of high school to the more independent, critical-thinking-based approach of higher education [29]. Many undergraduates:

- Require guidance in developing study habits, time management, and academic discipline.
- Often seek clear instructions and structured learning rather than self-directed exploration.
- May struggle with critical thinking and synthesizing complex information, as they are still developing these skills.
- Are accustomed to external motivation, such as grades and professor feedback, to drive their learning.

For TAs working with undergraduates, this means:

- Providing step-by-step guidance on assignments and expectations.
- Encouraging active engagement by fostering discussion and critical questioning.
- Offering extra academic support through review sessions, office hours, and study strategies.

Example: An undergraduate history student may need structured guidance on how to analyze primary sources, whereas a graduate history student is expected to interpret sources independently with minimal direction.

Graduate Students: Independent Inquiry and Critical Engagement

Graduate students, by contrast, have advanced cognitive abilities and approach learning with a higher level of academic autonomy [30]. They:

- Engage in self-directed research and inquiry, requiring minimal supervision.

- Are more likely to critique, analyze, and apply knowledge rather than memorize facts.

- Expect intellectual discussions, often challenging ideas rather than passively absorbing information.

- Are intrinsically motivated by research, professional growth, and subject mastery rather than grades alone.

For TAs, this means:

- Encouraging independent thought and peer-led discussions.

- Acting as a collaborator or facilitator rather than a direct instructor.

- Providing constructive feedback that promotes scholarly critique rather than just evaluating correctness.

Example: A graduate student in psychology conducting research on cognitive biases will need minimal guidance on theoretical frameworks but may require mentoring on refining research methodologies.

2. Expectations for Teaching and Learning Approaches

Undergraduate Students: Structure and Foundational Knowledge

Undergraduates often enter higher education with varying degrees of preparation and experience. Many:

- Prefer lectures, structured assignments, and frequent feedback to reinforce learning.

- Require clear explanations of concepts before engaging in higher-order thinking tasks.

- May hesitate to challenge or question authority, viewing professors and TAs as primary sources of knowledge.

- Benefit from learning scaffolding, where concepts are gradually built upon with support.

TA Strategies for Supporting Undergraduates:

- Use active learning techniques like group discussions, interactive exercises, and guided problem-solving.

- Provide frequent, constructive feedback to help students build confidence in their skills.

- Clearly outline learning objectives, deadlines, and expectations to reduce confusion.

Example: An undergraduate chemistry student might struggle with lab techniques and need step-by-step instructions, while a graduate student in chemistry is expected to design their own experiments and troubleshoot issues independently.

Graduate Students: Specialization and Advanced Scholarship

Graduate students are more self-sufficient and expect a higher degree of intellectual challenge [31]. They:

- Are deeply immersed in specialized fields and expect advanced discussions.

- May need less structured learning, preferring research-based or seminar-style learning.

- Expect to engage in academic debates and contribute original ideas rather than just mastering existing knowledge.

- Are more likely to seek mentorship from TAs, particularly in research and academic writing.

TA Strategies for Supporting Graduate Students:

- Encourage critical discourse and peer collaboration rather than lecturing.

- Guide students in exploring research gaps and theoretical applications.

- Provide tailored feedback that fosters deeper analytical thinking and originality.

Example: A graduate political science student writing a dissertation expects their TA to critique the originality of their arguments, whereas an undergraduate political science student might simply need help understanding key theories.

3. Motivation and Engagement Differences

Undergraduate Students: External Motivation and Career Exploration

Many undergraduates are still in the process of discovering their academic and career interests. Their motivation is often externally driven, meaning they are focused on:

- Grades, GPA, and degree completion as primary incentives.

- Career prospects and employability, sometimes choosing courses based on job market trends rather than intellectual curiosity.

- Balancing social life and academics, which can lead to disengagement or procrastination.

TA Strategies to Enhance Undergraduate Engagement:

- Relate coursework to real-world applications and career paths to make learning relevant.

- Use interactive and gamified learning to maintain interest.

- Provide extrinsic rewards, such as verbal encouragement and clear pathways to success.

Example: An undergraduate in an introductory economics class might be disengaged with abstract theories, but showing how these concepts apply to personal finance could increase interest.

Graduate Students: Intrinsic Motivation and Intellectual Passion

Graduate students tend to have a higher level of intrinsic motivation, meaning they are driven by:

- A passion for their field and intellectual curiosity.
- Professional and research aspirations, with a strong focus on academic contributions.
- A need for autonomy, preferring flexible, student-driven learning rather than passive instruction.

TA Strategies to Enhance Graduate Engagement:

- Encourage self-directed projects where students explore their own research questions.
- Facilitate seminar-style discussions that challenge existing theories and assumptions.
- Support professional development by guiding students toward academic publishing, conferences, and career networking.

Example: A graduate engineering student designing an AI model would be highly motivated to optimize algorithms for real-world applications, while an undergraduate engineering student may be focused on understanding fundamental coding principles.

4. Role of the TA in Undergraduate vs. Graduate Settings

Aspect	Undergraduate Students	Graduate Students
TA Role	Instructor, mentor, and source of guidance.	Facilitator, collaborator, and research mentor.
Teaching Style	Structured, directive, and foundational.	Discussion-based, research-driven, and analytical.
Assessment Approach	Frequent, objective-based, and structured.	Analytical, qualitative, and feedback-intensive.
Student Expectations	Clear instructions, structured support.	High intellectual engagement, scholarly depth.

Understanding these differences enables TAs to adjust their approach, communication, and instructional methods for each student group.

Conclusion

While both undergraduate and graduate students seek knowledge and academic growth, their needs, motivations, and learning styles differ significantly. Undergraduates require structured guidance, foundational knowledge, and external motivation, while graduate students thrive on intellectual independence, advanced inquiry, and research-driven engagement.

As a TA, adapting to these differences is key to facilitating meaningful learning experiences at both levels. By understanding student needs, fostering engagement, and employing tailored teaching strategies, TAs can maximize their impact in the classroom and contribute to a more effective and supportive academic environment.

Creating an Inclusive and Supportive Learning Environment

A truly effective learning environment is one where all students feel valued, respected, and empowered to participate. As a Teaching Assistant (TA), fostering inclusivity goes beyond simply acknowledging diversity—it requires intentional effort to create a classroom atmosphere where students from all backgrounds, abilities, and learning styles feel welcome, heard, and supported.

An inclusive classroom is not just about accommodating differences; it is about leveraging diversity to enhance learning. By fostering an equitable, respectful, and supportive environment, TAs can encourage higher levels of student engagement, deeper discussions, and improved academic performance.

This section explores the importance of inclusivity, strategies for fostering a supportive learning atmosphere, and techniques to ensure all students have access to educational opportunities.

1. The Importance of an Inclusive Learning Environment

In today's diverse educational landscape, students bring different perspectives, experiences, and learning needs to the classroom. These differences may stem from cultural background, race, gender identity, disability status, socioeconomic status, or prior educational experiences [32].

Why Does Inclusivity Matter?

1. Enhances Student Engagement: When students feel included, they are more likely to participate, ask questions, and contribute to discussions.

2. Supports Equity in Learning: Inclusivity ensures that all students, regardless of background, have equal access to learning opportunities.

3. Encourages Diverse Perspectives: A welcoming classroom allows for richer discussions, diverse viewpoints, and greater critical thinking.

4. Reduces Anxiety and Fear of Judgment: Students who feel safe and valued are more confident in their academic abilities.

TAs, as key figures in course facilitation, play an important role in creating this supportive environment by recognizing barriers to inclusivity and actively working to remove them.

2. Strategies for Fostering an Inclusive and Supportive Classroom

TAs can proactively design and facilitate learning experiences that accommodate diverse needs. Below are some key strategies to promote inclusivity and support for all students.

A. Setting the Tone for Respect and Open Dialogue

The classroom atmosphere is established from the very first interaction. TAs must ensure that students feel safe expressing their ideas without fear of ridicule or bias.

How to Set the Right Tone:

- **Establish Ground Rules for Respectful Discussion**
    - At the beginning of the semester, set clear expectations for classroom behavior (e.g., active listening, respecting different viewpoints, avoiding interruptions).
    - If students make inappropriate comments, intervene constructively to reinforce classroom respect.

- **Use Inclusive Language**
    - Be mindful of gender-neutral terms, avoid assumptions about backgrounds, and acknowledge the contributions of all students.
    - Example: Instead of addressing a group as "guys," use "everyone" or "class" to avoid unintentional exclusion.

- **Encourage All Voices to be Heard**
    - Some students may feel hesitant to speak up due to language barriers, shyness, or fear of being judged.
    - Implement participation structures such as small-group discussions, online forums, or anonymous question submissions to give all students a voice.

B. Recognizing and Accommodating Diverse Learning Styles

Students process and engage with information in different ways. Some may be visual learners, others auditory, and some kinesthetic (hands-on learners). Recognizing and integrating multiple learning modalities ensures that all students can thrive [33].

How to Address Different Learning Styles:

- **Incorporate Multiple Teaching Methods**
    - Visual learners benefit from slides, diagrams, and infographics.
    - Auditory learners absorb information better through discussions and verbal explanations.
    - Kinesthetic learners need hands-on activities, such as experiments or interactive exercises.

- **Use Universal Design for Learning (UDL) Principles**

    o Provide multiple ways for students to engage with content (e.g., readings, videos, and live discussions).

    o Offer alternative assessment formats, such as allowing students to choose between a written essay, presentation, or creative project.

C. Addressing Implicit Bias and Being Culturally Responsive

Implicit biases—unconscious attitudes or stereotypes—can inadvertently affect interactions with students. TAs must develop cultural awareness and sensitivity to ensure fair treatment of all students [34].

Steps to Address Bias:

- **Reflect on Personal Biases**

    o Regularly assess personal assumptions about students based on race, gender, disability, or academic performance.

    o Challenge stereotypes and strive to evaluate students on their individual merit.

- **Incorporate Diverse Perspectives in Course Content**

    o When leading discussions, highlight contributions from scholars of different backgrounds.

    o Use examples that reflect a variety of cultural, social, and global perspectives.

- **Acknowledge and Validate Student Experiences**

    o Encourage students to share their perspectives and lived experiences to enrich discussions.

    o If a student raises a concern about bias or exclusion, listen actively and take appropriate action.

D. Providing Academic and Emotional Support

Students may face personal or academic challenges that affect their performance. TAs should be aware of resources available to support students and know when to refer them for additional help.

Ways to Support Students:

- **Recognize Signs of Struggle**

    o If a student suddenly disengages, misses assignments, or expresses frustration, they may be struggling academically or personally.

    o Approach students privately to offer support and guidance.

- **Refer Students to Campus Resources**
    - o Academic tutoring centers, writing workshops, counseling services, disability support offices, and financial aid advisors are essential resources.
    - o TAs should familiarize themselves with these services and encourage students to seek help when needed.

- **Be Approachable and Accessible**
    - o Hold regular office hours and encourage students to seek assistance.
    - o Respond promptly and kindly to emails or requests for help.

Example: If a student struggling with coursework reveals they have a learning disability, the TA should recommend they visit the university's disability services office rather than trying to accommodate their needs without proper guidance.

3. Strategies for Inclusive Group Work and Participation

Classroom collaboration can be a valuable learning experience, but if not managed properly, it can also reinforce exclusionary dynamics. Some students may dominate discussions, while others may feel overlooked.

Best Practices for Inclusive Group Work:

- Assign diverse groups intentionally rather than allowing students to self-select, ensuring that different backgrounds and perspectives are represented.

- Rotate group roles so that leadership responsibilities are shared among all members.

- Encourage active listening and equal participation by setting clear expectations for contribution.

Best Practices for Inclusive Class Discussions:

- Use a variety of participation methods (verbal, written, online) to accommodate different comfort levels.

- Allow students time to think before responding—not all students process information at the same speed.

- Acknowledge all contributions with respect to reinforce that every opinion matters.

Conclusion

Creating an inclusive and supportive learning environment is a core responsibility of every Teaching Assistant. By fostering respect, recognizing diverse learning needs, addressing bias, and providing support, TAs play a critical role in ensuring equitable education for all students.

- An inclusive classroom promotes higher engagement, deeper learning, and a more positive academic experience.

- Recognizing individual learning styles, cultural diversity, and accessibility needs allows TAs to tailor their approach to meet student needs.

- A supportive TA is proactive in addressing challenges, creating an environment where every student feels welcome, valued, and capable of success.

Ultimately, an inclusive learning environment does not happen by accident—it is deliberately cultivated through intentional teaching practices, empathy, and a commitment to educational equity. By embracing these principles, TAs help shape classrooms that empower all students to thrive and reach their full potential.

Recognizing and Addressing Diverse Student Needs

In any higher education setting, students bring a rich diversity of backgrounds, experiences, abilities, and challenges that shape their learning processes. As a Teaching Assistant (TA), recognizing and addressing these diverse student needs is not just about accommodation—it is about fostering equity, engagement, and meaningful learning experiences for all students.

No two students learn the same way, and factors such as cultural background, learning disabilities, mental health, socioeconomic status, prior educational experience, and personal responsibilities influence how they engage with coursework. A TA who is attuned to these differences and actively works to provide support, flexibility, and inclusive teaching strategies plays a vital role in ensuring all students have the opportunity to succeed.

This section explores the types of diversity present in the classroom, how to identify students who may need additional support, and practical strategies for fostering an inclusive learning environment that meets the needs of all learners.

1. Understanding the Dimensions of Student Diversity

Diversity in student learning needs manifests in various ways, including cognitive, cultural, linguistic, socio-economic, and personal factors. Understanding these different dimensions helps TAs respond effectively to student challenges [35].

A. Cognitive and Learning Differences

Students have unique cognitive profiles that influence how they process, retain, and apply information. Some key differences include:

- **Learning Disabilities:** Students with conditions such as dyslexia, ADHD, or processing disorders may struggle with reading, writing, concentration, or organization.

- **Neurodivergence:** Some students may be on the autism spectrum or have executive functioning challenges that require structured support.

- **Varied Learning Preferences:** Some students are visual learners, while others benefit from auditory, kinesthetic, or experiential learning approaches.

TA Strategies for Supporting Cognitive Diversity:

- Use multi-modal instruction (visual aids, discussions, hands-on exercises).
  Allow extra processing time for students who may struggle with rapid information intake.
- Encourage alternative ways to demonstrate knowledge, such as oral responses or graphic representations.
- Work with the university's disability services office to implement appropriate accommodations.

Example: A student with ADHD might need clear and structured deadlines with reminders, while a student with dyslexia might benefit from audio-based materials rather than text-heavy content.

B. Cultural and Linguistic Diversity

Cultural background significantly influences student expectations, participation styles, and communication preferences. Many classrooms include international students, bilingual learners, and first-generation college students, each with unique challenges.

- **International Students:** May struggle with language barriers, different academic norms, and cultural adjustment.

- **English as a Second Language (ESL) Learners:** May need extra time for reading and writing assignments or benefit from clarification of idiomatic expressions used in lectures.

- **First-Generation College Students:** Often lack familiarity with academic expectations, office hours, or networking opportunities, requiring additional guidance.

TA Strategies for Supporting Cultural and Linguistic Diversity:

- Speak clearly and avoid unnecessary jargon or colloquialisms.
- Use visual aids and written reinforcement to support verbal instructions.
- Encourage peer mentoring and collaborative learning, allowing students to learn from each other.
- Be patient and rephrase concepts in multiple ways for ESL learners.
  Recognize that classroom participation styles vary by culture—not all students are comfortable with verbal debates.

Example: A TA in an economics class might notice that an international student hesitates to participate in class discussions. Instead of assuming disengagement, the TA could invite written reflections or smaller group discussions to create a more comfortable setting.

C. Socioeconomic and External Responsibilities

Not all students have the same access to financial, technological, or academic resources. Some face additional challenges such as:

- Working part-time or full-time while studying.

- Balancing childcare or family obligations.

- Limited access to textbooks, technology, or stable internet connections.

TA Strategies for Supporting Socioeconomic Diversity:

- Provide affordable or open-access resources when possible (e.g., free online readings instead of expensive textbooks).
- Be flexible with assignment deadlines for students balancing work and family commitments.
- Direct students to campus support services, such as financial aid, tutoring, or mental health counseling.
- Avoid assumptions—students struggling academically may not lack ability but may be facing external stressors.

Example: A TA might notice a student consistently missing deadlines. Instead of penalizing them outright, they could privately ask if the student needs support in managing workload and offer resources for time management.

D. Mental Health and Well-being

Mental health is a growing concern in higher education, with many students experiencing stress, anxiety, depression, or burnout. Academic pressures can exacerbate these challenges, making it harder for students to concentrate, participate, or complete assignments on time [35].

Signs a Student May Be Struggling with Mental Health:

- Sudden drop in academic performance or attendance.
- Expressions of overwhelm, hopelessness, or anxiety in class discussions or emails.
- Lack of engagement or excessive withdrawal from group work.

TA Strategies for Supporting Mental Well-being:

- Normalize mental health discussions—acknowledge stress as a common experience and encourage students to seek help.
- Be flexible and empathetic with assignment deadlines when possible.
- Know the university's counseling and mental health resources and refer students when necessary.
- Avoid playing the role of a therapist—listen with empathy, but set boundaries and refer students to professionals when needed.

Example: A TA receives an email from a student saying they "just can't handle the workload anymore." Instead of dismissing the concern, the TA could respond with support, encouragement, and a recommendation to visit campus mental health services.

2. Proactively Identifying and Addressing Student Needs

A TA doesn't need to wait for students to voice difficulties before offering support. Many students, particularly those facing stigma or uncertainty, may not self-advocate.

Proactive Strategies for Identifying Student Needs:

- **Observe classroom engagement:** Who is struggling with participation? Who seems confused but doesn't ask for help?
- **Check in with students**—especially those who show signs of academic or emotional distress.
- **Encourage office hours or email check-ins** as a safe space for students to ask questions privately.
- **Use anonymous surveys** to gather feedback on student needs and learning challenges.

Example: A TA teaching a statistics lab notices a group of students consistently lagging behind. Instead of assuming they aren't trying, the TA creates an optional review session where they can go over the material at a slower pace.

3. Cultivating a Culture of Support and Equity

Creating an inclusive classroom is not just about individual accommodations; it is about fostering a broader culture of support where all students feel respected and empowered to succeed.

Core Principles for an Inclusive TA Approach:

- Be patient and flexible—students learn at different paces.
- Be proactive in offering support, rather than waiting for students to ask.
- Foster a growth mindset, emphasizing improvement over perfection.
- Advocate for students when needed—help connect them to faculty or campus resources.
- Celebrate diversity in learning—frame student differences as strengths, not deficits.

Example: A TA in a literature class may integrate diverse authors and perspectives into class discussions, ensuring that students see their backgrounds represented in the curriculum.

Conclusion

Recognizing and addressing diverse student needs is not about lowering academic standards—it is about removing unnecessary barriers to success. By understanding the cognitive, cultural, socioeconomic, and emotional factors that shape student learning, TAs can create a classroom where all students feel valued and capable of achieving their full potential.

Through intentional teaching practices, proactive outreach, and a commitment to inclusivity, TAs become more than just instructional aides—they become advocates for student success and agents of positive change in higher education.

Chapter 3: Classroom and Lab Management

Figure 3.1. Teaching and Learning [113].

Effective classroom and lab management is essential for fostering a productive and engaging learning environment. Teaching Assistants (TAs) serve as both facilitators and enforcers of academic structure, ensuring that students remain focused, respectful, and actively involved in their coursework. Whether leading discussion sections, overseeing laboratory experiments, or assisting in large lecture-based courses, TAs must develop strategies to maintain order, encourage participation, and handle challenges that arise in both physical and virtual learning spaces.

Managing a classroom or lab setting extends beyond delivering content—it involves establishing clear expectations, structuring learning activities, promoting inclusivity, and handling disruptions with professionalism. A well-managed learning environment provides students with the structure and support they need to thrive, while also allowing for creativity, collaboration, and intellectual exploration [36]. For TAs, mastering these skills is crucial for building confidence as an educator and fostering a positive academic atmosphere.

This chapter explores key principles of classroom and lab management, equipping TAs with practical techniques to enhance student engagement and ensure smooth course facilitation. It covers essential topics such as setting expectations for behavior and participation, facilitating discussions and group work, handling student conflicts, and managing classroom disruptions. Additionally, the chapter delves into best practices for running lab sessions, ensuring safety, and guiding students through hands-on learning experiences.

Furthermore, this chapter will examine strategies for encouraging student accountability, maintaining academic integrity, and using technology to support classroom management. Whether dealing with disengaged students, addressing group dynamics, or resolving conflicts, TAs must approach each situation with professionalism, adaptability, and a student-centered mindset.

By the end of this chapter, TAs will be able to:

- Establish clear classroom and lab expectations that promote a structured learning environment.

- Implement strategies for facilitating discussions, group work, and interactive learning.

- Address student behavior challenges and classroom disruptions effectively.
- Manage lab sessions safely and efficiently, ensuring adherence to protocols.
- Use digital tools and learning management systems (LMS) to streamline classroom operations.
- Foster an inclusive and respectful classroom culture that supports student success.

An effective TA is more than just a content expert—they are a mentor, a facilitator, and a role model for students. Developing strong classroom and lab management skills allows TAs to create a supportive and structured learning environment where students feel motivated, respected, and empowered to excel.

Managing Discussion Sections and Lab Sessions Effectively

One of the most important responsibilities of a Teaching Assistant (TA) is to facilitate engaging and productive discussion sections and lab sessions. Unlike traditional lectures, where information is primarily delivered in a one-way format, discussion sections and lab sessions are interactive spaces where students can actively apply knowledge, develop critical thinking skills, and engage in collaborative learning.

Effective management of these sessions requires planning, adaptability, and strong facilitation skills to ensure that students remain engaged, understand key concepts, and participate meaningfully. Whether leading a discussion-based seminar or a hands-on laboratory session, a TA must balance structure with flexibility, authority with approachability, and collaboration with independence.

This section explores key strategies for successfully managing both discussion sections and lab sessions, addressing challenges that may arise, and fostering an environment where students thrive.

1. Structuring an Effective Discussion Section

Discussion sections provide students with the opportunity to delve deeper into course material, ask questions, and critically analyze concepts in a way that is not always possible in a lecture setting. However, without proper management, discussions can become unfocused, dominated by a few voices, or stagnant.

A. Establishing Clear Goals and Expectations

Before facilitating a discussion section, it is crucial to set clear objectives for each session and communicate expectations to students.

- **Define the Purpose of the Discussion:**
    - Are students analyzing a text, debating ethical dilemmas, solving technical problems, or reviewing key lecture concepts?

o   How should students prepare for the discussion? Should they bring questions, complete readings, or contribute written reflections?

- **Set Ground Rules for Participation:**

    o   Establish a respectful and inclusive environment where all voices are encouraged.

    o   Emphasize the importance of active listening and constructive dialogue.

    o   If necessary, set guidelines such as "No interruptions" or "Everyone should contribute at least once" to ensure balanced participation.

B. Facilitating Meaningful and Engaging Discussions

An effective discussion requires more than just asking, "Does anyone have questions?" TAs must proactively engage students and foster dynamic interactions.

Strategies for Encouraging Participation:

- **Use Open-Ended Questions:** Instead of "Did you understand the reading?", ask, "How does this theory apply to real-world examples?"
- **Encourage Student-Led Discussion:** Allow students to pose their own questions and respond to each other rather than relying solely on the TA.
- **Wait for Responses:** Give students time to think before moving on; don't rush to fill silences.
- **Call on Different Voices:** If a few students dominate, redirect the discussion to quieter students with prompts like, "I'd love to hear from someone who hasn't spoken yet."

Managing Common Discussion Challenges:

- **Silence and Lack of Participation:** Start with low-stakes warm-up questions or pair students to brainstorm before sharing with the larger group.
- **Overpowering Students Who Dominate the Discussion:** Acknowledge their contributions but redirect—"That's a great point. Let's hear what others think."
- **Disruptive or Inappropriate Comments:** Address immediately with diplomacy and firmness, emphasizing classroom respect.

C. Balancing Guidance with Student Autonomy

- Provide structure but allow room for exploration.

- Encourage peer-to-peer interaction rather than having students always direct responses toward the TA.

- Step in to clarify misunderstandings or steer discussions back on track when necessary.

Example: In a philosophy discussion on ethics, instead of summarizing arguments, a TA might ask students to debate real-world ethical dilemmas, encouraging them to apply theoretical concepts to contemporary issues.

2. Managing Lab Sessions Effectively

Lab sessions differ from discussion sections in that they are hands-on, experiment-driven environments where students actively engage with the scientific or technical aspects of a subject [37]. Managing a lab requires not just content expertise but also attention to safety, organization, and student collaboration.

A. Preparing for a Successful Lab Session

Labs require thorough preparation to ensure smooth execution. Before the session:

- **Review the Experiment or Procedure in Advance:** Ensure that all materials, equipment, and safety protocols are in place.

- **Anticipate Potential Problems:** Identify common mistakes students might make and plan solutions ahead of time.

- **Prepare a Clear Introduction:**
    - Explain the purpose of the experiment and what students should learn.
    - Outline step-by-step procedures and safety measures.
    - Clarify how students should record and analyze their data.

B. Establishing a Structured Lab Environment

Unlike discussion sections, where flexibility is key, labs require clear structure and procedural adherence.

Key Principles for Managing Lab Sessions:

- **Set Expectations from the Start:** Explain what successful lab work looks like—accuracy, collaboration, and proper data recording.
- **Prioritize Safety and Protocols:** Reinforce safety procedures and ensure students understand lab rules before beginning any experiment.
- **Encourage Active Engagement:** Don't just provide answers—ask guiding questions that prompt students to think critically about their results.
- **Monitor and Support Without Micromanaging:** Walk around the lab, check progress, and offer help without taking over students' work.

Common Challenges in Lab Management:

- **Students Rushing Through Procedures:** Emphasize the importance of accuracy over speed.
- **Groups Struggling with Equipment or Techniques:** Offer brief demonstrations before the session begins.
- **Students Making Critical Errors:** Instead of fixing mistakes for them, ask guiding questions: "What might have gone wrong in your setup?"

C. Encouraging Collaboration and Scientific Thinking

Labs are not just about following instructions—they are about developing problem-solving skills.

- Promote collaborative teamwork while ensuring that all students contribute equally.

- Challenge students to interpret their data rather than just recording it.

- Encourage them to connect lab results to theoretical concepts discussed in class.

Example: In a physics lab, instead of just verifying equations, a TA could ask, "How do these results compare to your predictions? What factors might have influenced the deviation?"

3. Effective Time Management in Discussion and Lab Sessions

Whether facilitating a discussion or a lab, time management is critical to ensuring all objectives are met without rushing or running out of time.

Time Management Strategies:

- Break the session into segments (e.g., introduction, activity, reflection).
- Set milestones to keep discussions on track or labs progressing smoothly.
- Use timers or cues to ensure one topic doesn't consume the entire session.
- Leave time for questions and debriefing to consolidate learning.

Example: In a discussion, a TA might structure the session as:

1. 5 minutes – Warm-up question.

2. 15 minutes – Small group discussion.

3. 20 minutes – Whole-class debate.

4. 10 minutes – Summary and takeaways.

4. Maintaining Student Engagement and Motivation

Students learn best when they are actively engaged and invested in the material. Whether in a discussion or a lab, a TA must foster curiosity and enthusiasm.

Strategies to Maintain Engagement:

- Use real-world applications to demonstrate relevance.
- Incorporate interactive elements, such as polling or case studies.
- Provide positive reinforcement and encouragement to boost confidence.
- Show enthusiasm—a TA's energy and passion are contagious!

Example: In a biology lab, a TA could ask, "How might these genetic principles apply in real-world medical research?" to help students see the broader significance of the experiment.

Conclusion

Managing discussion sections and lab sessions effectively requires planning, strong facilitation, and adaptability. A skilled TA:

- Sets clear goals and expectations to guide discussions and lab work.
- Encourages participation and critical thinking through strategic questioning.
- Balances structure with student autonomy, allowing exploration while maintaining focus.
- Uses time efficiently, ensuring sessions are productive and engaging.
- Supports all students, addressing learning needs and fostering an inclusive environment.

Ultimately, a TA is not just an instructor but a guide, mentor, and facilitator of deeper learning. By employing these strategies, TAs can create dynamic discussion sections and well-organized lab sessions that empower students to engage, explore, and succeed.

Encouraging Student Participation and Engagement

A well-managed classroom or lab is not just a space where information is delivered—it is an interactive, engaging, and dynamic environment where students feel motivated to contribute. As a Teaching Assistant (TA), fostering student participation and engagement is a critical responsibility that directly impacts learning outcomes, retention of material, and the overall classroom experience.

However, participation is not automatic—it must be actively cultivated. Many students may hesitate to engage due to lack of confidence, fear of making mistakes, cultural norms, or previous educational experiences that discouraged active involvement. A TA's role is to create a supportive environment that encourages interaction, critical thinking, and curiosity while ensuring that participation is meaningful and inclusive.

This section explores why student engagement matters, the barriers that prevent participation, and effective strategies to foster active learning in both discussion-based and lab settings.

1. Why Is Student Engagement Important?

Participation is not just about raising hands and speaking up—it is about engagement with ideas, peers, and course material. Active participation leads to:

- Deeper understanding of concepts – Students who articulate their thoughts reinforce and clarify their learning.

- Improved critical thinking – Discussing, questioning, and debating ideas develops analytical and problem-solving skills.

- Greater student motivation – Engaged students are more likely to persist through challenges and remain invested in their coursework.

- Better classroom dynamics – A lively, interactive class creates a sense of community where students support each other's learning.

A TA's goal is not just to increase the quantity of participation but to improve its quality, ensuring all students have the opportunity to engage, contribute, and benefit from active learning.

2. Understanding Barriers to Student Participation

Before implementing engagement strategies, it is essential to understand why some students hesitate to participate.

Common Barriers to Participation:

- Fear of being wrong or looking unintelligent – Some students worry about giving incorrect answers or being judged by their peers.
- Lack of confidence – Some students are naturally shy or introverted and may be hesitant to speak up.
- Unclear expectations – If students are unsure how to participate or what is expected, they may remain silent.
- Classroom power dynamics – Students may feel intimidated by the TA, professor, or more vocal classmates.
- Cultural differences – Some students come from educational backgrounds where silent listening is the norm rather than verbal participation.
- Disengagement or boredom – If the material feels irrelevant or is delivered in a passive, lecture-heavy format, students may mentally check out.

Once a TA recognizes these challenges, they can implement targeted strategies to break down barriers and foster engagement.

3. Strategies to Encourage Student Participation

A. Creating a Supportive and Inclusive Environment

Students are more likely to participate when they feel safe, respected, and encouraged.

- Establish Classroom Norms for Respectful Discussion

- Set expectations that all voices are valued and that mistakes are part of learning.
- Encourage constructive debate while ensuring that no student dominates or dismisses others' viewpoints.

- Validate All Contributions

- Acknowledge student responses with encouragement: "That's an interesting perspective! Can you expand on that?"
- If a student gives an incorrect answer, respond positively: "That's a great attempt—let's break it down together."

- Use Names and Personalized Engagement

- Address students by name to build rapport and encourage accountability.

- If a student is particularly quiet, engage them in one-on-one discussion before class to build their confidence.

B. Using Different Participation Methods to Engage All Students

Not all students are comfortable with speaking in front of a group, but participation can take many forms.

1. Think-Pair-Share

How It Works:

- Students think individually about a question.

- They pair up with a peer to discuss.

- They then share their discussion with the class.

Why It Works:
- Gives students time to process before responding.
- Encourages peer discussion, making participation feel less intimidating.
- Ensures that quieter students have a voice before group sharing.

2. Small Group Discussions or Breakout Rooms

How It Works:

- Students form small groups and discuss a topic, analyze a case study, or solve a problem.

- One group member presents key findings to the class.

Why It Works:
- Students feel more comfortable contributing in small groups.
- Discussions allow for collaborative learning and peer teaching.

3. Polling and Anonymous Responses

How It Works:

- Use tools like Poll Everywhere, Kahoot, or Google Forms for students to submit responses anonymously.

- Display results in real time to spark discussion.

Why It Works:
- Helps shy students engage without speaking aloud.
- Encourages honest opinions without fear of judgment.

4. Role-Playing or Case-Based Learning

How It Works:

- Students take on roles (e.g., scientist, historian, policymaker) and debate a real-world issue.
- Encourage students to apply theoretical knowledge to practical scenarios.

Why It Works:

- Encourages deep thinking and creativity.
- Appeals to students who prefer hands-on or interactive learning.

Example: In a political science discussion, students might role-play as different countries negotiating climate policies, applying real-world principles rather than just discussing theories.

C. Enhancing Lab Engagement and Hands-On Participation

In a lab setting, participation is more than just following instructions—it's about curiosity, inquiry, and problem-solving.

- Start with an Engaging Question

- Instead of just explaining procedures, ask: "What do you predict will happen in this experiment?"
- Encourage students to make hypotheses and justify their reasoning.

- Assign Rotating Roles in Group Labs

- **Lead Scientist:** Oversees procedures.
- **Data Recorder:** Takes notes and measurements.
- **Analyst:** Interprets results and draws conclusions.
- **Presenter:** Summarizes findings for the group.

- This ensures that every student is actively involved rather than one person doing all the work.

- Encourage Students to Troubleshoot Problems Themselves

- If an experiment isn't working, ask students to diagnose the issue before providing answers.
- Foster scientific thinking: "What variables might be affecting the outcome?"

4. Overcoming Common Participation Challenges

- What if the class is silent despite prompting?
- Use low-risk questions to start, such as polls, small groups, or written reflections.
- Allow students to submit questions anonymously to guide discussion.
- Use cold-calling gently: Instead of putting students on the spot, say, "Let's hear from someone we haven't heard from yet."

- What if only a few students participate while others remain passive?
- Redirect discussions: "That's a great point. Let's see if someone else has a different perspective."
- Create participation incentives (e.g., discussion contributions as part of grading).

- What if students are disengaged in labs?
- Make labs interactive and exploratory rather than just following instructions.
- Give students real-world applications—why does this experiment matter?

Conclusion

Encouraging student participation is about more than just getting students to talk—it's about creating an environment where they feel comfortable, motivated, and eager to engage. By implementing inclusive discussion techniques, interactive learning methods, and structured engagement strategies, TAs can transform passive classrooms into vibrant spaces of curiosity and collaboration.

A successful TA adapts to student needs, removes participation barriers, and fosters a culture of engagement where every student feels heard, valued, and excited to learn.

Conflict Resolution and Handling Disruptive Students

Classroom and lab environments thrive when they foster respect, collaboration, and open communication. However, disruptions and conflicts can arise due to student disagreements, lack of engagement, misunderstandings, or personal frustrations. As a Teaching Assistant (TA), you serve not only as an educator but also as a mediator responsible for maintaining a productive learning atmosphere.

Conflict resolution and classroom management require diplomacy, patience, and assertiveness. Whether dealing with a disruptive student, a heated classroom debate, or a conflict between students, a TA must de-escalate tensions, set clear expectations, and create a space where all students feel respected and heard.

This section explores common sources of conflict, strategies for handling disruptions, and techniques for fostering a positive learning environment that encourages constructive dialogue rather than confrontation.

1. Understanding the Nature of Classroom Conflict

Conflicts and disruptions in the classroom or lab can stem from various sources, including:

A. Student-Student Conflicts

- Disagreements during group work or lab collaborations.

- Differing opinions in discussions or debates that escalate into hostility.

- Cultural or communication barriers leading to misunderstandings or exclusion.

B. Student-TA Conflicts

- Students challenging grading policies or perceived unfair treatment.

- Resistance to constructive criticism or academic expectations.

- Power struggles where students test the TA's authority.

C. General Classroom Disruptions

- Side conversations that distract others.

- Frequent interruptions or disrespectful behavior.

- Unprepared students who derail discussions with off-topic comments.

- Chronic disengagement (e.g., students using phones, showing up late, or sleeping in class).

Recognizing the root cause of the conflict—whether interpersonal, academic, or behavioral—helps a TA determine the best approach for resolution.

2. Proactive Strategies to Prevent Disruptions

A. Set Clear Expectations from the Start

Prevention is the best strategy for handling classroom disruptions. At the beginning of the semester, establish:

- Classroom norms for respect, participation, and professionalism.
- A clear policy on behavior (e.g., "Disruptions impact everyone's learning, so we will maintain a respectful dialogue").
- Guidelines for resolving conflicts in group work and discussions.

Example: If students know in advance that interruptions will not be tolerated and disagreements must be handled constructively, they are less likely to engage in disruptive behavior.

B. Foster a Positive Classroom Culture

An environment of mutual respect and open communication helps prevent conflicts before they escalate.

- Encourage Inclusive Discussions

- Remind students that differing opinions enrich the learning experience.

- Use neutral language to frame disagreements: "That's an interesting perspective—let's explore both sides."

- Model Professionalism and Empathy

- Respond to challenges with calmness and confidence, rather than reacting emotionally.

- Demonstrate active listening by acknowledging student concerns before offering solutions.

- Use Humor and Engagement

- Light humor can defuse tension and refocus discussions without undermining authority.

- Engaging students in hands-on activities, debates, or structured discussions prevents disengagement and distractions.

3. Handling Common Classroom Disruptions

Even in a well-managed classroom, disruptions will happen. The key is addressing them early and constructively.

A. Addressing Minor Disruptions (Talking, Side Conversations, Disengagement)

- **Scenario:** A few students frequently whisper to each other during class discussions.

- **Nonverbal Cues:** Make eye contact, pause mid-sentence, or move closer to the students to signal awareness.
- **Direct Reminder:** Calmly say, "Let's make sure everyone has the opportunity to hear and participate."
- **Engagement Strategy:** Ask one of the students a question related to the discussion to refocus their attention.

B. Managing Dominating or Interrupting Students

- **Scenario:** One student interrupts frequently, dominating discussions and preventing others from speaking.

- **Redirect Participation:** "That's a great point. Let's hear from someone else before we continue."
- **Use Speaking Time Limits:** "Let's allow 60 seconds per response so we can get multiple perspectives."
- **One-on-One Discussion:** If the behavior persists, privately explain: "I appreciate your enthusiasm, but I want to ensure everyone gets a chance to contribute."

C. Dealing with Students Who Challenge Authority

- **Scenario:** A student **publicly disputes a grade or TA decision** in front of the class.

- **Stay Calm and Professional:** Avoid escalating the situation. Say, "That's an important concern. Let's discuss this privately after class."
- **Redirect to Policy:** "We have a grading review process—let's go through that properly to ensure fairness."
- **Avoid Arguments in Front of Peers:** Engaging in a debate in front of the class can set a precedent for undermining authority.

D. Responding to Hostile or Disruptive Behavior

- **Scenario:** A student becomes hostile, either towards a peer or the TA, using disrespectful language.

- **Stay Firm and Direct:** "That language is not appropriate for this discussion. Let's keep our conversation respectful."
- **De-escalate, Not Confront:** Avoid power struggles—use a calm, neutral tone rather than raising your voice.
- **Offer a Private Conversation:** "Let's step outside for a moment to talk about this."
- **Involve Faculty or Administration if Necessary:** If the behavior is threatening or persistent, escalate the issue to the professor or academic support services.

4. Resolving Student Conflicts in Group Work and Labs

Group work and labs can create tensions if students feel frustrated with teammates, disagree over responsibilities, or encounter personality clashes.

A. Encourage Conflict Resolution Skills

- Set expectations for collaborative problem-solving before conflicts arise.
- Teach students how to address concerns respectfully—e.g., "Instead of blaming, frame issues as 'I feel' statements."
- If tension arises, mediate the discussion and guide students to a resolution.

B. Addressing Unequal Work Distribution in Labs and Group Projects

- **Scenario:** One student complains that a teammate is not contributing in a lab.

- **Encourage Direct Communication:** Suggest they first speak with the group member directly.
- **Intervene If Needed:** If the issue persists, meet privately with the group to discuss redistributing responsibilities.
- **Use Structured Group Roles:** Assign specific lab duties to each student to clarify expectations.

5. Conflict Resolution Strategies for TAs

When conflicts escalate beyond minor disruptions, a TA must act as a mediator to restore classroom harmony.

A. The Five Steps of Conflict Resolution

- **Acknowledge the Issue** – Identify the root cause without placing blame.
- **Listen Actively** – Allow all sides to express their perspectives.
- **Clarify the Impact** – Explain how the conflict is affecting the class dynamic.
- **Propose Solutions** – Offer ways to resolve the conflict (e.g., policy reminders, structured

participation, mediation).

- **Follow Up** – Check in later to ensure resolution.

Example: If two students frequently argue in class, a TA might:

- Meet privately with each student.

- Encourage perspective-taking: "Can you see where the other person is coming from?"

- Set behavioral expectations moving forward.

Conclusion

Handling classroom disruptions and resolving conflicts requires calmness, confidence, and strategic intervention. A TA is not just a knowledge provider but also a facilitator of a respectful and engaging learning environment.

- Prevent conflicts by setting clear expectations and fostering mutual respect.

- Address minor disruptions swiftly before they escalate.

- Mediate student disagreements constructively, encouraging collaboration and compromise.

- Remain professional and neutral in all interactions, reinforcing an atmosphere of fairness and support.

By implementing these conflict resolution strategies, TAs can ensure that discussions, labs, and group work remain productive, inclusive, and intellectually stimulating—creating a space where all students can focus on learning rather than tension or disruption.

Strategies for Addressing Academic Anxiety and Boosting Confidence

Academic anxiety is a pervasive challenge in higher education, affecting students across disciplines and experience levels. It manifests in various ways, from fear of failure and test anxiety to reluctance in participating in discussions or tackling complex assignments. As a Teaching Assistant (TA), recognizing and addressing academic anxiety is essential for fostering a positive learning environment where students feel empowered, capable, and confident in their abilities [38].

A supportive TA can play a crucial role in reducing anxiety, encouraging resilience, and equipping students with strategies to manage their academic stress. By combining empathetic communication, structured guidance, and confidence-building techniques, TAs can help students transform fear into engagement and uncertainty into self-assurance.

This section explores the causes of academic anxiety, signs that a student may be struggling, and effective strategies for helping students develop confidence in their academic abilities.

1. Understanding Academic Anxiety

Academic anxiety stems from a variety of sources, including high performance expectations, fear of judgment, lack of preparation, previous negative experiences, and imposter syndrome [39]. It can significantly impact a student's motivation, ability to concentrate, and willingness to engage in learning activities [40].

A. Common Types of Academic Anxiety

- **Test and Performance Anxiety** – Fear of exams, presentations, or graded assessments, often leading to physical symptoms (racing heart, sweating, nausea) and mental blocks.

- **Participation Anxiety** – Hesitation to speak in class discussions or answer questions due to fear of saying the wrong thing or looking unintelligent.

- **Perfectionism and Fear of Failure** – Anxiety stemming from unrealistically high self-expectations, leading to procrastination or excessive self-criticism.

- **Imposter Syndrome** – The belief that one is not intelligent or talented enough and will eventually be "exposed" as undeserving of success.

- **Math or Science Anxiety** – A specific form of anxiety that causes avoidance of quantitative subjects, often due to negative past experiences.

B. Recognizing Signs of Student Anxiety

- Frequent late or missing assignments despite evident effort.
- Avoidance of speaking in discussions or asking for help even when struggling.
- Physical signs of distress, such as restlessness, sweating, or fidgeting during exams or class activities.
- Over-apologizing for mistakes or excessively doubting their own abilities.
- Negative self-talk, such as "I'm just bad at this" or "I'll never understand this."

Once a TA identifies these signs, they can implement strategies to help students regain confidence and manage their anxiety effectively.

2. Strategies for Reducing Academic Anxiety and Building Confidence

A student's confidence in learning is not an inherent trait—it can be cultivated through intentional strategies that reinforce self-efficacy and a growth mindset. TAs can employ the following techniques to create a low-pressure learning environment, encourage participation, and help students develop self-assurance in their academic abilities.

A. Creating a Low-Anxiety Learning Environment

- **Normalize Mistakes as Part of Learning**
  - Reinforce that errors are a natural part of the learning process rather than signs of incompetence.

- Model this behavior by sharing examples of your own learning struggles and how you overcame them.

- **Encourage a Growth Mindset**

  - Shift the focus from "I can't do this" to "I can't do this yet" by emphasizing progress over perfection.

  - Acknowledge effort and improvement rather than just correct answers.

- **Establish a Supportive Atmosphere**

  - Use positive reinforcement: Instead of saying "That's wrong," try, "You're on the right track—let's explore this further."

  - Encourage peer support and collaboration so students feel less isolated in their struggles.

Example: If a student struggles with public speaking, a TA might offer low-risk participation options, such as written responses, small-group discussions, or the ability to present informally before speaking to the whole class.

B. Helping Students Overcome Participation Anxiety

Many students hesitate to contribute in discussions due to fear of judgment, uncertainty about their answers, or a history of being discouraged from speaking up.

Techniques to Encourage Participation:

- **Start with Low-Stakes Engagement:**

  - Use think-pair-share activities where students first discuss in pairs before sharing with the group.

  - Offer anonymous response options, such as online discussion boards or polling tools.

- **Create Predictable Structures for Participation:**

  - Establish clear expectations that participation is encouraged but will be handled in a respectful, low-pressure way.

  - Rotate participation so no one feels put on the spot unexpectedly.

- **Acknowledge All Contributions Positively:**

  - Reframe answers to highlight their value, even if they are incorrect:

    - Instead of "That's not quite right," say: "That's an interesting approach—how might we adjust it?"

  - Connect student responses to the larger discussion so they feel their input is meaningful.

Example: If a student hesitates to answer, a TA could say, "I appreciate you thinking about this. Let's explore it together."

C. Strategies to Reduce Test and Performance Anxiety

Exams, presentations, and graded assessments often trigger heightened anxiety. TAs can implement techniques to help students prepare effectively and feel more in control of their performance.

- Teach Study and Exam Strategies

- Offer review sessions focused on effective study techniques (e.g., spaced repetition, active recall).
- Break down large topics into smaller, manageable learning objectives to reduce overwhelm.

- Provide Practice Opportunities

- Offer mock exams or sample problems so students can familiarize themselves with test formats.
- Use low-stakes quizzes or self-check activities to boost confidence.

- Help Students Develop Calming Techniques

- Encourage deep breathing exercises before tests.
- Teach positive self-talk techniques (e.g., replacing "I'm going to fail" with "I am prepared and capable").

Example: If student expresses test anxiety, a TA might suggest: "Try explaining key concepts to a friend as if you were teaching them. This can reinforce understanding and build confidence."

D. Addressing Perfectionism and Imposter Syndrome

Many students struggle with self-doubt, believing they are not smart enough or do not deserve their academic success.

Ways to Counteract Perfectionism and Self-Doubt:

- Encourage Process-Oriented Thinking:

- Instead of emphasizing grades, focus on growth, effort, and improvement.

- Challenge Negative Self-Talk:

- If a student says, "I'll never be good at math," counter with, "You've improved significantly—what strategies have helped you so far?"

- Remind Students That Struggle Is Normal

- Normalize that even experts face challenges and that setbacks are part of learning.

- Encourage Seeking Help Without Shame

- Remind students that asking questions is a sign of engagement, not weakness.

Example: A TA might share their own academic struggles: "I used to feel overwhelmed by writing assignments, but I learned that outlining my ideas first made the process easier."

3. Long-Term Confidence-Building Techniques

Confidence is built over time through consistent reinforcement, small wins, and positive experiences.

Help Students Track Progress:

- Encourage students to reflect on how much they've learned over the semester.

- Use progress journals or self-assessment checklists to highlight growth.

Foster a Collaborative Learning Community:

- Promote peer mentorship and study groups where students can support and learn from one another.

- Create opportunities for students to teach concepts to others, reinforcing their understanding and confidence.

Conclusion

Addressing academic anxiety and boosting confidence requires a holistic approach that combines emotional support, structured learning techniques, and positive reinforcement. A successful TA:

- Creates a supportive and inclusive classroom environment where students feel safe making mistakes.
- Encourages growth mindset thinking, helping students see learning as a process rather than a test of inherent ability.
- Implements practical strategies to reduce anxiety related to participation, exams, and self-doubt.

Ultimately, a TA who fosters confidence empowers students not just to succeed academically but to develop resilience, curiosity, and a lifelong love of learning.

Chapter 4: Teaching Strategies for TAs

Teaching is both an art and a science, requiring a blend of subject expertise, instructional design, and the ability to engage students effectively. As a Teaching Assistant (TA), developing strong teaching strategies is essential for fostering student learning, critical thinking, and academic success. Whether leading discussions, conducting lab sessions, assisting with lectures, or mentoring students one-on-one, TAs must employ diverse instructional techniques to accommodate various learning styles, course formats, and student needs.

Unlike traditional faculty members who often have years of teaching experience, many TAs are at the beginning of their instructional journey. This chapter aims to equip TAs with foundational teaching methodologies that will enhance their effectiveness in the classroom, lab, or virtual learning environment. It explores evidence-based strategies for facilitating discussions, promoting active learning, structuring effective lectures, and utilizing questioning techniques to stimulate critical thinking.

Figure 4.1. Teaching and Learning [113].

Additionally, this chapter will address the importance of flexibility in teaching—how to adapt lesson plans based on student engagement, adjust instructional techniques for hybrid or online learning settings, and incorporate technology to enhance student understanding. Teaching is not a one-size-fits-all approach, and successful TAs learn to modify their strategies to meet the needs of diverse student populations, including international students, students with disabilities, and non-traditional learners.

By the end of this chapter, TAs will be able to:
- Understand and implement different teaching methodologies for diverse learning environments.
- Facilitate discussions and active learning strategies to encourage student engagement.
- Deliver clear, structured, and interactive lectures or presentations.
- Use questioning techniques to promote higher-order thinking and critical analysis.
- Adapt teaching strategies for hybrid and online learning formats.
- Leverage technology and digital tools to enhance instructional delivery.

Effective teaching is not just about delivering information—it is about inspiring curiosity, encouraging student participation, and creating an environment where learners feel supported and motivated to succeed. By mastering these teaching strategies, TAs can transform their instructional approach, making a lasting impact on student learning and their own professional development as educators.

Facilitating Discussions and Active Learning Strategies

Effective teaching is not just about delivering content—it is about engaging students, encouraging critical thinking, and creating an environment where knowledge is actively constructed rather than passively received. As a Teaching Assistant (TA), one of the most powerful ways to enhance learning is through facilitated discussions and active learning strategies.

A well-structured discussion deepens understanding, refines analytical skills, and encourages diverse perspectives, while active learning transforms students from passive listeners into active participants. The key to success lies in thoughtful planning, strategic questioning, and creating an inclusive space where students feel comfortable contributing.

This section explores how TAs can facilitate engaging discussions, implement active learning techniques, and overcome common participation challenges to maximize student engagement.

1. The Role of Discussion in Learning

Discussions serve as a bridge between knowledge acquisition and application—they allow students to:

- Process and articulate ideas in their own words, reinforcing comprehension.
- Engage in critical thinking, evaluating concepts rather than just memorizing them.
- Learn from diverse viewpoints, gaining insight from their peers.
- Develop communication and argumentation skills, essential for academic and professional success.

However, discussions can easily become one-sided, dominated by a few students, or stagnate into surface-level conversations. A skilled TA must plan, guide, and adapt discussions to ensure that all students participate meaningfully.

2. Structuring Effective Discussions

A strong discussion does not happen by chance—it requires intentional design and facilitation.

A. Preparing for a Productive Discussion

1. **Set Clear Objectives**

o   What should students gain from the discussion?

o   Are you aiming to clarify concepts, debate viewpoints, analyze case studies, or connect theory to practice?

2. **Provide Pre-Class Preparation**

o   Assign thought-provoking readings or videos to give students a foundation for discussion.

o   Use pre-discussion questions to help students organize their thoughts beforehand.

3. **Create a Discussion Framework**

o   Establish guidelines for respectful engagement (e.g., active listening, disagreeing constructively).

o   Set expectations for how students should support their arguments (e.g., citing sources, using examples).

B. Facilitating Engaging and Inclusive Discussions

Once a discussion begins, the TA must balance structure with flexibility, ensuring that students stay on topic while allowing organic intellectual exploration.

1. Start with an Icebreaker or Warm-Up Question

- **Example:** "What was the most surprising insight from this week's reading?"
- Low-stakes questions reduce anxiety and get everyone talking early.

2. Use Strategic Questioning to Deepen Engagement

- **Open-Ended Questions** – Encourage elaboration:

  - - "Did you like the reading?"
  - - "What argument in the reading did you find most compelling, and why?"

- **Application Questions** – Connect learning to real-world scenarios:

  - - "How would this concept apply in your field of study?"

- **Devil's Advocate Questions** – Encourage debate and deeper thinking:

  - - "What's a counterargument to this theory?"

- **Hypothetical Questions** – Challenge students to explore new possibilities:

  - - "If this policy were implemented differently, what impact might it have?"

- **Socratic Questioning** – Push students to examine assumptions:

- - "How do we know this is true?"

3. Encourage Equal Participation

- **Challenge:** Discussions often become dominated by a few students, leaving others silent.

- **Solution:**
- Think-Pair-Share – Students reflect individually, discuss with a partner, then share with the group.
- Round-Robin Contributions – Each student provides one thought or reaction before open discussion begins.
- Small-Group Discussions – Students explore a topic in teams before presenting to the class.
- Anonymous Polling or Digital Responses – Shy students may engage more through online discussion boards or polling apps (e.g., Poll Everywhere, Padlet, Kahoot).

C. Managing Common Discussion Challenges

- **Silence & Lack of Participation**
- Ask low-risk questions first to ease students into the conversation.
- Allow students time to write down their thoughts before responding.
- Use small groups to build confidence before opening discussion to the full class.

- **Off-Topic or Unfocused Responses**
- Gently redirect – "That's an interesting point, but how does it connect to today's topic?"
- Summarize and refocus – "So far, we've explored X and Y. Let's now shift toward…"

- **Overpowering Students Who Dominate the Discussion**
- Acknowledge their enthusiasm but redirect – "Let's hear from someone who hasn't spoken yet."
- Set time limits per response to ensure balanced participation.

- Conflict or Heated Debates
- Encourage evidence-based reasoning – "Can you provide support for your perspective?"
- Reinforce respectful discourse – "We can disagree while still valuing each other's viewpoints."

3. Implementing Active Learning Strategies

Active learning is any instructional approach that engages students in the learning process through interaction, problem-solving, and hands-on experience [41]. Studies show that active learning improves retention, critical thinking, and student motivation [42].

Here are some effective active learning techniques TAs can incorporate into discussions and lab sessions:

A. Case-Based Learning

- Students analyze real-world scenarios related to course content.
- Encourages practical application and critical thinking.
- Works well in business, law, medicine, and policy-based courses.
- Example: "How would you handle this ethical dilemma as a public health official?"

B. Role-Playing & Simulations

- Students adopt different perspectives (e.g., policymakers, engineers, historians).
- Encourages empathy, critical thinking, and problem-solving.
- Example: In a history course, students might debate as key figures from a historical event.

C. Peer Teaching

- Students teach concepts to their peers, reinforcing their own understanding.
- Works well for review sessions and complex topics.
- Example: Assign students different topics to research and present to the class.

D. Flipped Classroom Approach

- Students engage with lecture materials before class, so class time is spent on active discussion and problem-solving.
- Encourages independent learning and preparation.
- Works well for technical and problem-based courses.

E. Gamification & Interactive Activities

- Use quizzes, problem-solving competitions, and collaborative challenges to enhance engagement.
- Works particularly well for STEM fields and review sessions.
- **Example:** Kahoot or Jeopardy-style quizzes to reinforce concepts.

4. Encouraging Reflection & Takeaways

At the end of a discussion or active learning session, students should consolidate their learning.

- Ask students to summarize key takeaways in one sentence.
- Use Exit Tickets – "What's one thing you learned today that changed how you think about the topic?"
- Encourage metacognition – "How did today's discussion challenge or reinforce your understanding?"

Conclusion

Facilitating discussions and implementing active learning strategies transforms the classroom into an engaging, student-centered space. A successful TA:

- Prepares discussions with clear objectives and structured questioning.
- Uses strategic facilitation techniques to encourage broad participation.
- Implements active learning methods that enhance understanding and retention.
- Manages challenges effectively, ensuring discussions remain inclusive and productive.

By mastering these techniques, TAs empower students to think critically, articulate their ideas confidently, and take an active role in their learning journey—creating a more enriching and interactive educational experience for all.

Effective Lecturing and Presentation Skills for TAs

Lecturing is one of the most fundamental teaching methods in higher education, yet delivering an effective lecture is far more than simply relaying information. A well-structured, engaging lecture captures students' attention, promotes active learning, and facilitates deep comprehension. As a Teaching Assistant (TA), you may be required to present material in discussion sections, lab sessions, review workshops, or even guest lectures.

However, delivering a compelling lecture requires more than content knowledge—it demands clarity, structure, engagement techniques, and the ability to adapt to student needs. A strong TA must balance authority with approachability, information with interaction, and structure with flexibility to ensure students not only absorb information but also actively engage with it.

This section explores strategies for structuring lectures, developing effective presentation skills, engaging students, and refining delivery techniques to maximize learning outcomes.

1. The Role of Lecturing in Higher Education

While active learning and discussions are vital, lecturing remains an essential tool for delivering foundational knowledge and guiding student understanding. A well-crafted lecture serves several key purposes:

- Introduces new concepts clearly and efficiently, providing students with a structured foundation.

- Synthesizes and contextualizes information, helping students connect different ideas.

- Models expert thinking, demonstrating how to approach complex problems in a discipline.

- Provides structured explanations, reducing confusion and guiding independent study.

However, traditional, one-way lectures—where the instructor speaks uninterrupted for long periods—can lead to passive listening, cognitive overload, and disengagement. The goal of an effective TA lecture is not just to inform but to engage, motivate, and inspire curiosity.

2. Structuring a Clear and Engaging Lecture

A lecture should be well-organized, easy to follow, and engaging to ensure students remain attentive and retain key concepts.

A. The Three-Part Structure of an Effective Lecture

Introduction: Setting the Stage

The first few minutes of a lecture are critical for capturing attention and establishing purpose. A strong introduction should:

- Provide a roadmap: Clearly outline what will be covered (e.g., "Today, we'll explore three key theories of motivation and apply them to real-world scenarios").
- Connect to prior knowledge: Link new material to what students already know.
- Pose a thought-provoking question or problem: Encourage curiosity.
- Clarify the lecture's relevance: Explain why the topic matters in academic or real-world contexts.

Example: Instead of starting with, "Today, we're covering supply and demand," a TA could begin with, "Have you ever wondered why concert ticket prices fluctuate? Understanding supply and demand can explain this phenomenon."

Main Body: Delivering Content Effectively

Once students are engaged, the main section should:

- Present information in manageable chunks: Avoid overwhelming students with excessive details.
- Use signposting: Guide students through the lecture (e.g., "Now that we've covered X, let's move to Y…").
- Integrate examples and real-world applications: Make abstract concepts more tangible.
- Incorporate visuals: Use slides, diagrams, charts, or multimedia to reinforce learning.
- Check for understanding: Pause periodically to ask students questions or encourage reflection.

- Example of Poor Delivery: A TA reads dense PowerPoint slides verbatim with no interaction.
- Example of Effective Delivery: A TA breaks down key points using analogies, engages students with a quick poll, and checks comprehension with a short discussion.

Conclusion: Reinforcing Key Takeaways

The final minutes of a lecture should:

- Summarize major points concisely (e.g., "In summary, we've explored how X affects Y…").
- Highlight key takeaways: Emphasize big-picture connections.
- Encourage reflection: Ask students to identify the most important idea they learned.
- Provide a call to action: Suggest further reading, applications, or questions for next time.

3. Mastering Presentation Skills for an Engaging Lecture

Beyond structuring content effectively, strong delivery and presence are essential for holding students' attention.

A. The TA's Presence: How You Communicate Matters

- Project Confidence and Authority

- Speak with clarity and conviction—avoid trailing off or using excessive filler words ("um," "like").

- Stand or move with purpose rather than pacing aimlessly.

- Maintain strong posture and eye contact to establish credibility.

- Use Effective Voice Modulation

- Vary tone, pace, and volume to maintain interest (avoid monotone speech).

- Use pauses strategically—silence can emphasize key points and allow students to process information.

- Engage Through Nonverbal Communication

- Use gestures naturally to highlight key ideas.

- Move purposefully around the room rather than staying static.

B. Crafting Effective Visual Aids (Slides & Media Use)

Avoid:
- Overloading slides with text.
- Using distracting animations or excessive bullet points.
- Reading slides word-for-word.

- Best Practices for Slides:
- Use concise text (no more than 5-6 bullet points per slide).
- Include relevant images, diagrams, or graphs to illustrate concepts.
- Ensure high contrast and readable fonts (avoid tiny text).
- Keep slides focused on key concepts, elaborating verbally rather than dumping information.

Example: Instead of a slide crammed with dense paragraphs, use:
- A single image or chart illustrating the key point.
- A headline phrase summarizing the concept.
- A verbal explanation to expand on details.

4. Keeping Students Engaged During Lectures

Even the best-structured lecture can fail if students become passive listeners. Effective TAs integrate active learning techniques to keep students mentally engaged.

A. Interactive Strategies to Maintain Attention

- Ask Open-Ended Questions – "Why do you think this experiment produced these results?"
- Use Think-Pair-Share – Students think individually, discuss with a partner, and share with the class.
- Incorporate Quick Polls – Use Kahoot, Google Forms, or in-class hand-raising to gauge understanding.
- Pause for Reflection – Ask, "What's one thing you've learned so far?"
- Use Real-World Applications – Frame concepts in ways students can relate to.

Example: Instead of simply explaining a historical event, a TA might ask, "If you were a policymaker at the time, how would you have handled this situation differently?"

5. Handling Challenges in Lecturing and Presenting

Even experienced lecturers face challenges, and TAs must be prepared to adapt and problem-solve.

- Students Are Disengaged
- Ask, "How does this concept relate to your field?" to personalize learning.
- Use interactive questions or relatable examples.
- Adjust pacing and energy level—monotony kills engagement.

- Students Don't Understand a Key Concept
- Pause and re-explain using a different example.
- Ask students, "How would you explain this in your own words?" to check comprehension.

- Technical Issues with Slides or Equipment
- Always prepare backup notes in case slides fail.
- If technology glitches, pivot to discussion-based explanation.

Conclusion

Effective lecturing and presentation skills combine structure, delivery, and engagement techniques to create a learning experience that is both informative and interactive. A skilled TA:

- Structures lectures with clear introductions, engaging delivery, and concise conclusions.
- Communicates confidently using strong voice modulation and body language.
- Uses well-designed slides and visuals to enhance understanding.
- Incorporates interactive elements to maintain student engagement.
- Adapts to student feedback, ensuring clarity and accessibility.

By mastering these lecturing strategies, TAs not only deliver content effectively but also inspire curiosity, critical thinking, and active participation—essential qualities for a meaningful learning experience.

Effective Lecturing and Presentation Skills for TAs

Teaching Assistants (TAs) play a critical role in the learning process, often serving as a bridge between students and course instructors. One of the most essential skills for a TA is the ability to deliver engaging, clear, and structured lectures or presentations. Effective lecturing goes beyond simply conveying information—it involves capturing students' attention, fostering comprehension, and encouraging active participation.

Understanding the Purpose of Lecturing

A well-delivered lecture is not just about sharing content; it should provide context, stimulate critical thinking, and facilitate meaningful discussions. The most effective TAs recognize that their lectures should:

- Clarify complex concepts that students may struggle with in readings or assignments.

- Connect theory to real-world applications to enhance relevance and engagement.

- Serve as a framework that helps students structure their learning process.

By understanding these objectives, TAs can design lectures that are not only informative but also impactful.

Structuring an Effective Lecture

A structured approach to lecturing ensures coherence and accessibility. A well-organized lecture typically follows this format:

1. **Introduction (Setting the Stage)**

   - Begin with a compelling hook: an intriguing question, a real-world example, or a brief anecdote.

   - Outline the objectives of the lecture, so students know what they should learn by the end.

   - Establish a connection to prior knowledge to activate students' existing understanding.

2. **Main Content (Delivering Key Ideas)**

   - Present information in manageable chunks, avoiding cognitive overload.

   - Use clear explanations, definitions, and examples to illustrate complex ideas.

   - Incorporate different modalities—visuals, case studies, problem-solving scenarios—to appeal to diverse learning styles.

   - Engage students through Socratic questioning or interactive discussions rather than relying solely on one-way communication.

3. **Conclusion (Reinforcing Learning)**

- o Summarize the key takeaways succinctly.

- o Allow students to reflect by posing thought-provoking questions or assigning a brief application task.

- o Offer a preview of upcoming topics to create continuity in learning.

Presentation Techniques for Impactful Delivery

In addition to structuring the content effectively, TAs must focus on their delivery style to maintain engagement and clarity. Key strategies include:

- **Voice Modulation and Clarity**: Speak at an appropriate volume, pace, and tone. Vary intonation to emphasize important points and maintain interest.

- **Nonverbal Communication**: Maintain eye contact, use purposeful gestures, and move around the classroom to create a dynamic presence.

- **Visual Aids and Technology**: Leverage slides, diagrams, videos, and digital tools to reinforce concepts without overwhelming students with excessive text.

- **Active Engagement Techniques**: Use think-pair-share, live polls, or Q&A sessions to encourage student participation.

Overcoming Common Challenges in Lecturing

Even experienced educators encounter challenges during lectures. TAs can enhance their lecturing effectiveness by anticipating and addressing the following:

- **Student Disengagement**: If students seem distracted or passive, incorporate interactive elements like group discussions or real-world problem-solving tasks.

- **Complex Topics**: Break down intricate concepts into step-by-step explanations and use analogies to make them more relatable.

- **Time Management**: Stick to the planned lecture structure while allowing flexibility for student inquiries and discussions.

Conclusion

Mastering the art of lecturing and presentation is a valuable skill that enhances both the TA's teaching effectiveness and students' learning experiences. By thoughtfully structuring lectures, employing engaging delivery techniques, and addressing potential challenges, TAs can transform their presentations into powerful learning opportunities. A great lecture is not one where the instructor talks the most, but one where students walk away having truly understood and connected with the material.

Using Questioning Techniques to Promote Critical Thinking

Effective questioning is one of the most powerful teaching strategies a Teaching Assistant (TA) can employ to foster critical thinking. Rather than simply assessing students' recall of information, well-crafted questions can challenge students to analyze, evaluate, and synthesize knowledge, leading to deeper engagement and understanding. By using questioning techniques strategically, TAs can encourage students to move beyond passive learning and actively construct their own knowledge.

The Role of Questioning in Critical Thinking

Questioning serves as a catalyst for intellectual curiosity, guiding students to:

- Analyze concepts by breaking them down into components.

- Evaluate different perspectives and arguments.

- Synthesize ideas to generate new insights.

- Apply knowledge to novel situations.

- Reflect on their reasoning and assumptions.

When used effectively, questioning techniques can transform classroom discussions into rich learning experiences where students develop their ability to think independently and articulate their reasoning with clarity.

Types of Questions and Their Purpose

Different types of questions serve different pedagogical purposes. TAs should vary their questioning techniques to scaffold students' learning experiences and gradually push them toward higher-order thinking.

1. **Lower-Order Questions (Foundational Thinking)**

   - **Recall Questions**: Assess basic memory of facts (e.g., *"What are the three branches of government?"*).

   - **Comprehension Questions**: Check understanding of concepts (e.g., *"Can you explain the main idea of this theory in your own words?"*).

   - These questions are essential for establishing foundational knowledge but should serve as a stepping stone to more complex inquiries.

2. **Higher-Order Questions (Critical Thinking)**

   - **Application Questions**: Encourage students to apply knowledge in different contexts (e.g., *"How would you apply this concept to a real-world problem?"*).

   - **Analysis Questions**: Require breaking down ideas into components (e.g., *"What are the key differences between these two perspectives?"*).

   - **Evaluation Questions**: Challenge students to form judgments (e.g., *"Which argument do you find more convincing, and why?"*).

- o **Synthesis Questions**: Encourage creativity and integration of ideas (e.g., *"How could these theories be combined to create a new approach?"*).

By moving from lower-order to higher-order questions, TAs can progressively challenge students to develop deeper analytical and reasoning skills.

Strategies for Effective Questioning

To maximize the impact of questioning techniques, TAs should be intentional in their approach:

1. **Use Open-Ended Questions**

   - o Open-ended questions encourage exploration and multiple viewpoints rather than simple "yes" or "no" answers.

   - o Example: Instead of asking, *"Was the experiment successful?"*, ask *"What factors influenced the outcome of the experiment, and how might they be adjusted?"*

2. **Encourage Wait Time**

   - o Give students time to think before answering, rather than expecting immediate responses.

   - o A brief pause of 5–10 seconds after asking a question allows students to formulate more thoughtful answers.

3. **Use the Socratic Method**

   - o Challenge students by responding to their answers with further probing questions.

   - o Example: If a student states an opinion, follow up with *"What evidence supports that conclusion?"* or *"How does that perspective compare with the opposing view?"*

4. **Foster a Safe and Supportive Environment**

   - o Encourage all students to participate without fear of judgment.

   - o Reinforce that there are often multiple valid answers and that the goal is exploration, not just correctness.

5. **Encourage Peer-to-Peer Questioning**

   - o Have students formulate and ask their own questions to promote collaborative learning.

   - o Example: Assign small groups to develop discussion questions and engage in a structured debate.

6. **Use Real-World Scenarios**

   - o Frame questions in the context of real-world issues to enhance engagement.

    o   Example: *"How would you apply this ethical principle in a business setting?"*

Overcoming Common Challenges in Questioning

Even skilled TAs may encounter obstacles in facilitating critical thinking through questioning. Some common challenges include:

- **Student Reluctance to Participate**: Some students may hesitate to answer out of fear of being wrong. Solution: Use think-pair-share activities, where students first discuss in pairs before responding to the class.

- **Overreliance on a Few Voices**: Often, the same students dominate discussions. Solution: Use strategies like calling on students randomly or using participation-based grading.

- **Questions That Are Too Broad or Vague**: If a question is too general, students may struggle to respond. Solution: Frame questions with enough specificity to guide responses while still allowing for open-ended thought.

Conclusion

Using questioning techniques effectively is a skill that distinguishes an exceptional TA from an average one. Thoughtful, well-structured questions have the power to transform passive learning into an active process where students critically engage with material, question assumptions, and develop independent thought. By fostering an environment of inquiry and discussion, TAs can instill in students the essential habit of thinking critically—an ability that will serve them well beyond the classroom.

Adapting Teaching Methods for Hybrid and Online Learning Environments

The evolution of education has seen a significant shift toward hybrid and online learning models, requiring Teaching Assistants (TAs) to develop new strategies that foster engagement, comprehension, and academic success across digital and in-person settings. Unlike traditional face-to-face instruction, hybrid and online learning environments present unique challenges and opportunities that demand flexibility, creativity, and a keen understanding of digital pedagogy.

Understanding the Hybrid and Online Learning Landscape

Hybrid and online learning environments differ from conventional classroom settings in several key ways:

- **Hybrid Learning**: A combination of in-person and online instruction, where students engage in both synchronous (real-time) and asynchronous (self-paced) learning activities [43].

- **Fully Online Learning**: Courses delivered entirely in a digital format, with interactions occurring through virtual platforms, discussion boards, and multimedia content [43].

To be effective in these environments, TAs must adapt their teaching methods to ensure that students receive the same level of support, clarity, and interaction as they would in a traditional classroom.

Key Strategies for Hybrid and Online Teaching

1. Designing an Inclusive and Accessible Learning Experience

One of the primary responsibilities of a TA in an online or hybrid setting is ensuring that all students—regardless of their learning style, time zone, or technological access—can participate fully. This requires:

- **Providing Multiple Modes of Engagement**: Some students learn best through video lectures, while others prefer text-based content or interactive discussions. Offering a variety of resources, such as recorded lectures, reading materials, and discussion forums, ensures accessibility.

- **Ensuring Digital Accessibility**: Use captions for videos, readable fonts and color contrast in presentations, and screen-reader-friendly materials to accommodate diverse learning needs.

- **Encouraging Asynchronous Participation**: Not all students can attend live sessions due to work or time differences. Providing discussion forums, recorded lectures, and flexible assignment deadlines helps create an equitable learning environment.

2. Facilitating Engagement in Virtual Classrooms

One of the biggest challenges of hybrid and online learning is maintaining student engagement. Unlike in physical classrooms, where body language and real-time feedback can guide instruction, digital environments require intentional strategies to keep students active and involved.

- **Leveraging Interactive Technology**: Utilize polling tools (e.g., Poll Everywhere, Kahoot), collaborative documents (e.g., Google Docs, Miro), and breakout rooms to facilitate real-time engagement.

- **Encouraging Active Participation**: Ask open-ended questions during live sessions, incorporate peer-to-peer discussions, and assign group projects that require students to interact.

- **Setting Clear Communication Norms**: Establish expectations for participation in discussion boards, virtual office hours, and live sessions to ensure that students remain engaged.

3. Enhancing Instructor Presence in Digital Spaces

A key challenge of online learning is the sense of isolation that students may experience. TAs can mitigate this by maintaining an active and visible presence:

- **Regular Check-Ins**: Send weekly announcements summarizing key topics and upcoming deadlines.

- **Prompt and Personalized Feedback**: Respond to questions in discussion boards and provide detailed, constructive feedback on assignments to foster a sense of connection.

- **Virtual Office Hours and Q&A Sessions**: Offer scheduled times where students can meet for additional support via video conferencing tools like Zoom or Microsoft Teams.

4. Adapting Assessment and Feedback Methods

Assessment in hybrid and online learning requires a shift from traditional testing methods to more flexible, student-centered approaches:

- **Frequent Low-Stakes Assessments**: Instead of relying solely on midterms and finals, incorporate quizzes, reflective journals, and peer feedback activities to gauge understanding throughout the course.

- **Project-Based and Collaborative Assessments**: Encourage students to work on group projects, case studies, or multimedia presentations that demonstrate their knowledge in practical ways.

- **Use of Digital Tools for Feedback**: Leverage video feedback, annotated comments on documents, or voice recordings to provide a more personalized and engaging assessment experience.

5. Managing the Challenges of Hybrid Instruction

Hybrid learning, where some students participate in person while others join remotely, introduces unique logistical challenges that require thoughtful coordination:

- **Balancing Attention Between In-Person and Online Students**: Use dual-camera setups, live chat monitors, and discussion moderators to ensure that remote students remain fully included in class discussions.

- **Aligning Asynchronous and Synchronous Components**: Ensure that online students receive equivalent materials, activities, and opportunities to interact with peers and instructors.

- **Leveraging Learning Management Systems (LMS)**: Platforms like Canvas, Blackboard, and Moodle provide tools for organizing course content, discussions, and assignments in a centralized location, making it easier for hybrid students to stay on track.

Conclusion

Adapting teaching methods for hybrid and online learning environments requires a shift in approach, but with thoughtful planning, TAs can create engaging, inclusive, and effective learning experiences. By embracing digital tools, fostering interaction, and maintaining strong instructor presence, TAs can bridge the gap between physical and virtual classrooms, ensuring that all students—regardless of where or how they learn—receive the support and guidance needed to succeed.

Chapter 5 – Assessment and Feedback

Figure 5.1. Teaching and Learning [113].

Assessment is a cornerstone of the learning process, providing students with insights into their progress while allowing instructors to measure comprehension, performance, and skill development. For Teaching Assistants (TAs), grading and feedback responsibilities require a careful balance of fairness, accuracy, and constructive guidance. Beyond simply assigning grades, effective assessment involves evaluating student work objectively, providing meaningful feedback, and fostering a growth mindset that encourages continuous learning.

This chapter explores the key principles of assessment and feedback, equipping TAs with the skills to evaluate student work effectively while maintaining academic integrity. It covers different types of assessments, including formative (ongoing) and summative (final) evaluations, and the role of rubrics in maintaining consistency in grading. Additionally, this chapter highlights best practices for delivering feedback that is timely, specific, and actionable—helping students improve their understanding and performance.

One of the most challenging aspects of assessment is managing student concerns about grades and handling disputes professionally. This chapter provides strategies for addressing grade-related questions, guiding students through the appeal process, and fostering open, constructive conversations about academic performance. Moreover, it discusses the role of digital grading tools and AI-assisted evaluation systems in streamlining assessment while ensuring objectivity and efficiency.

By the end of this chapter, TAs will be able to:
- Develop fair and transparent grading methods using rubrics and structured evaluation criteria.
- Differentiate between formative and summative assessments to support student learning.
- Provide constructive, meaningful feedback that encourages student growth and improvement.
- Handle grade disputes and student concerns with professionalism and clarity.
- Utilize technology to enhance grading efficiency while maintaining fairness and integrity.
- Promote academic integrity and identify potential issues such as plagiarism.

Effective assessment is more than just measuring student performance—it is an opportunity to support learning, encourage self-reflection, and help students achieve their full potential. By mastering the strategies outlined in this chapter, TAs can become instrumental in creating a fair, supportive, and academically rigorous learning environment.

Grading Responsibilities and Developing Fair Evaluation Methods

Grading is one of the most significant responsibilities of a Teaching Assistant (TA), as it directly impacts students' academic progress and overall learning experience [44]. Effective grading is not just about assigning numerical scores—it requires fairness, consistency, and a deep understanding of how assessment can shape student motivation and learning outcomes [45]. TAs must navigate this responsibility with professionalism, ensuring that evaluation methods align with course objectives, institutional policies, and principles of academic integrity.

Understanding the Role of a TA in Grading

TAs may have varying levels of involvement in grading, depending on the course structure and instructor preferences. Their grading responsibilities often include:

- Scoring Assignments, Exams, and Quizzes: Using established rubrics or guidelines to assess student work objectively.

- Providing Constructive Feedback: Offering specific, actionable comments that help students understand their strengths and areas for improvement.

- Maintaining Grading Consistency: Ensuring uniform application of grading criteria across all students.

- Addressing Student Inquiries on Grades: Explaining grading decisions and guiding students on how to improve future performance.

- Handling Grade Disputes and Appeals: Communicating grading rationale transparently and following institutional protocols for grade reconsiderations.

Given these responsibilities, it is crucial for TAs to adopt grading methods that promote fairness, accuracy, and student engagement with the learning process.

Developing Fair and Effective Evaluation Methods

Fair grading is not just about precision; it is about creating a system that objectively assesses student performance while recognizing individual learning differences [46]. Below are key strategies to develop a fair and effective evaluation framework.

1. Establishing Clear Grading Criteria

One of the most effective ways to ensure fairness is by developing transparent grading standards that outline expectations before students begin an assignment.

- **Use Detailed Rubrics**: A rubric provides a structured framework for grading by defining specific performance levels for different criteria.

  - Example: For an essay, categories might include argument clarity, evidence use, organization, grammar, and originality.

- **Align Criteria with Learning Objectives**: Every graded component should correspond to the course's intended learning outcomes, ensuring that assessment measures what it is supposed to.

- **Communicate Expectations Clearly**: Share rubrics and grading policies with students in advance to eliminate confusion and subjective interpretations.

2. Ensuring Consistency and Objectivity in Grading

To minimize bias and maintain fairness, TAs should implement strategies that promote consistent grading across all students.

- **Grade Blindly When Possible**: Removing student names during grading can help reduce unconscious bias.

- **Grade in Batches**: Instead of grading assignments sequentially, evaluate responses to the same question or section for all students before moving on to the next. This helps ensure uniform standards are applied [47].

- **Use Anchor Responses**: Reviewing a few sample assignments before grading the entire set can help establish a reference for grading standards [48].

- **Collaborate with Other TAs or Instructors**: Periodic discussions with other graders can help ensure consistency across different graders and sections.

3. Balancing Rigor and Compassion

While maintaining high academic standards is essential, fairness in grading also means recognizing individual student challenges and being open to flexibility where appropriate.

- **Recognize Effort and Improvement**: If a student shows significant improvement over time, consider providing opportunities to demonstrate learning beyond a single graded attempt.

- **Accommodate Special Circumstances**: Follow institutional policies on deadline extensions and accommodations for students facing exceptional difficulties, such as illness or personal hardships.

- **Encourage Revisions**: When appropriate, allow students to revise assignments based on feedback, reinforcing the idea that learning is an evolving process.

4. Providing Meaningful and Constructive Feedback

Grades alone are insufficient for student development—clear and constructive feedback is essential for guiding learning and improvement [49]. Effective feedback should be:

- **Specific**: Rather than vague comments like "Good job" or "Needs improvement," highlight precise areas for growth. Example: *"Your thesis is strong, but the argument could be clearer if you provided more supporting examples in paragraph three."*

- **Balanced**: A mix of positive reinforcement and areas for improvement helps maintain motivation.

- **Timely**: Providing feedback promptly allows students to apply insights to future work while the material is still fresh.

- **Actionable**: Offer concrete suggestions on how students can enhance their work rather than just pointing out flaws.

5. Handling Grade Disputes and Student Concerns

Occasionally, students may question their grades or seek clarification on how their work was evaluated. TAs should handle such interactions professionally and transparently.

- **Be Prepared to Explain Grading Decisions**: Keep detailed notes on why certain scores were assigned, referring to rubrics and grading guidelines.

- **Encourage Constructive Dialogue**: Instead of treating grade disputes as conflicts, frame them as opportunities for learning. Example: *"Let's go over the rubric together so we can discuss where improvements can be made."*

- **Follow Institutional Policies**: Ensure that any grade appeals are managed in accordance with university guidelines to maintain fairness and accountability.

Conclusion

Grading is more than just an administrative task—it is a crucial aspect of the learning process that requires fairness, clarity, and a commitment to student growth. By establishing clear criteria, ensuring consistency, balancing academic rigor with compassion, and providing detailed feedback, TAs can create an evaluation process that not only assesses student performance but also supports their ongoing learning journey. Ultimately, fair and effective grading fosters a classroom environment where students feel motivated, informed, and confident in their ability to improve.

Providing Constructive and Meaningful Feedback to Students

Feedback is one of the most powerful tools in the learning process, shaping students' understanding, guiding their improvement, and fostering motivation [50]. For Teaching Assistants (TAs), providing feedback is not merely about correcting mistakes or assigning grades; it is about engaging students in a dialogue that deepens their comprehension, encourages self-reflection, and helps them develop the skills necessary for academic success. Effective feedback should be timely, specific, balanced, and actionable, enabling students to recognize their strengths while addressing areas that need improvement.

The Purpose and Impact of Constructive Feedback

Effective feedback serves multiple functions in education:

- **Enhancing Learning and Understanding**: It helps students grasp complex concepts, clarify misunderstandings, and refine their approach to coursework.

- **Encouraging Self-Assessment and Critical Thinking**: Thoughtful feedback promotes metacognition, allowing students to evaluate their own work and identify strategies for improvement.

- **Boosting Confidence and Motivation**: When delivered constructively, feedback reassures students of their progress and encourages a growth mindset.

- **Facilitating Academic and Professional Skill Development**: Detailed feedback strengthens analytical, writing, and problem-solving abilities, which are essential beyond the classroom.

Characteristics of Effective Feedback

For feedback to be meaningful, it must be:

1. **Timely**

   - Providing feedback soon after the submission of work ensures that students can recall their thought processes and apply the suggestions to future assignments.

   - Feedback delays can lead to disconnection from the learning objectives, making it less useful for student growth.

2. **Specific and Clear**

   - Vague comments like "Needs improvement" or "Good job" do not guide students toward understanding what was done well or how they can improve.

   - Example: Instead of saying, *"Your argument is unclear,"* provide targeted guidance: *"Your thesis is strong, but your supporting evidence in paragraph three could be more explicitly linked to your main argument."*

3. **Balanced (Strengths and Areas for Improvement)**

   - Effective feedback highlights what the student has done well while also pointing out areas for refinement.

   - Example: *"Your analysis of the data is well-structured and thorough. To improve clarity, consider breaking your discussion into smaller sections with subheadings."*

4. **Actionable and Forward-Looking**

   - Feedback should offer clear, practical steps for improvement.

   - Example: Instead of stating, *"Your writing lacks cohesion,"* provide a strategy: *"Try using transition phrases such as 'Building on this idea…' to create a smoother flow between paragraphs."*

5. **Encouraging and Growth-Oriented**

- o Feedback should reinforce that improvement is possible through effort and revision.

- o Example: *"Your engagement with the source material is strong. In your next essay, try integrating more direct quotations to strengthen your argument."*

Strategies for Delivering Meaningful Feedback

1. The "Sandwich" Method (Praise – Constructive Criticism – Encouragement)

A well-known strategy for delivering feedback is the sandwich method, which provides a structured way to balance positive reinforcement with constructive suggestions:

- Start with a Strength: Acknowledge an aspect of the work that was done well.

- Provide a Constructive Critique: Offer targeted suggestions for improvement.

- End with Encouragement: Reinforce the student's potential and provide motivation for applying the feedback.

Example:
"Your argument is well-researched and clearly structured. However, some of your points could be supported with more specific evidence. Consider integrating examples from the readings to strengthen your claims. Keep up the great work—I can see your analytical skills improving!"

2. Use Rubrics and Criteria-Based Feedback

- Grading rubrics provide a transparent evaluation framework, helping students understand how their work aligns with learning objectives.

- When using a rubric, go beyond simply assigning scores; explain how the student's work meets or falls short of specific criteria.

Example: Instead of just marking "3/5" on an organization criterion, provide context:
"Your essay follows a logical sequence, but some transitions between paragraphs could be clearer. Using signpost words like 'therefore' and 'however' will improve flow."

3. Provide Feedback in Different Formats

Different students respond best to different modes of feedback. Consider varying the format based on the nature of the assignment:

- Written Comments: Useful for essays and reports, but should be specific and legible.

- Audio or Video Feedback: Personalized recorded feedback can be more engaging and allows for tone and emphasis.

- Live Feedback Sessions: One-on-one discussions allow students to ask clarifying questions and engage in deeper reflection.

4. Foster a Dialogue, Not Just a One-Way Critique

Encourage students to reflect on and respond to feedback by:

- Asking follow-up questions: *"What do you think could be improved in your analysis?"*

- Allowing revisions: Giving students the opportunity to rework their assignments based on feedback reinforces continuous learning.

5. Tailor Feedback to Student Needs and Learning Styles

- Some students may need more direct guidance, while others benefit from open-ended questions that encourage independent problem-solving.

- Consider cultural and linguistic differences, especially when providing feedback to non-native speakers, by ensuring that language is clear and supportive.

Common Pitfalls to Avoid in Feedback

- Being Overly Harsh or Vague: Feedback should challenge students, but not in a discouraging way. Avoid statements that feel punitive rather than constructive.

- Providing Too Much Feedback at Once: Overwhelming students with excessive corrections can be counterproductive. Focus on the most critical areas for improvement.

- Ignoring Emotional Impact: Feedback should be phrased in a way that maintains a student's confidence while pushing them toward growth.

Conclusion

Providing constructive and meaningful feedback is an essential skill for TAs, one that has the power to shape students' academic journeys and long-term learning habits. When feedback is timely, specific, balanced, and actionable, it not only helps students improve their work but also fosters a mindset of continuous growth and self-improvement [51]. A well-crafted comment or suggestion can be the turning point that transforms a student's struggle into an opportunity for deeper learning. By engaging in thoughtful, personalized, and constructive feedback practices, TAs can play a pivotal role in guiding students toward academic success and intellectual confidence.

Academic Integrity: Identifying and Addressing Plagiarism

Academic integrity is the cornerstone of a fair and credible educational system, ensuring that students engage in original thinking, proper research practices, and ethical scholarship. One of the most significant challenges to academic integrity is plagiarism, which undermines the learning process and devalues the efforts of honest students. As a Teaching Assistant (TA), understanding how to identify, prevent, and address plagiarism is essential in fostering a culture of academic honesty and guiding students toward ethical research and writing practices.

Understanding Plagiarism

Plagiarism occurs when an individual presents someone else's work, ideas, or words as their own without proper attribution. It can take many forms, ranging from deliberate deception to unintentional mistakes due to a lack of understanding of citation rules [52].

Types of Plagiarism

1. **Direct Plagiarism**

    - Copying entire passages, sentences, or paragraphs from a source without quotation marks or proper attribution.

    - Example: A student submits an essay that includes verbatim content from a scholarly article without citation.

2. **Self-Plagiarism**

    - Reusing one's own previous work (e.g., submitting a paper written for one course to another without permission) [53].

    - Example: A student repurposes a research paper from a prior semester without informing the instructor.

3. **Paraphrasing Plagiarism**

    - Restating someone else's ideas in different words without citation, often keeping the structure and key concepts intact.

    - Example: A student rewrites a passage from a textbook in their own words but does not credit the original author.

4. **Patchwriting**

    - A mix of copied phrases and slight rewording that fails to create an original piece [54].

    - Example: A student substitutes a few words in a copied sentence without significant rephrasing or citing the source.

5. **Mosaic Plagiarism**

    - Blending multiple sources together without proper acknowledgment, making it appear as though the work is original [55].

    - Example: A student takes portions from different articles and stitches them into their paper without citations.

6. **Accidental Plagiarism**

    - Failing to cite properly due to unfamiliarity with citation styles or mismanagement of sources [56].

  o Example: A student forgets to include quotation marks around a direct quote, mistakenly treating it as their own writing.

Detecting Plagiarism

Identifying plagiarism requires vigilance and familiarity with student writing styles, as inconsistencies can often signal potential academic misconduct. TAs should be aware of the following indicators:

- **Inconsistencies in Writing Style**: A sudden shift in vocabulary, tone, or complexity within a single piece of work may suggest copied content.

- **Disjointed Flow of Ideas**: When a paper lacks coherence, it may indicate that different sections were taken from multiple sources.

- **Mismatched Citations or Formatting**: Incorrect or missing references can suggest improperly borrowed material.

- **Unusual Sentence Structure or Unexplained Concepts**: If a student includes advanced terminology or ideas not covered in class, it may warrant further investigation.

- **Use of Online Plagiarism Detection Tools**: Software such as Turnitin, Grammarly, or Copyscape can help identify copied text by comparing submissions against academic papers, websites, and databases [57].

Addressing Plagiarism

Once plagiarism is identified, it is crucial to address it appropriately, considering both intent and institutional policies. Handling plagiarism effectively involves education, fair consequences, and reinforcing academic integrity principles.

Step 1: Investigate the Case

- Verify whether plagiarism has occurred by cross-referencing the suspicious content with original sources.

- Differentiate between intentional misconduct and accidental errors due to citation misunderstandings.

Step 2: Follow Institutional Policies

- Most universities have academic integrity guidelines outlining procedures for handling plagiarism cases.

- Depending on severity, consequences may range from a warning and resubmission to formal disciplinary action.

Step 3: Educate Rather than Punish (When Appropriate)

- If the plagiarism appears unintentional, use the opportunity to teach the student proper citation techniques.

- Provide guidance on using quotation marks, paraphrasing effectively, and employing citation management tools (e.g., Zotero, Mendeley).

Step 4: Encourage Ethical Academic Practices

- Offer workshops or additional resources on plagiarism prevention.

- Promote the importance of integrity by discussing real-world consequences (e.g., damaged credibility in academia and professional fields).

- Suggest tools like Purdue OWL, citation generators, and style guides (APA, MLA, Chicago) to help students format their references correctly.

Preventing Plagiarism Through Proactive Teaching

TAs play a crucial role in reducing plagiarism by fostering an environment where students understand and value original work. Strategies for prevention include:

- **Clarifying Expectations**: At the beginning of the semester, discuss academic integrity policies and what constitutes plagiarism.

- **Teaching Proper Citation Skills**: Offer mini-sessions on paraphrasing, summarizing, and correct citation practices.

- **Assigning Incremental Writing Tasks**: Breaking assignments into drafts and requiring annotated bibliographies can prevent last-minute copying [58].

- **Encouraging Original Thought**: Design assignments that require personal reflection, case studies, or unique applications of knowledge to minimize opportunities for plagiarism.

- **Using Technology to Support Integrity**: Encourage students to check their own work with plagiarism detection software before submission.

Conclusion

Maintaining academic integrity is essential for fostering a culture of honesty, intellectual growth, and ethical scholarship. As a TA, identifying and addressing plagiarism requires a balance of vigilance, fairness, and education. While punitive measures may sometimes be necessary, proactive teaching strategies can significantly reduce plagiarism cases by equipping students with the skills and knowledge to produce original, well-cited work. By promoting ethical academic practices, TAs not only help students succeed in their coursework but also prepare them for responsible engagement in their future academic and professional careers.

Managing Student Complaints About Grades and Assignments

Grading is one of the most sensitive aspects of academic assessment, and students occasionally challenge their scores due to concerns about fairness, misunderstanding of evaluation criteria, or personal frustration. As a Teaching Assistant (TA), handling student complaints about grades and assignments requires professionalism, patience, and a clear understanding of both course policies and institutional guidelines. Effective management of grade-related concerns not only resolves individual disputes but also fosters a culture of transparency, accountability, and trust between students and educators.

Understanding the Nature of Student Complaints

Students may express dissatisfaction with their grades for a variety of reasons, including:

1. **Perceived Unfairness** – Believing that their work was graded too harshly or that inconsistencies exist in grading.

2. **Misinterpretation of the Assignment Requirements** – Feeling that they met the criteria but received an unexpected grade.

3. **Comparisons with Peers** – Assuming that another student received a higher grade for similar work.

4. **Lack of Clarity in Feedback** – Being unsure why they lost points or how to improve future work.

5. **Desire for a Higher Grade Without Justification** – Hoping to negotiate a better grade without a substantive basis.

Regardless of the reason, every complaint should be handled with fairness and professionalism, ensuring that students feel heard while maintaining the integrity of the grading process.

Key Strategies for Managing Grade Complaints

1. Establish Clear Grading Policies from the Start

Preventing grade disputes begins before assignments are even submitted. As a TA, you can minimize confusion by:

- Providing Detailed Rubrics: A well-structured rubric clarifies expectations and grading criteria.

- Explaining Grading Policies in Advance: Reinforce that grades are based on objective assessment, not personal judgment.

- Emphasizing Constructive Feedback: Ensure that feedback is clear, specific, and actionable, so students understand why they received a particular score.

When students know what to expect, they are less likely to feel blindsided by their grades.

2. Responding to Grade Complaints Professionally

When a student approaches you with a grading concern, it is important to maintain professionalism and create a productive dialogue. Use the following approach to handle complaints effectively:

Step 1: Acknowledge the Concern Respectfully

Even if a complaint seems unwarranted, listen to the student with an open mind. A dismissive response may escalate frustration.

- **Example Response**:
  "I understand that grades are important, and I appreciate you taking the time to discuss your concerns. Let's go through your assignment together."

Step 2: Review the Graded Work Together

Walk the student through the grading rubric and feedback provided. Point out where the work meets expectations and where improvements were needed.

- If the complaint is valid: If an error in grading is found, acknowledge it and follow the appropriate procedures for grade adjustments.

- If the grading is justified: Explain how the student's work aligns with the rubric and course expectations.

Step 3: Encourage Constructive Reflection

Instead of focusing solely on the grade, shift the conversation to what the student can do to improve in future assignments.

- **Example Response**:
  "Your analysis was strong, but your evidence wasn't clearly linked to your argument. Let's talk about strategies to strengthen this connection in your next paper."

Step 4: Maintain Firmness but Fairness

While it is essential to be empathetic, do not give in to unwarranted pressure. Ensure that grade adjustments are based on merit, not persistence.

- If a student repeatedly insists on a grade change without justification, calmly reinforce that grades are based on objective evaluation.

- If the student is aggressive or argumentative, remain composed and remind them of institutional policies regarding grade appeals.

3. Handling Grade Disputes with Larger Implications

Occasionally, a student's complaint may indicate a broader issue, such as grading inconsistencies or unclear assignment instructions. In such cases:

- Consult the Instructor or Course Coordinator: If multiple students raise similar concerns, it may be necessary to clarify expectations with the lead instructor.

- Ensure Consistency Across Sections: If multiple TAs are grading the same assignment, coordinate with them to align grading standards.

- Document Complaints and Resolutions: Keeping a record of grade disputes ensures transparency and provides reference points in case of formal appeals.

4. Guiding Students Through the Formal Grade Appeal Process

If a student remains dissatisfied after discussing their concerns with you, they may choose to pursue a formal grade appeal. In such cases:

- Direct the Student to Institutional Guidelines: Universities have formal policies for grade disputes, typically requiring a written appeal with specific justifications.

- Encourage a Professional Approach: Advise students to focus on factual concerns rather than emotional arguments.

- Provide Documentation If Needed: If requested, supply records of feedback, grading rubrics, and correspondence related to the dispute.

By guiding students through the proper channels, you ensure that concerns are addressed fairly while upholding academic policies.

Common Pitfalls to Avoid When Handling Grade Complaints

- Taking Complaints Personally: Grading disputes are rarely personal; they stem from student concerns about their academic performance. Maintain objectivity.

- Providing Inconsistent Justifications: Ensure that your explanations align with grading criteria, avoiding arbitrary justifications.

- Overexplaining or Becoming Defensive: Provide clear, concise responses without excessive justification. Defensiveness can escalate conflicts.

- Granting Grade Changes Without Merit: While it is easier to concede to persistent students, doing so undermines grading fairness for the entire class.

- Failing to Document Complaints: Keeping records of grading concerns helps protect against misunderstandings and ensures accountability.

Conclusion

Managing student complaints about grades and assignments is an inevitable part of being a TA. Handling these concerns with professionalism, clarity, and fairness not only ensures academic integrity but also helps students learn from their mistakes and improve their work. By establishing clear grading policies, responding to complaints with empathy and logic, and maintaining consistency in evaluation, TAs can foster a constructive learning environment where students feel heard while respecting the integrity of the grading process. Ultimately, a well-handled grade dispute can be a teaching moment—one that helps students develop resilience, accountability, and a deeper understanding of academic expectations.

Chapter 6: Leveraging Technology in Teaching Assistance

Technology has revolutionized education, transforming the way instructors deliver content, assess student learning, and facilitate communication. For Teaching Assistants (TAs), understanding and effectively utilizing digital tools is no longer optional—it is a fundamental skill that enhances instructional efficiency, engagement, and accessibility. Whether managing an online course, grading assignments through digital platforms, or using artificial intelligence (AI) to personalize student learning, technology provides countless opportunities to optimize the teaching and learning experience.

This chapter explores how TAs can leverage technology to streamline course management, enhance student engagement, and support academic success. It covers essential digital tools such as Learning Management Systems (LMS) like Canvas, Blackboard, and Moodle, which serve as the backbone of modern education by centralizing assignments, communication, and assessments. Additionally, this chapter delves into AI-powered grading systems, digital

Figure 6.1. Teaching and Learning [113].

collaboration platforms, and tools designed to provide personalized learning support.

A critical aspect of using technology in education is ensuring accessibility for all students, including those with disabilities. This chapter provides best practices for making digital content inclusive, incorporating assistive technologies, and adhering to institutional and legal guidelines for digital accessibility. Furthermore, it discusses the ethical implications of using AI and automation in education, emphasizing the balance between technological efficiency and the human element of teaching.

By the end of this chapter, TAs will be able to:
- Utilize Learning Management Systems (LMS) effectively for course organization, assignments, and grading.
- Implement AI-powered tools to enhance grading efficiency and personalized learning support.
- Use digital platforms to facilitate student collaboration and engagement.
- Ensure digital accessibility and inclusivity for students with disabilities.
- Address ethical considerations in technology-enhanced teaching.

- Adapt to emerging educational technologies to stay current in the evolving landscape of digital learning.

As education continues to evolve, TAs who embrace technology will be better equipped to support instructors, streamline administrative tasks, and create engaging and inclusive learning environments. By mastering the tools and strategies outlined in this chapter, TAs will enhance not only their effectiveness in the classroom but also their professional growth in an increasingly technology-driven world.

Introduction to Learning Management Systems (LMS) (Canvas, Blackboard, Moodle)

In the modern educational landscape, Learning Management Systems (LMS) play a pivotal role in facilitating instruction, streamlining administrative tasks, and enhancing the overall learning experience. For Teaching Assistants (TAs), mastering an LMS is essential, as it serves as the central hub for managing course materials, assignments, assessments, communication, and student progress tracking. Platforms such as Canvas, Blackboard, and Moodle are widely used in universities and colleges, each offering unique functionalities while sharing core features that support both instructors and students [59].

The Role of Learning Management Systems in Education

An LMS is more than just a repository for course content—it is a dynamic environment designed to support teaching, learning, and administrative efficiency. These platforms provide a structured framework for:

- **Course Organization**: Hosting syllabi, lecture materials, reading lists, and multimedia content in an accessible format.

- **Assignment Management**: Allowing students to submit work digitally while enabling TAs to provide timely feedback and grading.

- **Assessment and Quizzes**: Automating quizzes and exams with customizable settings, including multiple-choice, open-ended, and time-restricted tests.

- **Communication and Collaboration**: Facilitating discussions, announcements, and messaging between students and instructors.

- **Analytics and Student Tracking**: Providing insights into student engagement, assignment completion rates, and performance trends.

By leveraging these features, TAs can enhance efficiency, improve student engagement, and support a seamless learning experience in both in-person and online courses.

Overview of Popular LMS Platforms

While various LMS platforms exist, three of the most widely adopted systems in higher education are Canvas, Blackboard, and Moodle. Each has distinct features and advantages, yet they share common functionalities that TAs must understand to effectively assist in course management.

1. Canvas

Canvas is a modern, intuitive, and user-friendly LMS that has gained popularity for its streamlined interface and integration with external tools [60].

- **Key Features**:
    - Drag-and-drop content organization for ease of navigation.
    - SpeedGrader for efficient grading with inline comments, rubrics, and video feedback.
    - Deep integration with third-party applications such as Google Drive, Turnitin, and Zoom.
    - Mobile-friendly design, allowing students and TAs to access course content on the go.
    - Robust analytics tools to track student participation and engagement.
- **Why TAs Should Use It**:
    - The intuitive design reduces the learning curve, making it easy to manage discussions, grade assignments, and post announcements.
    - Automated notifications help keep students informed about due dates and instructor feedback.

2. Blackboard

Blackboard is one of the longest-standing LMS platforms, known for its comprehensive tools and versatility in supporting various teaching modalities [61].

- **Key Features**:
    - Customizable course structures with modules, folders, and adaptive release of content.
    - Robust assessment capabilities, including auto-graded quizzes and in-depth feedback options.
    - Integrated virtual classroom tools (Blackboard Collaborate) for synchronous learning.
    - A gradebook that allows for weighted grading, categories, and performance tracking.

- o Support for SCORM-compliant content, enabling interactive learning experiences [61].

- **Why TAs Should Use It**:

  - o Blackboard is commonly used in large institutions, making it a valuable skill for academic professionals.

  - o The platform's grading and reporting tools provide detailed insights into student progress.

3. Moodle

Moodle is an open-source LMS that offers extensive customization options, making it ideal for institutions that require flexibility in course design and administration [62].

- **Key Features**:

  - o Modular design that allows institutions to tailor course layouts and learning paths.

  - o Discussion forums, peer feedback tools, and interactive learning modules.

  - o Strong focus on collaborative learning, with built-in group work functionalities.

  - o Gamification features such as badges and progress tracking to enhance engagement [63].

  - o Offline access options, allowing students to download materials and work asynchronously.

- **Why TAs Should Use It**:

  - o Moodle is widely used in online and blended learning environments, offering rich interaction tools.

  - o Its customizable nature enables innovative teaching approaches tailored to diverse learning needs.

Essential LMS Functions Every TA Should Master

Regardless of the platform, TAs should develop proficiency in core LMS functionalities to effectively support instructors and students. Key areas to focus on include:

1. Managing Course Content

- Uploading and organizing lecture slides, readings, and multimedia materials.

- Structuring content using modules or folders to ensure logical progression.

- Embedding links, videos, and interactive tools to enhance engagement.

2. Facilitating Assignments and Grading

- Setting up assignment submission portals with clear due dates and instructions.

- Using built-in grading tools such as rubrics, inline commenting, and batch feedback.

- Leveraging plagiarism detection software integrations (e.g., Turnitin) to ensure academic integrity.

3. Engaging Students Through Communication Tools

- Posting announcements and reminders to keep students informed.

- Moderating discussion forums and responding to student inquiries.

- Setting up virtual office hours through integrated video conferencing tools.

4. Tracking Student Progress and Providing Support

- Monitoring student participation and engagement through analytics dashboards.

- Identifying struggling students and offering targeted support.

- Running reports to analyze trends in performance and attendance.

Best Practices for TAs Using an LMS

To maximize the effectiveness of an LMS, TAs should adopt best practices that enhance student experience and instructional efficiency:

- **Stay Organized**: Maintain a clear and structured layout for course materials to prevent confusion.

- **Be Proactive with Communication**: Use announcements and discussion boards to provide timely updates and clarify common student questions.

- **Utilize Automation Features**: Schedule assignments, quizzes, and reminders to streamline administrative tasks.

- **Encourage Student Interaction**: Promote participation in discussion forums and collaborative activities.

- **Regularly Check for Updates**: Familiarize yourself with new features and integrations that can enhance the learning experience.

Conclusion

Learning Management Systems such as Canvas, Blackboard, and Moodle serve as indispensable tools in modern education, enabling efficient course management, assessment, and student engagement. As a TA, developing expertise in LMS platforms enhances your ability to support instructors, provide timely feedback, and create a seamless learning experience for students. By mastering essential LMS functions and adopting best practices, TAs can play a vital role in ensuring that courses run smoothly, students stay engaged, and academic success is maximized in both in-person and digital learning environments.

Using Digital Tools for Grading, Assignments, and Communication

The integration of digital tools in education has transformed the way Teaching Assistants (TAs) manage grading, assignments, and communication, making these tasks more efficient, transparent, and accessible. Technology enables TAs to streamline administrative responsibilities while enhancing student engagement, feedback quality, and overall course management. Mastering the use of these digital tools allows TAs to provide timely support, ensure consistency in grading, and foster better interaction with students and instructors.

1. Digital Tools for Grading: Enhancing Efficiency and Fairness

Grading is one of the most time-consuming yet critical responsibilities of a TA. Digital grading tools not only speed up the evaluation process but also help maintain consistency, accuracy, and fairness. These tools offer features such as automated scoring, rubrics, and inline feedback, which improve both the grading experience and student learning outcomes [64].

Key Digital Grading Tools and Their Features

1.1 Learning Management System (LMS) Grading Tools

Most **Learning Management Systems (LMS)**, such as Canvas, Blackboard, and Moodle, provide built-in grading features that help TAs evaluate student work efficiently.

- **SpeedGrader (Canvas)**: Allows inline grading, rubric-based assessment, and video or audio feedback.

- **Grade Center (Blackboard)**: Offers weighted grading, custom grading scales, and integration with plagiarism detection tools.

- **Moodle Grading Interface**: Supports flexible grading schemes, competency-based assessment, and feedback templates.

1.2 Automated and AI-Powered Grading Tools

Artificial Intelligence (AI) and automation have made grading more efficient, especially for objective assessments such as multiple-choice quizzes and coding assignments.

- Gradescope: Uses AI-assisted grading for written responses, allowing TAs to grade faster while ensuring consistency across responses.

- Turnitin and Grammarly: Analyze student writing for originality and grammar, helping maintain academic integrity while improving student writing skills.

- AutoGrader (for Coding Assignments): Tools like Codio and CodePost allow automated evaluation of programming assignments based on predefined test cases.

1.3 Rubrics and Feedback Tools

- Google Classroom & Microsoft Teams: Allow the creation of rubrics for assignments, making grading transparent for students.

- Kaizena: Enables voice and text feedback for essays and written work, helping students understand areas of improvement more effectively.

Best Practices for Digital Grading:

- Use rubrics to ensure consistency and fairness in grading.
- Provide clear and constructive feedback using inline comments and annotation tools.
- Leverage automated tools for objective assessments but manually review subjective components to ensure fairness.
- Maintain digital records of student performance to track progress and identify struggling students.

2. Digital Tools for Assignments: Submission, Organization, and Plagiarism Detection

The traditional method of collecting physical assignments has largely been replaced by digital submission systems, which improve accessibility, organization, and feedback quality. Digital assignment tools help in managing deadlines, preventing plagiarism, and ensuring secure storage of student work.

2.1 Assignment Submission Platforms

Most LMS platforms offer **digital dropboxes** where students can submit assignments in various formats, including Word documents, PDFs, and multimedia files.

- Canvas Assignments & Blackboard Submission Portals: Enable scheduled submissions, file uploads, and grading integration.

- Google Classroom & Microsoft Teams: Allow seamless assignment collection with cloud storage, eliminating the risk of lost work.

- Dropbox & OneDrive for Education: Facilitate shared folders for student submissions, particularly for large file formats.

2.2 Plagiarism Detection and Academic Integrity Tools

Ensuring **originality and academic integrity** is crucial when managing assignments. Plagiarism detection software helps TAs identify copied content and guide students toward ethical academic practices.

- Turnitin: Compares submissions against academic databases and online sources, highlighting potential plagiarism.

- SafeAssign (Blackboard): Analyzes content originality within an LMS environment.

- Grammarly & QuillBot: Help students refine writing clarity and originality while preventing unintentional plagiarism.

2.3 Collaborative Assignment Tools

For group projects and interactive assignments, digital tools enable **real-time collaboration** and seamless submission tracking.

- Google Docs & Microsoft Word Online: Allow multiple students to work on the same document simultaneously.

- Miro & Padlet: Digital whiteboards for brainstorming, visual organization, and group activities.

- Perusall: Facilitates collaborative reading and annotation, encouraging deeper engagement with course materials.

Best Practices for Managing Digital Assignments:

- Set clear deadlines and enable automated reminders to keep students on track.

- Use plagiarism detection tools not just for penalization but also as a teaching tool for academic integrity.

- Encourage the use of version control in collaborative assignments (e.g., Google Docs' revision history).

- Provide multi-format feedback (text, audio, video) to cater to diverse learning styles.

3. Digital Tools for Communication: Engaging and Supporting Students

Effective communication is critical in any teaching role, and digital tools provide TAs with various channels to interact with students, address their concerns, and foster engagement. Whether it is responding to queries, conducting office hours, or facilitating discussions, the right communication platform can enhance accessibility, responsiveness, and student participation.

3.1 LMS-Based Communication Features

- Announcements (Canvas, Blackboard, Moodle): Keep students updated on deadlines, changes, and important course information.

- Discussion Forums: Facilitate asynchronous discussions where students can engage in peer learning and ask questions.

- Messaging Systems: Enable private communication between students and TAs, ensuring confidentiality when discussing grades or personal concerns.

3.2 Virtual Office Hours and Video Conferencing

Virtual meetings have become essential for supporting students remotely. Platforms such as:

- Zoom & Microsoft Teams: Support live Q&A sessions, breakout rooms for small-group discussions, and screen sharing for concept explanations.

- Google Meet: Allows direct integration with Google Classroom for quick access to one-on-one or group meetings.

- Calendly & Google Calendar Scheduling: Streamline office hour appointments by letting students book time slots without email exchanges.

3.3 Instant Messaging & Community Platforms

For more informal yet structured communication:

- Slack & Discord: Provide organized chat channels for different topics, promoting collaborative discussions.

- Edmodo & Piazza: Education-focused Q&A platforms where students can ask questions, get peer responses, and receive instructor clarification.

Best Practices for Digital Communication:
- Establish communication norms (e.g., response time expectations, preferred platforms).
- Use structured discussion boards to encourage peer-to-peer learning.
- Maintain professional tone and boundaries, especially in informal communication platforms.
- Offer multiple channels of communication to accommodate different student preferences.

Conclusion

Digital tools have revolutionized the way Teaching Assistants handle grading, assignments, and communication, making these processes more efficient, transparent, and student-centered. By leveraging LMS platforms, automated grading tools, plagiarism detection software, and communication systems, TAs can enhance both their own workflow and the overall student learning experience. Mastering these tools not only makes grading and administrative tasks more manageable but also enables TAs to provide timely support, deliver high-quality feedback, and foster engagement in both face-to-face and online learning environments. When used effectively, digital tools empower TAs to act as facilitators of learning, ensuring that students receive the guidance and support they need to succeed.

Best Practices for Using AI Tools for Personalized Learning Support

The integration of Artificial Intelligence (AI) in education has opened new possibilities for personalized learning, enabling Teaching Assistants (TAs) to provide targeted support that enhances student engagement, comprehension, and performance. AI-driven tools can adapt to individual learning styles, identify areas of struggle, and offer customized recommendations, making education more accessible, efficient, and student-centered. However, leveraging AI effectively requires a strategic approach that balances technological capabilities with pedagogical best practices.

This section explores best practices for using AI tools to support personalized learning while ensuring ethical considerations, effectiveness, and a human-centered approach.

1. Understanding the Role of AI in Personalized Learning

AI-driven learning tools enhance the traditional teaching assistant role by providing adaptive, data-driven, and interactive learning experiences [65]. The key benefits of AI in personalized learning include:

- Adaptive Learning Paths: AI can analyze student performance and adjust the difficulty level or recommend additional resources based on individual progress.

- Automated Feedback and Assessment: AI-powered tools can provide instant feedback on assignments, quizzes, and essays, helping students learn from their mistakes in real time [66].

- Predictive Analytics for Student Support: AI can identify at-risk students by detecting patterns in engagement, participation, and performance, allowing TAs to intervene early [67].

- 24/7 Learning Assistance: Chatbots and AI tutors can assist students outside of traditional class hours, answering frequently asked questions and guiding them through coursework.

While AI can enhance learning, it should be used as a complement to human interaction, not a replacement for personalized instructor support.

2. Best Practices for Using AI Tools in Personalized Learning

To maximize the effectiveness of AI in education, TAs should implement the following best practices:

2.1 Selecting the Right AI Tools for Learning Support

Different AI-powered platforms serve unique purposes, and choosing the right tool is essential for effective personalization.

- AI-Powered Tutors (e.g., Coursera's AI Coach, ScribeSense)
  - Provide personalized explanations and targeted practice questions based on student progress.

- Intelligent Writing Assistants (e.g., Grammarly, QuillBot)
  - Help students refine their writing by offering grammar, style, and clarity suggestions.

- Adaptive Learning Platforms (e.g., Knewton, Carnegie Learning)
  - Modify lesson difficulty based on student responses, reinforcing concepts before progressing.

- AI Chatbots for Student Support (e.g., IBM Watson Tutor, ChatGPT-powered course assistants)
  - Answer frequently asked questions and guide students through course material.

Best Practice: Choose AI tools that align with the course's objectives, student needs, and institutional policies on technology use.

2.2 Using AI to Enhance, Not Replace, Human Interaction

While AI can automate repetitive tasks and provide individualized learning recommendations, human engagement remains critical to student success.

- Use AI for routine queries but offer personal interactions for complex discussions, mentorship, and emotional support.

- Ensure AI-generated feedback is supplemented with TA insights, especially for nuanced academic writing and critical thinking exercises.

- Encourage students to critically evaluate AI-generated content rather than relying on it passively.

Best Practice: AI should act as an enhancement tool, not a substitute for human mentorship, creativity, and intellectual engagement.

2.3 Personalizing Learning Without Encouraging Dependence on AI

AI should empower students to become independent learners rather than creating over-reliance on automated assistance.

- Encourage students to use AI as a study aid, not a content generator—for example, using AI to get explanations rather than expecting AI to write assignments for them.

- Teach students critical thinking skills so they can evaluate AI-generated responses for accuracy and bias.

- Balance AI-driven recommendations with self-reflection activities, ensuring students engage actively in their learning process.

Best Practice: Guide students on how to use AI responsibly and ethically, ensuring they develop analytical and self-directed learning skills.

2.4 Leveraging AI for Early Intervention and Academic Support

AI tools can predict learning difficulties and flag students who may require additional support [68].

- Monitor student progress through AI-generated analytics to identify patterns of struggle or disengagement.

- Use AI-driven assessment tools to pinpoint knowledge gaps and tailor remedial instruction accordingly.

- Engage with students who show signs of low participation by offering additional support based on AI insights.

Best Practice: Combine AI analytics with human judgment to provide proactive interventions before students fall behind.

2.5 Addressing Ethical Considerations and AI Limitations

AI, while powerful, comes with ethical concerns and limitations that TAs must navigate responsibly.

- Data Privacy: Ensure that AI tools comply with institutional and legal standards for student data protection (e.g., FERPA, GDPR) [69].

- Bias in AI: AI algorithms may reflect biases present in training data, potentially leading to inequitable learning recommendations.

- Over-Reliance on AI-Graded Work: Automated grading tools may misinterpret nuances in student responses, requiring human oversight.

Best Practice: Use AI ethically and transparently, ensuring students understand its limitations and know how to use it responsibly.

3. Practical Applications of AI for TAs

3.1 Enhancing Student Feedback with AI

- Use AI-powered grading tools (e.g., Gradescope) to provide faster feedback on objective assessments.

- Encourage students to refine their writing using AI-enhanced proofreading tools before submitting assignments.

- Use AI-generated learning analytics dashboards to tailor feedback based on student performance trends.

3.2 Supporting Diverse Learning Needs

- AI-driven speech-to-text tools help students with disabilities access course content more effectively.

- Multilingual AI translation tools can assist non-native English speakers in understanding course materials.

- Adaptive learning platforms provide extra practice and scaffolding for students who need additional support.

3.3 Automating Repetitive Tasks to Free Up TA Time

- Use AI chatbots for answering frequently asked student questions, reducing email overload.

- Automate content summarization and transcription to make lectures more accessible.

- Implement AI-powered scheduling assistants to manage virtual office hours efficiently.

4. Conclusion

The effective use of AI tools in personalized learning support can enhance student engagement, streamline administrative tasks, and improve learning outcomes. However, best practices must be followed to ensure AI serves as an aid rather than a replacement for human instruction. By selecting the right AI tools, maintaining ethical standards, balancing AI with human mentorship, and promoting critical engagement with AI-generated content, TAs can leverage AI to create a more inclusive, efficient, and personalized educational experience.

Ultimately, AI should act as a force multiplier, allowing TAs to focus on high-value interactions, mentorship, and personalized guidance, while technology handles routine tasks and provides data-driven insights. When used effectively, AI empowers both TAs and students to navigate the learning process with greater efficiency, adaptability, and success.

Ensuring Digital Accessibility for Students with Disabilities

As technology becomes an integral part of education, ensuring digital accessibility is essential for creating an inclusive learning environment where all students—regardless of ability—can engage with course materials, participate in discussions, and complete assessments without barriers. For Teaching Assistants (TAs), understanding and implementing digital accessibility is not just about compliance with institutional policies or legal frameworks such as the Americans with Disabilities Act (ADA) and Section 508 of the Rehabilitation Act; it is about fostering equity, inclusivity, and meaningful engagement in both in-person and online courses.

Ensuring digital accessibility requires intentional design choices, the use of assistive technologies, and proactive support strategies to meet the diverse needs of students with disabilities. This section explores best practices for making digital learning spaces more accessible, addressing common challenges, and leveraging technology to remove barriers.

1. Understanding Digital Accessibility in Education

Digital accessibility ensures that students with disabilities can:

- Access course content in multiple formats (e.g., text, audio, video, and interactive elements).

- Navigate digital platforms independently using assistive technologies.

- Engage with assignments, discussions, and assessments without technological limitations.

- Receive equitable opportunities to succeed in their academic work.

Students may have disabilities that affect vision, hearing, mobility, cognitive processing, or learning, and each category presents unique accessibility considerations. For example:

- A visually impaired student may require screen readers or alternative text descriptions for images.

- A deaf or hard-of-hearing student may need captions or transcripts for video lectures.

- A student with mobility impairments may need keyboard navigation options rather than mouse-dependent interactions.

- A student with dyslexia may benefit from text-to-speech tools and customizable font settings.

By anticipating diverse needs and incorporating accessibility principles from the start, TAs can help create a barrier-free learning experience that benefits all students.

2. Best Practices for Digital Accessibility

2.1 Designing Accessible Course Materials

Ensuring that course materials are accessible from the outset reduces the need for last-minute accommodations and fosters a more inclusive learning experience.

Text-Based Content Accessibility

- Use clear, structured formatting (e.g., headings, bullet points, and short paragraphs) to make documents easier to navigate.

- Ensure that all PDFs and documents are screen-reader friendly by enabling text recognition (avoid scanned images of text).

- Choose accessible fonts (e.g., Arial, Verdana, or OpenDyslexic) and avoid small font sizes or excessive italics.

- Use high contrast between text and background to improve readability (e.g., black text on a white or light background).

Image and Multimedia Accessibility

- Provide alt text (alternative text) for all images, graphs, and charts so screen readers can describe them.

- Ensure descriptive captions for complex visual content such as infographics and data visualizations.

- Avoid using color alone to convey meaning (e.g., differentiate with text labels or patterns).

Video and Audio Accessibility

- Include closed captions or subtitles for all videos to support students who are deaf or hard of hearing.

- Provide full transcripts for video and audio content to allow text-based engagement.

- Ensure audio clarity and minimize background noise in recorded lectures or podcasts.

- Offer adjustable playback speeds for videos to accommodate different learning paces.

Best Practice: Always check whether your Learning Management System (LMS) (e.g., Canvas, Blackboard, Moodle) supports automated captioning and alternative text descriptions, and encourage students to utilize these features.

2.2 Ensuring Accessible Digital Tools and Platforms

TAs frequently interact with LMS platforms, discussion boards, and third-party educational tools, and must ensure these systems are navigable for all students.

Choosing Accessible Learning Platforms

- Use LMS platforms with built-in accessibility features, such as Canvas Ally (which checks course material accessibility).

- Ensure that all interactive elements (quizzes, discussion forums, polls, simulations) are keyboard-navigable.

- Avoid tools that require fine motor skills alone (e.g., drag-and-drop activities without keyboard alternatives).

Ensuring Website and Link Accessibility

- Provide descriptive hyperlinks instead of vague terms like *"Click Here"* (e.g., use *"Read the Accessibility Guidelines for Canvas"* instead).

- Check that external resources comply with Web Content Accessibility Guidelines (WCAG) [70].

- Ensure web pages are responsive for different devices, especially for students using screen magnifiers.

Keyboard and Screen Reader Navigation

- Avoid relying solely on mouse-dependent navigation; ensure that all key features are accessible via keyboard shortcuts.

- Test content with screen readers (e.g., NVDA, JAWS, VoiceOver) to verify compatibility.

Best Practice: Encourage students who use assistive technologies to provide feedback on accessibility barriers they may encounter in course materials.

2.3 Supporting Students with Assistive Technologies

Assistive technologies help students interact with digital learning environments in ways that align with their abilities. TAs should be familiar with common assistive tools that students may use.

Vision Impairment

- Screen readers (e.g., JAWS, NVDA, VoiceOver) convert on-screen text to speech [71].

- Braille displays translate digital content into braille for visually impaired students.

- Magnification software enlarges on-screen text and images.

Hearing Impairment

- Real-time transcription tools (e.g., Otter.ai, Rev, Live Caption) provide instant subtitles for lectures.

- Video relay services (VRS) allow students to communicate using sign language interpreters.

Cognitive and Learning Disabilities

- Text-to-speech software (e.g., Kurzweil, Read&Write) helps students with dyslexia process text-based content [72].

- Speech-to-text tools (e.g., Dragon NaturallySpeaking) assist students who struggle with written communication.

- Distraction reduction apps (e.g., Focus@Will, Pomodoro timers) aid students with ADHD in maintaining concentration.

Best Practice: When recommending digital resources, ensure they integrate well with assistive technologies that students may already be using.

2.4 Providing Proactive TA Support for Digital Accessibility

TAs play a critical role in advocating for accessibility and supporting students with disabilities throughout the course. Key responsibilities include:

- Regularly testing digital materials for accessibility before students encounter barriers.

- Encouraging open communication so students feel comfortable requesting accommodations.

- Being flexible with assessment formats, allowing alternative ways for students to demonstrate their learning (e.g., oral responses instead of written essays for students with dysgraphia).

- Collaborating with Disability Services Offices to ensure students receive necessary accommodations.

- Providing accessible office hours (e.g., offering virtual sessions with captions for students who cannot attend in person).

Best Practice: If unsure whether a digital tool or platform is accessible, test it yourself using screen readers, keyboard navigation, or color contrast checkers (e.g., WebAIM Contrast Checker).

3. Conclusion

Ensuring digital accessibility is not just about compliance—it is about creating equitable learning experiences where every student, regardless of ability, can fully participate and succeed. By implementing inclusive design principles, leveraging assistive technologies, and proactively supporting students, TAs can remove digital barriers and enhance student learning.

Accessibility benefits not only students with disabilities but also those with diverse learning preferences, non-native speakers, and students facing temporary impairments. By embracing universal design for learning (UDL) principles, TAs can contribute to a more inclusive, adaptive, and student-centered educational environment—one where technology serves as a bridge to learning, rather than a barrier.

Chapter 7: Research, Scholarship, and Teaching Integration

Figure 7.1. Teaching and Learning [113].

Student success extends beyond academic performance—it encompasses well-being, resilience, and the ability to navigate challenges in higher education. As a Teaching Assistant (TA), your role is not only to facilitate learning but also to support students in managing academic pressures, maintaining motivation, and overcoming personal and institutional obstacles. Many students face difficulties such as time management struggles, test anxiety, mental health challenges, or balancing coursework with work and personal responsibilities. Understanding how to provide guidance and connect students with the appropriate resources can make a significant difference in their academic journey.

This chapter explores the various dimensions of student success and well-being, equipping TAs with strategies to identify struggling students, provide appropriate academic support, and promote a healthy, inclusive, and productive learning environment. It covers best practices for mentoring and advising students, fostering a growth mindset, and encouraging resilience in the face of academic setbacks. Additionally, the chapter delves into issues such as test anxiety, stress management, and mental health awareness, helping TAs recognize when students may need additional support beyond the classroom.

Beyond individual student concerns, TAs also play a crucial role in fostering an inclusive and supportive learning community. This chapter discusses ways to create a positive classroom culture, address imposter syndrome, and ensure that all students—regardless of background, learning style, or personal challenges—feel valued and supported in their academic pursuits.

By the end of this chapter, TAs will be able to:
- Recognize the academic and personal challenges students face and provide appropriate support.
- Mentor and guide students in developing resilience, motivation, and effective study habits.
- Identify signs of academic stress, test anxiety, and mental health struggles.
- Direct students to campus resources for academic advising, counseling, and student support services.

- Foster an inclusive and supportive learning environment that promotes well-being.
- Encourage students to adopt self-regulated learning strategies and a growth mindset.

Higher education is a transformative period for students, and the guidance of a supportive TA can significantly enhance their academic experience. By developing skills in student mentorship and well-being support, TAs can help students not only succeed academically but also develop lifelong skills in resilience, confidence, and self-directed learning.

Supporting Students in Academic Research

Academic research is a fundamental aspect of higher education, equipping students with critical thinking skills, intellectual curiosity, and the ability to engage in scholarly discourse. As a Teaching Assistant (TA), supporting students in research extends beyond simply guiding them to sources—it involves fostering analytical thinking, teaching methodological rigor, and helping students navigate the complexities of academic inquiry. Effective research support empowers students to ask meaningful questions, evaluate sources critically, synthesize information, and contribute to academic conversations with originality and depth.

This section explores the key responsibilities of TAs in guiding students through the research process, equipping them with essential research skills, and addressing common challenges that students encounter.

1. Understanding the Role of the TA in Research Support

While faculty members set the foundation for research-based assignments, TAs serve as the primary point of contact for students, offering hands-on guidance and clarification. Their role includes:

- Helping students define research questions and refine their focus.

- Teaching information literacy skills—evaluating sources, avoiding misinformation, and understanding scholarly credibility.

- Guiding students in using academic databases and research tools effectively.

- Providing support in structuring research papers, synthesizing findings, and citing sources correctly.

- Addressing challenges such as overcoming writer's block, managing research anxiety, and avoiding plagiarism.

TAs bridge the gap between students and faculty expectations, ensuring that students develop the confidence and skills necessary to engage in independent scholarly work.

2. Helping Students Develop Research Questions and Topics

The foundation of any strong research project lies in a well-defined research question. Many students struggle with broad, vague, or unfocused topics, leading to papers that lack depth and coherence.

Best Practices for Refining Research Questions

- Encourage specificity: Guide students from broad topics to focused, researchable questions.

    - Example: Instead of *"How does technology affect education?"*, refine to *"How has AI-assisted tutoring impacted student engagement in higher education since 2020?"*

- Teach the importance of feasibility: Ensure students choose topics with accessible sources and manageable scope.

- Promote inquiry-driven research: Encourage students to frame their research as a problem to be explored, rather than just collecting existing information.

    - Example: *"Why have remote work policies disproportionately affected women in STEM fields?"*

TA Tip: If students struggle with topic selection, suggest mind-mapping exercises or exploratory searches in databases like JSTOR, Google Scholar, or ProQuest to identify emerging discussions in their field.

3. Teaching Information Literacy and Source Evaluation

In an age of abundant (and sometimes misleading) information, students must develop information literacy skills to distinguish credible academic sources from unreliable material.

Key Strategies for Teaching Source Evaluation

- Introduce the CRAAP Test (Currency, Relevance, Authority, Accuracy, Purpose) to help students assess sources critically.

- Differentiate between primary, secondary, and tertiary sources, ensuring students understand when each is appropriate.

- Encourage students to use peer-reviewed journals, academic books, and institutional research reports, rather than relying solely on general web searches.

- Warn against common pitfalls, such as confirmation bias (seeking only sources that support preconceived opinions) and over-reliance on a single source.

Recommended Digital Research Tools:
- Google Scholar – For finding scholarly articles, with citation tracking and advanced search filters.
- JSTOR, PubMed, and IEEE Xplore – For accessing discipline-specific journals.

- Zotero & Mendeley – For managing citations and organizing research sources.
- Semantic Scholar – An AI-driven database that highlights influential research in a given field.

TA Tip: Encourage students to use library research consultations when they need deeper guidance on finding scholarly materials.

4. Assisting Students in Synthesizing Research and Constructing Arguments

Gathering sources is only the first step—students must learn how to analyze and synthesize information, rather than summarizing sources without critical engagement.

Best Practices for Teaching Synthesis

- Encourage thematic grouping of sources: Instead of writing source-by-source summaries, students should identify common patterns or debates across literature.

    o Example: If researching climate change policies, group sources into categories like *economic impact, policy effectiveness, and public perception.*

- Teach students to engage with sources rather than merely report on them:

    o Ask: *How do these studies build upon or challenge one another?*

    o Encourage comparative analysis: *What gaps exist in the literature?*

- Guide students in constructing a coherent argument:

    o Ensure that research papers have a clear thesis statement, rather than a disconnected collection of ideas.

    o Help them integrate sources to support claims rather than replace their own analysis.

TA Tip: Use reverse outlining as a strategy—have students outline their drafts after writing, helping them visualize whether their paper flows logically.

5. Addressing Common Student Research Challenges

A. Managing Research Anxiety and Overwhelm

Many students feel intimidated by large research projects, unsure where to begin or how to manage time effectively.

Solutions:
- Break the research process into smaller steps, setting manageable deadlines (topic selection, literature review, thesis development, etc.).
- Teach time management strategies, such as the Pomodoro technique or scheduling research blocks.
- Recommend research logs to help students track sources, ideas, and progress systematically.

B. Avoiding Plagiarism and Promoting Academic Integrity

Unintentional plagiarism often results from poor paraphrasing skills or misunderstanding citation norms [72].

Solutions:
- Teach proper paraphrasing—have students summarize key points in their own words before referring to the original text.
- Explain the difference between quoting, summarizing, and paraphrasing, ensuring students attribute sources correctly.
- Encourage students to use citation management tools (e.g., EndNote, Zotero) to keep track of references.
- Direct students to university writing centers for further plagiarism prevention resources.

C. Formatting and Citation Challenges

Many students struggle with APA, MLA, or Chicago style citations, leading to formatting errors or accidental plagiarism [73].

Solutions:
- Direct students to official style guides and online resources (e.g., Purdue OWL).
- Encourage the use of citation generators (e.g., Citation Machine, BibTeX) but stress the importance of verifying results.
- Offer quick formatting tutorials or refer students to institutional writing support services.

6. Encouraging Independent Research and Lifelong Inquiry

A TA's role extends beyond helping students complete a single assignment—it involves cultivating a mindset of curiosity, critical inquiry, and scholarly engagement.

- Encourage students to explore interdisciplinary research and attend academic conferences or guest lectures.

- Foster discussions on research ethics, data reliability, and the evolving nature of knowledge.

- Support students in considering publication opportunities in undergraduate research journals or conferences.

- Inspire curiosity by relating research skills to real-world applications (e.g., policy-making, industry innovation, public discourse).

Conclusion

Supporting students in academic research requires a balance of guidance, encouragement, and skill-building. By teaching students how to formulate research questions, evaluate sources critically, synthesize ideas, and write with scholarly rigor, TAs play an essential role in fostering academic independence and intellectual growth. Ultimately, the goal is not just to help students complete a research paper, but to equip them with the skills to engage with knowledge, think critically, and contribute meaningfully to their disciplines—a foundation that extends far beyond the classroom.

Encouraging Student Participation in Research Projects

Engaging students in academic research projects is a transformative experience that deepens their intellectual curiosity, enhances critical thinking skills, and prepares them for future scholarly or professional pursuits. Participation in research allows students to move beyond passive learning, actively contributing to knowledge creation while developing essential skills such as analytical reasoning, problem-solving, and effective communication. However, many students hesitate to get involved in research due to a lack of confidence, uncertainty about the process, or limited awareness of available opportunities.

As a Teaching Assistant (TA), you play a crucial role in fostering student engagement in research by identifying opportunities, mentoring students through the research process, and making scholarly work approachable, relevant, and rewarding. By integrating research participation into coursework and encouraging students to see themselves as contributors to their fields, TAs can help cultivate the next generation of scholars, innovators, and critical thinkers.

1. Understanding the Benefits of Student Research Participation

Before encouraging students to engage in research, it is essential to articulate why research participation is valuable. Many students perceive research as an exclusive activity for advanced scholars, failing to recognize its accessibility and practical benefits. Highlighting these advantages can motivate students to actively seek research opportunities.

Academic and Intellectual Growth

- Encourages deep learning beyond memorization, fostering critical thinking and problem-solving skills.

- Develops information literacy—students learn how to evaluate sources, synthesize findings, and construct well-supported arguments.

- Helps students formulate research questions and think methodically about evidence-based inquiry.

Professional and Career Development

- Enhances resume and graduate school applications—research experience demonstrates intellectual curiosity, initiative, and analytical skills.

- Provides students with opportunities to publish papers, present at conferences, and collaborate with faculty mentors.

- Builds expertise in data analysis, academic writing, and technical skills, which are highly valued in various industries.

Personal and Collaborative Skills

- Increases self-confidence by allowing students to contribute original ideas to their discipline.

- Develops teamwork and communication skills, especially when working on research teams or co-authoring papers.

- Encourages persistence and adaptability, as research often involves challenges and iterative learning.

By framing research as a meaningful and achievable pursuit, TAs can help demystify the process and inspire students to engage with research beyond the classroom.

2. Identifying and Promoting Research Opportunities

Many students hesitate to participate in research because they do not know where to begin or believe they lack the necessary qualifications. TAs can play an active role in connecting students with research opportunities by directing them to faculty projects, institutional programs, and independent study options.

Institutional Research Programs and Initiatives

- Encourage students to explore undergraduate research programs such as:

  - Honors research tracks

  - Summer research internships

  - Independent study courses for academic credit

- Direct students to faculty-led research groups, departmental research initiatives, or interdisciplinary projects.

- Inform students about grant-funded research assistantships, where they can gain experience while earning stipends.

External Research Opportunities

- Guide students toward national and international research programs, such as:

  - The National Science Foundation (NSF) Research Experiences for Undergraduates (REU)

  - Internships at research institutions or industry labs

  - Conference travel grants and undergraduate presentation forums

Encouraging Classroom-to-Research Pathways

- Help students identify research-worthy questions based on their coursework and interests.

- Encourage students to expand class essays or projects into full research papers.

- Connect students with faculty mentors who align with their research interests.

TA Tip: Many students assume research is limited to STEM fields. Help them see that research exists in all disciplines, from historical analysis and literary studies to business case studies and policy research.

3. Fostering Student Confidence and Overcoming Barriers

Even when opportunities are available, many students hesitate to engage in research due to self-doubt, fear of failure, or lack of mentorship. TAs can help students build confidence and develop a growth mindset by addressing common concerns.

Barrier 1: "I'm not qualified to do research."

Many students believe research is only for graduate students or high-achieving scholars.

- Solution: Normalize research as a learning process, not just an elite activity. Encourage students by explaining that research skills develop over time—they do not need to be experts to start.

Barrier 2: "I don't know where to start."

Students may struggle to navigate research databases, find faculty mentors, or develop research ideas.

- Solution: Provide step-by-step guidance, such as:

- Helping students refine a research question.
- Teaching them how to use Google Scholar, JSTOR, and institutional databases.
- Recommending introductory readings to help them contextualize their topic.

Barrier 3: "I'm afraid of failing or making mistakes."

Students often fear that research requires perfect results, which can prevent them from taking the first step.

- Solution: Emphasize that failure is part of the research process. Mistakes, unexpected findings, and iterative learning are fundamental to scholarly inquiry. Encourage students to see setbacks as opportunities for deeper understanding.

TA Tip: Share personal experiences about research challenges you faced and how you overcame them. Authentic storytelling can reduce intimidation and encourage persistence.

4. Integrating Research Participation into Coursework

Encouraging research participation does not always require separate projects—TAs can integrate research elements into existing coursework to make scholarly inquiry more accessible.

Research-Based Assignments

- Assign mini-research projects that require students to investigate a question beyond textbook materials.

- Use literature review assignments to introduce students to academic sources and research synthesis.

- Encourage students to design surveys, experiments, or case studies relevant to their discipline.

Encouraging Conference and Publication Engagement

- Suggest that students submit class projects or research papers to undergraduate journals.

- Inform students about campus or regional research symposiums where they can present findings.

- Offer workshops on abstract writing and presentation skills to prepare students for research dissemination.

Facilitating Group Research Collaborations

- Pair students with similar interests to co-author projects or conduct team research.

- Create research mentorship groups where experienced students guide newcomers.

- Encourage peer feedback sessions to help students refine their ideas and methodologies.

TA Tip: Organize a "Research Roundtable" where students can share their ideas in an informal setting, allowing them to discuss topics without pressure.

5. Long-Term Impact: Encouraging Lifelong Research Engagement

Beyond coursework, research experience equips students with skills that extend into graduate studies, professional careers, and lifelong learning. TAs can help students recognize how research experience contributes to:

- Stronger graduate school applications: Research experience is a key differentiator for competitive applications [74].

- Enhanced professional skills: Research sharpens analytical thinking, data interpretation, and written communication, which are valuable in many industries.

- Continued intellectual curiosity: Research fosters a lifelong habit of questioning, exploration, and innovation.

Encouraging students to see research as a dynamic, ongoing process rather than a one-time task helps them develop intellectual confidence and curiosity beyond the classroom.

Conclusion

Encouraging students to engage in research projects requires more than simply presenting opportunities—it involves mentorship, confidence-building, and skill development. By demystifying research, addressing barriers, and integrating scholarly inquiry into coursework, TAs can help students recognize their potential as researchers and knowledge creators. When students see themselves as active contributors to academic and professional fields, they gain a deeper appreciation for learning, critical inquiry, and the pursuit of knowledge that extends beyond the university setting.

Understanding Citation Styles and Avoiding Plagiarism

Academic integrity is the foundation of ethical scholarship, and one of the most critical responsibilities of a Teaching Assistant (TA) is to guide students in understanding proper citation practices and avoiding plagiarism. Citing sources correctly is not merely a technical requirement but a fundamental aspect of scholarly discourse—it acknowledges intellectual contributions, provides credibility to arguments, and allows for academic transparency. However, many students struggle with citation styles and, in some cases, unintentionally commit plagiarism due to lack of familiarity with proper attribution.

As a TA, your role involves helping students navigate different citation styles, teaching them when and how to cite sources, and fostering a deep understanding of academic integrity. This section explores key citation styles, common citation challenges, and effective strategies to prevent plagiarism.

1. Why Citation Matters in Academic Writing

Citation serves multiple purposes beyond avoiding plagiarism—it is an integral part of research ethics and scholarly communication. When students properly credit their sources, they:

- Demonstrate credibility and academic integrity by acknowledging the work of others.

- Support their arguments with evidence, showing that their research is grounded in established knowledge.

- Allow readers to verify information, enabling others to follow citations and explore sources further.

- Engage in the scholarly conversation, contributing to ongoing discussions within their field.

By emphasizing the value of citations beyond mere compliance, TAs can help students appreciate citation as a critical research skill rather than just a formatting requirement.

2. Overview of Common Citation Styles

Different academic disciplines follow distinct citation styles, each with unique formatting rules. TAs should be familiar with the most commonly used citation formats and be prepared to guide students accordingly.

2.1 APA (American Psychological Association) – Used in Social Sciences

- Focus: Author-date system, emphasizing recent research and empirical evidence.

- Example (In-text Citation): *(Smith, 2023, p. 45)*
- Example (Reference List):
    - Smith, J. (2023). *Understanding research ethics*. Academic Press.
- Common Usage: Psychology, Sociology, Education, Business, Nursing.

2.2 MLA (Modern Language Association) – Used in Humanities

- Focus: Author-page system, prioritizing literary and textual analysis.
- Example (In-text Citation): *(Smith 45)*
- Example (Works Cited Page):
    - Smith, John. *Understanding Research Ethics*. Academic Press, 2023.
- Common Usage: Literature, Philosophy, Art History, Cultural Studies.

2.3 Chicago/Turabian – Used in History and Publishing

- Focus: Two systems—(1) Notes and Bibliography (used in humanities) and (2) Author-Date (used in sciences).
- Example (Footnote Citation):
    - [1] John Smith, *Understanding Research Ethics* (Academic Press, 2023), 45.
- Example (Bibliography):
    - Smith, John. *Understanding Research Ethics*. Academic Press, 2023.
- Common Usage: History, Theology, Political Science, Publishing.

2.4 IEEE (Institute of Electrical and Electronics Engineers) – Used in Engineering and Computer Science

- Focus: Numerical citation system, prioritizing technical research.
- Example (In-text Citation): *[1]*
- Example (Reference List):
    - [1] J. Smith, *Understanding Research Ethics*, Academic Press, 2023.
- Common Usage: Engineering, Computer Science, Information Technology.

2.5 AMA (American Medical Association) – Used in Medicine and Health Sciences

- Focus: Numerical system, emphasizing medical research.
- Example (In-text Citation): *1*
- Example (Reference List):

       ○

> 1. Smith J. *Understanding Research Ethics*. Academic Press; 2023.

- Common Usage: Medicine, Public Health, Biomedical Research.

TA Tip: Encourage students to consult their course syllabus or ask their professor to confirm the appropriate citation style for their field.

3. Avoiding Plagiarism: Common Issues and Solutions

Plagiarism occurs when a student uses someone else's ideas, words, or work without proper attribution. While some plagiarism is intentional, many instances result from misunderstanding citation rules, paraphrasing incorrectly, or poor research habits.

3.1 Types of Plagiarism

A. Direct Plagiarism (Copy-Pasting Without Citation)

- Example: Copying a paragraph from an article and inserting it into a paper without quotation marks or attribution.

- Solution: Teach students to always use quotation marks and provide a citation when using someone else's exact words.

B. Paraphrasing Plagiarism (Changing a Few Words Without Citing the Source)

- Example: Altering some words in a passage but keeping the structure and meaning intact without crediting the original author.

- Solution: Emphasize that paraphrasing still requires citation, and encourage students to fully rewrite content in their own words.

C. Patchwriting (Mosaic Plagiarism)

- Example: Combining phrases from multiple sources without original analysis.

- Solution: Encourage synthesis of ideas rather than merely reshuffling existing content.

D. Self-Plagiarism (Reusing One's Own Work)

- Example: Submitting a previous essay for a different class without permission.

- Solution: Teach students that reusing their own work requires citation and instructor approval.

E. Accidental Plagiarism (Unintentional Citation Errors)

- Example: Forgetting to cite a source or using an incorrect citation format.

- Solution: Promote meticulous note-taking and citation management tools (e.g., Zotero, Mendeley, EndNote).

4. Strategies to Teach Proper Citation and Prevent Plagiarism

4.1 Teaching Effective Paraphrasing

- Use the "Read, Restate, Write" Method: Have students read a passage, explain it in their own words without looking at the original, then write a paraphrase.

- Provide Side-by-Side Examples: Show correct and incorrect paraphrasing with proper citations.

- Encourage Summarization: Guide students to focus on main ideas rather than copying sentence structure.

4.2 Using Technology to Aid Citation

- Introduce students to citation management tools (e.g., Zotero, BibTeX, RefWorks) for organizing references.

- Encourage students to use plagiarism detection software (e.g., Turnitin, Grammarly) to check for citation errors before submission.

- Teach students how to use built-in citation features in Google Scholar and academic databases.

4.3 Creating a Culture of Academic Integrity

- Set Clear Expectations: Explain what constitutes plagiarism and reinforce citation policies early in the semester.

- Encourage Discussions on Ethical Scholarship: Lead class discussions on why proper citation matters in academic discourse.

- Offer Writing Workshops: Collaborate with university writing centers to provide citation and research support.

TA Tip: Encourage formative feedback—allow students to submit drafts for review before final submission, helping them refine citation practices.

5. Conclusion

Understanding citation styles and avoiding plagiarism are fundamental skills for academic success. As a TA, your role is not just to enforce citation rules but to educate students on ethical research practices, critical thinking, and scholarly communication. By equipping students with citation tools, teaching effective paraphrasing, and fostering an awareness of academic integrity, you help them develop skills that will serve them throughout their academic and professional careers. Proper citation is more than a technical requirement—it is a commitment to ethical scholarship and intellectual respect [75].

Balancing TA Responsibilities with Personal Academic Research

Serving as a Teaching Assistant (TA) while pursuing one's own academic research is both a rewarding and demanding endeavor. TAs must navigate the dual responsibilities of supporting students and faculty while also advancing their own scholarly work—a challenge that requires strategic time management, clear prioritization, and strong professional boundaries. Successfully balancing these roles not only enhances teaching effectiveness and research productivity but also fosters long-term career growth in academia or beyond.

This section explores key strategies for managing TA duties alongside personal research, addressing challenges, and optimizing both teaching and scholarly commitments.

1. Understanding the Dual Role of a TA and Researcher

TA positions provide valuable opportunities for pedagogical development, mentorship, and collaboration. At the same time, personal research is a critical component of academic progress, contributing to one's intellectual growth, publication record, and career trajectory.

The challenge lies in balancing these interconnected but distinct roles:

- Teaching Responsibilities: Grading assignments, conducting discussion sections, holding office hours, assisting faculty with course administration.

- Research Commitments: Conducting literature reviews, designing experiments, writing and revising manuscripts, attending conferences.

Both roles require significant time and cognitive effort, making it essential to establish strategies that prevent burnout while ensuring success in both teaching and research domains.

2. Time Management Strategies for TAs

Effective time management is crucial for juggling multiple responsibilities without sacrificing the quality of either teaching or research.

2.1 Prioritization and Scheduling

- Use a weekly planner or digital task manager (e.g., Trello, Notion, Todoist) to allocate dedicated blocks of time for both TA duties and research.

- Set clear priorities each week—identify urgent vs. important tasks (e.g., grading deadlines vs. research milestones).

- Align your schedule with your peak productivity hours—if you work best in the morning, reserve that time for research and allocate afternoons for teaching-related tasks.

2.2 Implementing Time-Blocking Techniques

- Structured Work Sessions: Use the Pomodoro Technique (25-minute focused sessions with 5-minute breaks) to maintain efficiency.

- Theme Your Days: Dedicate specific days or times for teaching-related tasks (grading, office hours) and others for research-intensive work (writing, data analysis).

2.3 Avoiding Task Overload

- Set realistic expectations—avoid taking on excessive commitments that interfere with research progress.

- Communicate with faculty supervisors about TA workload boundaries, ensuring you are not overburdened with administrative or grading duties.

- Utilize batch processing—group similar tasks together (e.g., responding to student emails at designated times rather than throughout the day).

TA Tip: Identify your "non-negotiables"—essential tasks that must be completed daily or weekly, such as writing for research or attending lab meetings.

3. Maximizing Research Productivity While TAing

Balancing teaching with research does not mean compromising academic progress. Instead, adopting strategic research habits ensures steady progress, even amidst TA responsibilities.

3.1 Setting Research Goals and Milestones

- Break large research tasks into smaller, manageable goals (e.g., "Write literature review section" rather than "Finish dissertation chapter").

- Use SMART goals (Specific, Measurable, Achievable, Relevant, Time-bound) to stay on track.

- Keep a research progress tracker (Google Sheets, Notion, or a research journal) to monitor achievements and setbacks.

3.2 Writing Efficiently Under Time Constraints

- Schedule consistent writing sessions, even if brief—daily writing (even 30 minutes) accumulates over time.

- Use writing sprints (uninterrupted 45-minute blocks) to maximize productivity.

- Set artificial deadlines (e.g., complete a draft before a peer review session) to maintain momentum.

3.3 Leveraging Synergies Between Teaching and Research

- Use teaching to reinforce research skills—explaining concepts to students can enhance understanding of your own research area.

- Incorporate research into teaching—draw examples from your field to make course content more engaging.

- Engage students in your research—undergraduate research assistants or project-based learning can help integrate your teaching and research.

TA Tip: Keep a dedicated research hour in your schedule each day, ensuring consistent progress even during busy teaching weeks.

4. Maintaining Work-Life Balance and Avoiding Burnout

Balancing TA responsibilities with research can be overwhelming, making self-care and well-being essential.

4.1 Setting Boundaries

- Establish communication boundaries—limit student emails to work hours and avoid grading outside scheduled times.

- Learn to say no to additional commitments that may derail research progress.

- If struggling, communicate with advisors or department heads to adjust TA responsibilities as needed.

4.2 Stress Management and Self-Care

- Incorporate physical activity (e.g., walking, yoga, stretching) to combat sedentary academic work.

- Maintain a social support network—connect with peers, colleagues, and mentors who understand academic challenges.

- Schedule unplugged time to avoid burnout—set aside time for hobbies or relaxation.

4.3 Recognizing When to Seek Support

- If struggling with time constraints or workload, discuss possible accommodation strategies with faculty supervisors.

- Utilize campus resources—many universities offer academic coaching, wellness programs, and mental health services.

TA Tip: Consider co-working sessions with fellow TAs or researchers—peer accountability can boost motivation and efficiency.

5. Long-Term Benefits of Balancing Teaching and Research

While challenging, balancing TA responsibilities with research cultivates skills that are essential for academic and professional success.

- Improved Time Management: Learning to juggle multiple responsibilities prepares you for faculty roles or research-intensive careers.

- Enhanced Communication and Leadership Skills: Teaching experience refines the ability to explain complex ideas clearly, a valuable skill in academia and industry.

- Professional Networking: Engaging with students, faculty, and researchers builds relationships that may lead to collaborative projects, conference invitations, or job opportunities.

- Stronger Research Output: Developing structured research habits while teaching ensures steady academic productivity, increasing the likelihood of publishing and securing research funding.

Ultimately, the ability to balance teaching and research effectively is a hallmark of a successful academic career—one that fosters both intellectual contribution and student mentorship.

6. Conclusion

Balancing TA responsibilities with personal academic research requires deliberate planning, strategic time management, and strong professional boundaries. By prioritizing tasks, integrating teaching with research, and maintaining a sustainable work-life balance, TAs can excel in both roles without compromising their scholarly progress. More than a challenge, this dual role is an opportunity to develop essential skills in organization, mentorship, and academic leadership—laying the foundation for a successful career in academia or beyond.

By fostering teaching excellence and research productivity simultaneously, TAs not only contribute to their own academic success but also enrich the learning experiences of their students, creating a dynamic and impactful educational environment.

Chapter 8: Inclusivity and Student Support

Being a Teaching Assistant (TA) is not just about supporting students—it is also an opportunity for personal and professional growth. Serving as a TA provides hands-on experience in teaching, mentoring, academic leadership, and communication, all of which are transferable skills valuable in both academia and the workforce. Whether a TA plans to pursue a career in education, research, industry, or administration, the role offers a unique foundation for developing expertise in instructional strategies, student engagement, and academic professionalism.

This chapter focuses on how TAs can maximize their professional development opportunities during their tenure. It explores essential skills such as effective communication, classroom leadership, conflict resolution, and time management. Additionally, the chapter discusses how TAs can build their academic credentials through networking, conference participation, research collaborations, and teaching portfolio development.

Figure 8.1. Teaching and Learning [113].

Beyond immediate TA responsibilities, this chapter also examines long-term career planning. It provides insights into how TAs can leverage their experiences for future job applications, teaching positions, or graduate studies. Furthermore, it addresses the importance of self-reflection, feedback, and continuous learning to improve teaching effectiveness and professional competence.

By the end of this chapter, TAs will be able to:
- Develop key professional skills such as leadership, communication, and conflict resolution.
- Build a strong teaching portfolio to showcase instructional experience and expertise.
- Leverage networking opportunities and professional organizations for career growth.
- Balance TA responsibilities with research, coursework, and personal development.
- Utilize feedback and self-assessment to enhance teaching effectiveness.
- Explore career pathways in academia, industry, and other professional sectors.

Becoming a TA is more than just a job—it is a stepping stone toward future opportunities. By actively engaging in professional development, seeking mentorship, and continuously refining their skills, TAs can maximize their impact in the classroom while preparing for rewarding careers in their chosen fields.

Understanding Diverse Student Backgrounds and Learning Challenges

Higher education is a diverse and dynamic environment where students come from various cultural, socioeconomic, and educational backgrounds. As a Teaching Assistant (TA), recognizing and understanding this diversity is essential for fostering an inclusive, supportive, and equitable learning experience. Students bring with them unique perspectives, learning styles, and challenges, all of which shape how they engage with course material, interact with instructors, and navigate academic expectations.

By adopting an awareness-driven, empathetic, and proactive approach, TAs can help ensure that all students—regardless of background or ability—have the resources and support they need to succeed. This section explores the dimensions of student diversity, the common learning challenges students may face, and best practices for fostering an inclusive and supportive educational environment.

1. The Spectrum of Student Diversity in Higher Education

Students enter the classroom with distinct experiences, abilities, and perspectives, which influence their approach to learning. These factors can be broadly categorized into:

1.1 Cultural and Linguistic Diversity

- Many students come from different cultural and national backgrounds, bringing varied communication styles, perspectives, and academic expectations.

- International and multilingual students may face challenges in language comprehension, participation, and writing conventions.

- Cultural attitudes toward authority and classroom engagement may differ—some students may be hesitant to challenge ideas or speak up in discussions due to cultural norms.

1.2 Socioeconomic Background and Educational Preparation

- Students from under-resourced schools or first-generation college backgrounds may have had limited access to advanced coursework, academic mentorship, or research opportunities.

- Economic disparities may affect access to technology, textbooks, and study resources, making digital accessibility and open educational resources (OER) crucial.

- Some students may be working full-time jobs, supporting families, or facing food and housing insecurity, impacting their ability to focus solely on academics.

1.3 Neurodiversity and Learning Disabilities

- Many students have neurodiverse learning profiles, including dyslexia, ADHD, autism spectrum conditions, or processing disorders.

- Traditional lecture-based or text-heavy instruction may not align with their preferred modes of learning, requiring multi-modal teaching strategies.

- Providing structured learning environments, clear communication, and flexible assessment methods can help neurodiverse students thrive.

1.4 Mental Health and Emotional Well-being

- Students today face increasing pressures related to academic performance, financial stress, social expectations, and mental health challenges [76].

- Anxiety, depression, and imposter syndrome can significantly impact student participation, focus, and motivation [77].

- TAs should be aware of campus mental health resources and encourage a compassionate, stigma-free classroom atmosphere.

1.5 Physical Disabilities and Accessibility Needs

- Some students may require mobility accommodations, assistive technology, or flexible participation options (e.g., captioned videos, alternative formats for readings).

- Ensuring that all digital content is accessible (screen-reader friendly, transcripts available, high-contrast visuals) can support students with visual or auditory impairments.

- Many students with disabilities may not disclose their needs unless accessibility barriers arise, making proactive inclusion strategies essential.

2. Common Learning Challenges and How to Address Them

Beyond demographic diversity, students may face learning-specific challenges that impact their engagement and success in the classroom.

2.1 Language Barriers and Communication Difficulties

- Challenge: Students for whom English is a second language (ESL) may struggle with academic jargon, complex sentence structures, or oral participation.

- Solution:
    - Provide written summaries of lectures, discussion points, and key takeaways.
    - Encourage peer collaboration to foster language development through interaction.
    - Avoid penalizing minor grammatical errors in assignments where content understanding is the primary focus.

2.2 Difficulty with Abstract or Theoretical Concepts

- Challenge: Some students struggle with abstract reasoning, high-level theoretical discussions, or complex problem-solving.

- Solution:
    - Use real-world applications, case studies, and hands-on demonstrations to ground abstract ideas.
    - Break down complex theories into smaller, digestible parts, connecting them to familiar concepts.

2.3 Executive Functioning and Time Management Challenges

- Challenge: Some students have difficulty with organization, prioritization, or staying on top of deadlines, particularly those with ADHD or high external stressors.

- Solution:
    - Provide structured timelines, reminders, and clear expectations for assignments.
    - Encourage students to use calendars, task lists, or productivity tools to track their progress.
    - Offer flexible office hours where students can seek guidance on planning their workload.

2.4 Imposter Syndrome and Academic Confidence Issues

- Challenge: Many students—especially first-generation, minority, or non-traditional students—experience self-doubt and fear that they do not belong in academic spaces [78].

- Solution:
    - Foster an inclusive classroom culture where diverse perspectives and learning styles are valued.
    - Provide affirmative, growth-oriented feedback that highlights improvement and effort, not just final results.
    - Normalize challenges by sharing examples of successful scholars who struggled early in their academic journeys.

2.5 Anxiety in Participation and Assessment

- Challenge: Some students hesitate to speak in class due to social anxiety, fear of being wrong, or discomfort with public speaking [79].

- Solution:

- o Use low-stakes participation methods (e.g., small-group discussions, online forums) to ease students into engagement.

- o Offer alternative ways to demonstrate understanding, such as written reflections instead of oral presentations.

- o Frame mistakes as a natural part of learning, encouraging intellectual risk-taking without fear of judgment.

3. Best Practices for Supporting a Diverse Student Body

TAs can implement inclusive teaching strategies to proactively address diverse learning needs and create an equitable classroom environment.

3.1 Cultivating an Inclusive Classroom Culture

- Use Inclusive Language: Be mindful of culturally diverse names, pronouns, and gender identities.
- Encourage a Growth Mindset: Reinforce that intelligence is developed through effort, practice, and feedback, not innate ability.
- Acknowledge Diverse Perspectives: Actively incorporate multicultural viewpoints and examples in discussions.

3.2 Implementing Universal Design for Learning (UDL)

- Provide Multiple Means of Engagement:

- Offer various participation formats (verbal, written, group-based).
  - Offer Flexible Assessment Methods:

- Use a mix of essays, projects, quizzes, and oral presentations to allow diverse ways to demonstrate knowledge.
  - Ensure Digital Accessibility:

- Use closed captions, alt text for images, and high-contrast visuals in presentations [79].

3.3 Supporting Mental Health and Well-being

- Recognize signs of academic distress and provide compassionate support.
- Direct students to campus counseling, disability services, or academic resources.
- Encourage work-life balance, emphasizing that well-being is a crucial part of academic success.

4. Conclusion

Understanding diverse student backgrounds and learning challenges is essential for fostering an inclusive, equitable, and supportive academic environment. TAs play a pivotal role in recognizing the unique needs of students, implementing adaptive teaching strategies, and removing barriers to learning. By embracing cultural awareness, flexible teaching methods, and proactive student support, TAs can contribute to a learning environment where all students—regardless of background, ability, or challenges—feel valued, empowered, and capable of success.

Ultimately, an inclusive classroom is not just about accommodating differences—it is about celebrating and leveraging them to enrich the learning experience for all.

Creating Culturally Responsive and Inclusive Learning Environments

In today's diverse academic landscape, fostering a culturally responsive and inclusive learning environment is essential to ensuring that all students—regardless of their background—feel valued, respected, and empowered to succeed. As a Teaching Assistant (TA), you play a crucial role in shaping classroom dynamics, facilitating discussions, and supporting students from a wide range of cultural, linguistic, and socioeconomic backgrounds. By embracing culturally responsive teaching (CRT) strategies, you can help create an engaging, equitable, and student-centered educational experience where diverse perspectives are not only acknowledged but celebrated.

This section explores the principles of culturally responsive teaching, strategies for fostering inclusivity, and best practices for promoting equitable learning opportunities for all students.

1. Understanding Culturally Responsive Teaching (CRT)

Culturally responsive teaching (CRT) is an educational approach that recognizes the diverse cultural wealth that students bring to the classroom and integrates it into teaching practices to enhance learning outcomes. Rather than treating diversity as a challenge, CRT leverages cultural differences as strengths, ensuring that all students can connect with and engage meaningfully with course content.

Key Principles of Culturally Responsive Teaching

- Cultural Awareness & Sensitivity – Recognizing and respecting the diverse cultural identities, values, and experiences of students.
- Equity & Representation – Ensuring that course materials and teaching strategies reflect a range of perspectives and experiences.
- Student-Centered Pedagogy – Acknowledging that students learn best when they see themselves reflected in their education.
- Inclusive Classroom Climate – Creating a safe and supportive space where all voices are valued and students feel comfortable expressing their identities.

CRT is not just about adding diverse perspectives to a syllabus—it is about adopting an inclusive mindset, fostering cross-cultural understanding, and adapting teaching methods to meet the needs of all students.

2. Strategies for Building a Culturally Inclusive Learning Environment

To create a culturally responsive and inclusive classroom, TAs should implement strategies that promote engagement, equity, and respect for diverse perspectives.

2.1 Acknowledging and Valuing Cultural Diversity

- Learn about the cultural, linguistic, and academic backgrounds of your students.

- Use inclusive language that respects gender, ethnicity, nationality, and identity.

- Encourage students to share their unique experiences and perspectives in class discussions.

- Avoid assumptions or stereotypes about students based on their backgrounds.

Example: Instead of assuming that all students have the same prior knowledge, create opportunities for students to share how their cultural backgrounds shape their understanding of a topic.

2.2 Diversifying Course Content and Examples

- Incorporate a wide range of perspectives, authors, and case studies into discussions and materials.

- Use multicultural examples in lectures to show the global relevance of concepts.

- Highlight historically marginalized voices and challenge dominant narratives in the discipline.

Example: In a history course, instead of only discussing Western perspectives on major events, include non-Western viewpoints, indigenous knowledge systems, and historically underrepresented scholars.

2.3 Encouraging Inclusive Participation and Engagement

- Recognize that different cultures have different norms regarding classroom participation. Some students may be hesitant to speak up due to cultural expectations, while others may feel comfortable engaging in debate.

- Provide multiple participation methods—such as written reflections, small group discussions, and online forums—to ensure all students can contribute.

- Use wait time after asking a question to allow students who may need more time to process and respond.

- Avoid favoring outspoken students and ensure that all voices are heard.

Example: In a discussion-heavy class, use think-pair-share activities before calling on students, allowing time for quieter students to gather their thoughts before speaking.

2.4 Adapting Teaching Methods for Cultural Inclusivity

- Offer flexible learning approaches to accommodate diverse learning preferences (e.g., visual, auditory, kinesthetic).

- Be mindful of different communication styles—some students may be more direct, while others may be more reserved due to cultural norms.

- Recognize that students may interpret feedback differently based on cultural expectations—provide clear, constructive, and culturally sensitive feedback.

Example: Some students may view direct criticism as discouraging, while others see it as essential for improvement. Frame feedback constructively, focusing on growth and actionable improvements.

2.5 Addressing Implicit Bias and Challenging Stereotypes

- Reflect on your own implicit biases and how they may impact interactions with students.

- Challenge stereotypical narratives and create a classroom space where diverse perspectives are valued.

- Encourage critical thinking by discussing how cultural assumptions shape knowledge production in different disciplines.

Example: If a student's name is difficult to pronounce, make an effort to learn and say it correctly rather than shortening it or asking for an alternative name. This small act demonstrates respect for cultural identity.

2.6 Recognizing and Supporting Students Facing Cultural or Language Barriers

- Offer additional academic support for students who may struggle with language barriers (e.g., directing them to writing centers or language tutors).

- Provide accessible materials, including transcripts, closed captions, and glossaries for technical terms.

- Foster peer mentorship programs where students from similar backgrounds can support each other.

- Be patient with students who may need extra time to formulate responses in English if it is not their first language.

Example: If a multilingual student is struggling with written assignments, suggest tools like Grammarly or online writing labs while reassuring them that language proficiency does not define intelligence or capability.

3. Creating a Safe and Inclusive Classroom Climate

3.1 Establishing Community Agreements for Respectful Dialogue

- Develop classroom norms that promote respect, active listening, and constructive discussion.

- Model inclusive and respectful language in all interactions.

- Address microaggressions or exclusionary behavior immediately to maintain a welcoming environment.

Example: At the start of the semester, collaborate with students to establish guidelines for respectful discussions, ensuring that diverse viewpoints are expressed without fear of discrimination or dismissal.

3.2 Providing Equitable Support for All Students

- Be proactive in identifying barriers to student success and offer tailored support where needed.

- Direct students to campus resources (e.g., diversity and inclusion offices, counseling services, academic tutoring).

- Offer office hours at flexible times to accommodate students with work, caregiving, or other responsibilities.

Example: Recognize that some students may face unique challenges—such as first-generation college students navigating unfamiliar academic systems—and offer mentorship or guidance.

4. Long-Term Impact: The Power of Culturally Responsive Teaching

When TAs commit to cultural responsiveness and inclusivity, the benefits extend beyond the classroom:

- Students feel valued, respected, and empowered to participate in academic discourse.
- Instructors gain deeper insights into student experiences and learning needs.
- Classrooms become more dynamic, globally informed, and intellectually rich spaces.
- TAs develop essential leadership, mentorship, and cross-cultural communication skills that are valuable in academia and beyond.

By fostering a culture of inclusion and equity, TAs help create an educational environment where all students—regardless of background—can succeed, grow, and contribute meaningfully to their academic communities.

5. Conclusion

Creating a culturally responsive and inclusive learning environment is not a one-time effort but an ongoing commitment to recognizing diversity, challenging biases, and adapting teaching methods to support all students. As a TA, you have the opportunity to cultivate a space where students from all backgrounds feel seen, heard, and respected. By implementing inclusive teaching strategies, diversifying course content, and fostering meaningful cross-cultural engagement, you play a crucial role in shaping an academic environment that is truly equitable, accessible, and enriching for all learners.

Supporting Students with Disabilities and Mental Health Concerns

Creating an inclusive and supportive learning environment requires recognizing and addressing the diverse needs of students, particularly those with disabilities and mental health concerns. As a Teaching Assistant (TA), you play a crucial role in ensuring that all students—regardless of physical, cognitive, or emotional challenges—receive equitable opportunities to succeed in their academic journey.

By understanding the barriers students face, implementing inclusive teaching strategies, and fostering a culture of accessibility and mental well-being, TAs can contribute to a learning environment that is not only accommodating but also empowering. This section explores best practices for supporting students with disabilities and mental health concerns, balancing academic rigor with compassion and equity.

1. Understanding the Challenges Faced by Students with Disabilities and Mental Health Concerns

Students with disabilities and mental health challenges often navigate academic environments that are not always designed with accessibility in mind [80]. The challenges they face can be broadly categorized into:

1.1 Physical Disabilities and Mobility Challenges

- Students with mobility impairments may require accessible seating, assistive technology, or extended time for assignments and exams.

- Classroom spaces and online learning platforms must be navigable for individuals using wheelchairs, mobility aids, or voice-controlled devices.

1.2 Sensory Disabilities (Visual and Hearing Impairments)

- Students who are blind or have low vision may require screen readers, braille materials, or high-contrast content.

- Students who are deaf or hard of hearing may depend on captioned lectures, sign language interpreters, or assistive listening devices.

1.3 Learning Disabilities and Neurodivergence

- Dyslexia, ADHD, autism spectrum conditions, and other cognitive processing disorders may affect reading comprehension, attention, organization, or social interactions.

- Students with executive functioning challenges may struggle with time management, complex assignments, or high-pressure exams.

1.4 Mental Health Concerns and Psychological Disabilities

- Anxiety, depression, PTSD, and other mental health conditions can impact concentration, participation, motivation, and attendance.

- The pressures of academia—deadlines, social stress, performance anxiety—may exacerbate pre-existing mental health challenges [81].

- Some students may experience panic attacks, social withdrawal, or emotional distress that interfere with their academic engagement.

TA Tip: Remember that disabilities and mental health conditions are often invisible. A student may be struggling internally, even if they appear fine externally.

2. Best Practices for Supporting Students with Disabilities

2.1 Creating an Accessible Learning Environment

- Use accessible digital materials: Ensure readings, slides, and course websites are compatible with screen readers and formatted for high contrast.

- Provide multiple means of engagement: Offer written, auditory, and visual formats for lectures, assignments, and discussions.

- Use clear and structured content: Break down information using headings, bullet points, and summaries to aid comprehension.

- Ensure classroom and online spaces are accessible: Check for barrier-free seating, captioned videos, and text-to-speech compatibility.

2.2 Accommodating Different Learning Needs

- Give students options for assessments (e.g., verbal vs. written presentations, extended deadlines).

- Encourage self-paced learning with recorded lectures and flexible deadlines when possible.

- Use Universal Design for Learning (UDL) principles to make learning accessible for all students, not just those with accommodations.

- Be flexible with participation—some students with anxiety or speech disorders may prefer alternative engagement methods like discussion boards.

Example: A student with ADHD may benefit from structured deadlines, check-ins, and an organized syllabus that clearly outlines expectations.

2.3 Working with Disability Services and Accommodations

- Familiarize yourself with campus disability support services and encourage students to utilize them.

- Respect confidentiality—students are not required to disclose their disability to their TA but may choose to share accommodation letters from the disability office.

- Work collaboratively with faculty to ensure accommodations (e.g., extended test time, note-taking support) are met without singling out students.

TA Tip: Do not assume a student is struggling due to lack of effort—barriers to learning may not always be visible, and support should be proactive, not reactive.

3. Best Practices for Supporting Students with Mental Health Concerns

3.1 Creating a Supportive and Low-Stress Learning Environment

- Normalize discussions about mental health and encourage students to seek support without stigma.

- Use compassionate communication—phrases like *"I understand that this may be a difficult time for you"* can make students feel seen.

- Encourage a growth mindset—frame mistakes as learning opportunities, not failures.

- Avoid punitive measures for missed participation—instead, check in with struggling students privately.

Example: If a student frequently misses deadlines due to depression, instead of penalizing them outright, offer structured extensions or flexible deadlines when feasible.

3.2 Recognizing Signs of Mental Health Struggles

- Sudden drop in participation or academic performance.

- Frequent absences or missed assignments.

- Expressions of hopelessness, anxiety, or extreme stress.

- Social withdrawal or disengagement.

- Signs of distress during office hours or in emails.

TA Tip: You are not a mental health counselor, but you can guide students to appropriate campus resources.

3.3 Encouraging Students to Seek Professional Support

- Know where to refer students for counseling, disability services, and mental health crisis intervention.

- Frame seeking help as a strength, not a weakness—many students avoid mental health services due to stigma.

- Offer academic guidance, not therapy—if a student discloses personal struggles, listen empathetically but encourage them to reach out to professionals.

Example:
If a student expresses overwhelming anxiety about coursework, you might say:
"I appreciate you sharing this with me. I want you to succeed, and I encourage you to check out the campus counseling center, which has resources for stress and academic anxiety. I can also work with you to break assignments into smaller, manageable steps."

4. Practical Steps for TAs to Promote Inclusivity

4.1 Communicate an Open-Door Policy

- Make it clear that students can approach you for academic guidance without judgment.
- Reinforce that struggling with coursework does not mean they don't belong in academia.

4.2 Offer Flexible Office Hours

- Consider virtual office hours for students who may have anxiety about face-to-face meetings.
- Provide multiple ways for students to ask questions (email, discussion boards, anonymous Q&A).

4.3 Advocate for Institutional Change

- If you notice systematic accessibility barriers in the course, communicate with faculty to improve inclusivity.
- Advocate for better accommodations, flexible grading policies, and mental health days where appropriate.

5. Conclusion

Supporting students with disabilities and mental health concerns is not just about compliance—it is about fostering a learning environment where every student has an equal opportunity to succeed. As a TA, your role is to implement accessible teaching strategies, encourage mental well-being, and create a space where students feel valued and supported.

By normalizing accommodations, practicing empathy, and guiding students toward appropriate resources, you can contribute to an academic culture that prioritizes inclusion, equity, and student success.

Ultimately, when students with disabilities and mental health challenges receive the support they need, they are not only able to thrive academically but also to develop confidence, resilience, and a sense of belonging in their educational journey.

Resources Available for Students Needing Academic and Personal Support

Higher education can be a transformative yet challenging experience, and students often require academic and personal support to navigate their journey successfully. As a Teaching Assistant (TA), your role extends beyond delivering course content—you also serve as a mentor, guide, and advocate, helping students access the resources they need to thrive. Whether students are facing academic struggles, personal hardships, financial difficulties, or mental health concerns, directing them to appropriate resources can make a significant difference in their success and well-being.

This section provides an overview of the types of support services available to students, how to guide students toward these resources, and best practices for creating a supportive and inclusive learning environment.

1. Understanding the Range of Student Support Services

Universities offer a variety of resources designed to help students overcome academic challenges, manage personal hardships, and develop essential skills for success. These resources generally fall into the following categories:

1.1 Academic Support Services

Students often encounter difficulties with coursework, study habits, research, and writing. Academic support services provide tutoring, workshops, and skill-building sessions to help students succeed.

- Writing Centers – Assist with essays, research papers, and academic writing skills.
- Tutoring Services – Offer subject-specific tutoring for struggling students.
- Library and Research Assistance – Provide guidance on academic databases, citations, and research strategies.
- Study Skills Workshops – Teach time management, note-taking, and test preparation strategies.
- Peer Mentorship Programs – Pair students with experienced peers for guidance and support.

TA Tip: If a student is struggling with assignments, recommend study groups, tutoring sessions, or writing consultations.

1.2 Mental Health and Well-Being Resources

The pressures of academic life, social expectations, and personal stressors can significantly impact students' mental health and well-being. Many institutions offer confidential counseling and mental health services to support students [82].

- Counseling and Psychological Services (CAPS) – Provide one-on-one therapy, group therapy, crisis counseling, and referrals.
- Mindfulness and Stress Management Workshops – Teach relaxation techniques, meditation, and coping strategies.
- Support Groups – Offer spaces for students experiencing grief, anxiety, depression, or cultural adjustment challenges.
- 24/7 Crisis Hotlines – Provide immediate support for students in distress.

Example: If a student expresses feelings of being overwhelmed or burnt out, suggest they reach out to the counseling center for mental health support.

1.3 Disability and Accessibility Services

Students with physical, sensory, cognitive, or psychological disabilities may require academic accommodations to support their learning experience.

- Disability Services Office – Provides official accommodations, note-taking support, alternative exam formats, and assistive technology.
- Accessible Learning Tools – Includes screen readers, captioned lectures, and ergonomic software.
- Extended Deadlines and Testing Accommodations – Supports students with learning disabilities, ADHD, or medical conditions.

TA Tip: If a student discloses a disability but is unaware of available accommodations, guide them toward the Disability Services Office to explore their options.

1.4 Career and Professional Development Support

Many students seek guidance on internships, career planning, and job applications as they prepare for post-graduation opportunities.

- Career Services Center – Assists with resume building, mock interviews, job search strategies, and career coaching.
- Internship and Job Placement Assistance – Connects students with industry opportunities and networking events.
- Graduate School Advising – Offers guidance on applying to master's and doctoral programs.
- Alumni Mentorship Programs – Pairs students with professionals in their field for career guidance.

Example: If a student is unsure about their career path, recommend scheduling a career counseling session or attending career fairs on campus.

1.5 Financial Aid and Emergency Assistance

Financial barriers can significantly impact academic performance and student well-being. Universities often provide financial resources and emergency aid to help students manage tuition, housing, and basic needs.

- Financial Aid Office – Assists with scholarships, grants, student loans, and tuition payment plans.
- Emergency Student Relief Funds – Provides short-term financial assistance for students facing unexpected financial hardships.
- Food Pantries and Housing Assistance – Helps students experiencing food insecurity or housing instability.
- Work-Study and On-Campus Job Opportunities – Connects students with part-time jobs to help cover expenses.

TA Tip: If a student is struggling financially, direct them to scholarship opportunities, emergency grants, or student work programs.

2. How TAs Can Support Students in Accessing Resources

As a TA, you are not expected to solve students' problems directly, but you can help by guiding them toward the appropriate resources. Here's how:

2.1 Creating Awareness of Available Resources

- Include a list of student resources in the course syllabus or Learning Management System (LMS).

- Announce available support services at the beginning of the semester and remind students periodically.

- Use office hours as a space to check in on students' needs and offer guidance.

Example: At the start of the semester, provide a Resource Guide with links to academic support, counseling, and financial aid services.

2.2 Recognizing When a Student Needs Support

TAs often serve as the first point of contact when students face difficulties. Some signs that a student may need additional support include:
- Frequent absences or declining performance.
- Missed assignments or disengagement in class.
- Expressions of stress, anxiety, or hopelessness.
- Sudden changes in behavior or emotional distress.

Example: If a student suddenly stops attending class, check in with a compassionate email:
"I noticed you haven't been in class lately—just wanted to check in and see if everything is okay. Let me know if I can help connect you with any resources."

2.3 Maintaining Boundaries While Offering Support

- Listen empathetically, but do not act as a therapist or advisor.

- Provide guidance without making assumptions—let students choose whether they want to access resources.

- Respect privacy—do not share a student's situation without their permission, unless there is a safety concern.

Example: If a student discloses financial hardship, avoid personal opinions and instead say:
"I understand that financial challenges can be stressful. The Financial Aid Office has emergency relief funds available—I'd be happy to help you find more information."

3. Encouraging a Culture of Support and Inclusivity

TAs can help normalize help-seeking behavior and create an academic culture where students feel comfortable accessing support.

- Emphasize that seeking help is a sign of strength, not weakness.
- Use inclusive and affirming language to make students feel welcome.

- Share success stories of students who have benefited from academic and personal support services.
- Model a balanced approach to well-being—if students see that you value self-care and time management, they may feel encouraged to do the same.

Example: If students seem overwhelmed before finals, remind them:
"The university offers stress management workshops, tutoring, and extended library hours during exam season—don't hesitate to use these resources!"

4. Conclusion

Ensuring that students are aware of and have access to academic and personal support resources is an essential part of fostering an inclusive, equitable, and supportive learning environment. As a TA, you can empower students to overcome challenges by connecting them with resources that address academic struggles, mental health concerns, financial barriers, and career planning.

By proactively sharing information, recognizing when students need help, and creating a supportive classroom culture, TAs play a crucial role in promoting student success and well-being—both inside and outside the classroom. Ultimately, when students feel supported, they are more likely to thrive academically, professionally, and personally.

Chapter 9: Professional Communication and Conduct

Figure 9.1. Teaching and Learning [113].

Serving as a Teaching Assistant (TA) is not just an academic responsibility—it is an opportunity to develop essential skills that can pave the way for future roles in higher education, research, industry, and beyond. Many TAs aspire to become faculty members, researchers, instructional designers, or professionals in corporate, government, or nonprofit sectors. Regardless of the career path chosen, the experiences gained as a TA—such as leadership, communication, mentorship, and classroom management—are invaluable in shaping one's professional journey.

This chapter explores how TAs can strategically leverage their experiences to prepare for future roles. It provides insights into transitioning from a TA position to a faculty or research role, developing strong academic credentials, and expanding professional networks. Additionally, it discusses alternative career pathways for those who wish to apply their teaching and leadership skills outside of academia, including roles in corporate training, educational consulting, policy-making, and instructional design.

Moreover, this chapter highlights the importance of continuous learning and skill development. From publishing research and presenting at conferences to securing fellowships and developing expertise in pedagogy, the path forward for TAs is filled with opportunities for growth and professional advancement.

By the end of this chapter, TAs will be able to:

- Identify and pursue academic career paths, including faculty and research positions.

- Develop a strong academic and professional portfolio for future opportunities.

- Explore alternative career options outside of academia that value teaching and mentoring experience.

- Network effectively with faculty, peers, and industry professionals to expand career prospects.

- Continue professional development through certifications, workshops, and advanced training.

- Apply leadership, instructional, and research skills to future roles in various industries.

Whether a TA plans to continue in academia or transition to a different field, the skills and knowledge gained from teaching can serve as a powerful foundation for lifelong success. By planning strategically and seeking opportunities for professional growth, TAs can position themselves for rewarding careers that align with their passions and expertise.

Communicating Professionally with Faculty, Students, and Peers

Effective professional communication is a cornerstone of success in a Teaching Assistant (TA) role, shaping relationships with faculty, students, and colleagues while ensuring clarity, respect, and efficiency in academic settings. TAs serve as intermediaries between students and instructors, and their ability to communicate professionally can impact classroom dynamics, faculty collaboration, and the overall educational experience.

Professional communication extends beyond using formal language—it involves active listening, adapting communication styles for different audiences, and maintaining ethical standards in verbal, written, and digital interactions. This section explores best practices for communicating with faculty, students, and peers, handling challenging conversations, and fostering an inclusive and respectful academic environment.

1. The Foundations of Professional Communication

Professional communication in academia is built upon three key principles:

- Clarity – Deliver messages concisely and unambiguously to prevent misunderstandings.
- Respect – Maintain courteous and inclusive language, regardless of the audience.
- Adaptability – Tailor communication to different contexts (e.g., formal with faculty, approachable with students).

By adhering to these principles, TAs can establish credibility, strengthen relationships, and create a positive learning environment.

2. Communicating with Faculty: Navigating the TA-Faculty Relationship

Faculty members serve as mentors, supervisors, and academic leaders, and effective communication with them is essential for ensuring alignment between teaching expectations and TA responsibilities.

2.1 Best Practices for Communicating with Faculty

- Use Professional Email Etiquette

    - Always use a formal greeting (e.g., *Dear Professor [Last Name]*).

    - Keep messages clear, concise, and grammatically correct.

    - Summarize key points upfront to avoid lengthy emails.

    - End with a professional closing (e.g., *Best regards, [Your Name]*).

Example Email to Faculty:

Subject: Follow-Up on Grading Guidelines for Midterm Assignments

Dear Professor Smith,

I hope you are doing well. I am reaching out for clarification on the grading criteria for the midterm essays. Would you prefer comments to be focused on content depth, writing mechanics, or both? Additionally, should we apply a grading rubric or provide individualized qualitative feedback?

Please let me know at your convenience. Thank you for your guidance.

Best regards,
[Your Name]

- **Be Proactive and Solution-Oriented**

    - If you anticipate challenges (e.g., student complaints, grading inconsistencies, scheduling conflicts), communicate early and propose solutions.

    - Keep faculty updated on student progress or concerns while respecting student confidentiality.

- **Maintain Professional Boundaries**

    - Recognize hierarchical structures in academia while maintaining confidence in your role.

    - Approach feedback or disagreements diplomatically (e.g., *"I understand your perspective on grading rigor   would you be open to discussing an alternative rubric for consistency?"*).

TA Tip: Schedule regular check-ins with faculty to align on expectations, share concerns, and clarify responsibilities.

3. Communicating with Students: Balancing Approachability and Authority

TAs act as mentors, facilitators, and academic guides for students, requiring a balance between approachability and professionalism. Clear and respectful communication can build trust, enhance engagement, and prevent misunderstandings.

3.1 Best Practices for Communicating with Students

- **Set Communication Expectations Early**

    - Clarify office hours, response times, and preferred communication methods at the start of the semester.

    - Use Learning Management Systems (LMS) (Canvas, Blackboard) for announcements rather than personal messaging platforms.

- **Use a Professional Yet Supportive Tone**

- Avoid overly casual language (e.g., "Hey guys, what's up?"). Instead, use warm but formal phrasing (e.g., "Hello everyone, I hope your week is going well.").
    - Address students by name and with respect to establish rapport.

- **Respond to Emails and Questions Efficiently**
    - Acknowledge inquiries promptly, even if a full response takes time (e.g., *"I appreciate your email and will get back to you with details by tomorrow."*).
    - Provide clear and direct responses, avoiding unnecessary complexity.

- **Maintain Boundaries While Being Supportive**
    - Do not share personal opinions on grades, faculty, or other students.
    - If students request personal favors (e.g., grade inflation, deadline extensions without reason), refer to course policies rather than making independent decisions.
    - Redirect students to campus resources for non-academic concerns (e.g., counseling, disability services).

Example Response to a Student Inquiry About Grades:

Subject: Question Regarding Midterm Grade

Hi [Student Name],

Thank you for reaching out. I understand your concern about your midterm grade. I recommend reviewing the feedback provided on your assignment and comparing it to the grading rubric. If you would like to discuss specific areas for improvement, feel free to attend my office hours on [day/time].

Best,
[Your Name]

TA Tip: Avoid engaging in confrontational email exchanges. If a student disputes a grade or policy, suggest a face-to-face or virtual meeting to discuss concerns constructively.

4. Communicating with Peers and Fellow TAs: Fostering Collaboration

TAs often work in teams, requiring collegial communication and coordination to ensure consistency in grading, instruction, and student support.

4.1 Best Practices for Communicating with Peers

- **Respect Different Roles and Responsibilities**
    - Recognize that some TAs may have different duties (e.g., grading vs. teaching) and align expectations accordingly.

- o   Be collaborative rather than competitive—share best practices and resources.

- **Coordinate Grading and Teaching Consistently**

  - o   If multiple TAs are grading the same assignments, establish standardized rubrics and grading norms to ensure fairness.

  - o   Hold team meetings to align on student concerns, grading trends, and best practices.

- **Handle Conflicts Professionally**

  - o   If disagreements arise (e.g., grading disputes, workload concerns), address them diplomatically rather than through public complaints or email confrontations.

  - o   Use neutral and constructive language (e.g., *"I noticed we have slightly different grading approaches. Would you be open to discussing a way to ensure consistency?"*).

Example of a Professional Team Email:

Subject: Coordination of Final Exam Grading

Hi Team,

As we begin grading the final exams, I wanted to check if we are using a standardized approach to ensure consistency. Would it be helpful to review a few sample responses together before finalizing scores? Let me know your thoughts!

Best,
[Your Name]

TA Tip: Be a team player. If a fellow TA is struggling, offer collaborative solutions rather than criticism.

5. Handling Difficult Conversations with Professionalism

Academic settings can involve challenging conversations, including student complaints, grading disputes, or disagreements with faculty. Handling these conversations with professionalism is essential for maintaining credibility and respect.

- Stay Calm and Objective – Avoid emotional responses and focus on facts.
- Acknowledge Concerns and Offer Solutions – Validate concerns without making promises beyond your authority.
- Know When to Escalate Issues – If a conflict is beyond your role, refer the issue to the faculty supervisor.

Example Response to a Student Grade Dispute:
"I understand your concern about the grade. I am happy to go over the rubric and feedback with

6. Conclusion

Professional communication is an essential skill for TAs, impacting relationships with faculty, students, and peers. By practicing clear, respectful, and adaptable communication strategies, TAs can foster collaboration, enhance student engagement, and navigate academic responsibilities with confidence. Ultimately, strong communication skills lay the foundation for a productive and professional teaching experience.

Handling Student Concerns, Complaints, and Requests Appropriately

In the academic environment, Teaching Assistants (TAs) serve as a bridge between students and faculty, often acting as the first point of contact for student concerns, complaints, and requests. Students may approach TAs with questions about grading, conflicts with course material, extension requests, or broader academic concerns, making it essential for TAs to handle these interactions professionally, equitably, and with a balance of empathy and authority.

Effectively managing student concerns requires clear communication, adherence to institutional policies, and maintaining a professional yet approachable demeanor. This section explores best practices for addressing student complaints and requests, strategies for conflict resolution, and techniques for maintaining fairness and boundaries in student interactions.

1. Understanding the Nature of Student Concerns, Complaints, and Requests

Students may reach out with various types of concerns, each requiring a different approach. These typically fall into the following categories:

1.1 Academic Concerns

- Grading Disputes – Students may challenge a grade or request a reassessment.
- Assignment Clarity – Students may seek clarification on instructions, rubrics, or expectations.
- Course Material Difficulties – Some students struggle to grasp complex concepts and may need additional guidance.

1.2 Administrative and Procedural Issues

- Deadline Extensions – Students may request extra time due to illness, personal circumstances, or workload concerns.
- Make-up Exams and Attendance Issues – Students may need accommodations for missed tests or mandatory class sessions.
- Group Project Conflicts – Interpersonal issues within team assignments may require mediation.

1.3 Personal or Well-being-Related Concerns

- Mental Health and Stress – Students experiencing anxiety, burnout, or emotional distress may seek guidance.

- Financial or Accessibility Challenges – Some students may struggle with resources and require institutional support.

TA Tip: Not all student concerns fall within your scope of authority. Recognizing when to handle an issue yourself and when to refer a student to faculty or campus resources is key to maintaining professional boundaries.

2. Best Practices for Addressing Student Concerns and Complaints

2.1 Establishing an Open and Professional Communication Channel

- Encourage students to reach out early—set expectations in your syllabus or during the first class session.

- Provide multiple communication options—such as office hours, email, or discussion forums, while maintaining boundaries (e.g., avoiding personal messaging platforms).

- Set realistic response times—acknowledge student concerns promptly, even if a full resolution takes time.

Example Email Response to a Student Concern:

Subject: Follow-Up on Your Concern Regarding Assignment Feedback

Hi [Student Name],

Thank you for reaching out. I understand your concerns about your assignment grade. I'd be happy to go over the feedback in more detail during my office hours on [day/time] or via email.

If you would like to discuss this further with the professor, I can also help facilitate that conversation. Let me know what works best for you.

Best,
[Your Name]

2.2 Handling Grade Disputes with Fairness and Transparency

Grading complaints are among the most common student concerns and require a structured, impartial approach.

Best Practices for Addressing Grade Disputes:

- Remain Objective and Data-Driven – Use the grading rubric to explain how the student's work was assessed.
- Encourage Self-Review – Ask students to compare their work against the rubric before discussing further.
- Document the Discussion – Keep records of grading disputes in case further intervention is needed.
- Know Your Limits – If a grading decision is beyond your authority, refer the student to the faculty member.

Example Conversation Approach for a Grade Dispute:
"I understand that you're concerned about your grade. Let's go through the rubric together and compare it with your submission. If you still feel that there is an issue, we can discuss the next steps, including bringing it to the professor for further review."

TA Tip: If multiple students raise the same grading concern, there may be an issue with the clarity of the rubric or assignment instructions—communicating this to faculty can help improve future assessments.

2.3 Managing Requests for Deadline Extensions and Accommodations

Students may request deadline extensions for various reasons, including personal emergencies, mental health struggles, or workload concerns. While some flexibility can be beneficial, it is crucial to ensure fairness and adherence to course policies.

Best Practices for Handling Extension Requests:

- Refer to Course Policies – Ensure consistency by applying the same standards to all students.
- Assess the Validity of the Request – Distinguish between genuine emergencies (e.g., illness, family crisis) and last-minute requests due to poor planning.
- Offer Alternative Solutions – If an extension isn't possible, suggest strategies for partial submission or extra credit opportunities.
- Encourage Proactive Communication – Students should request extensions before the deadline, not after missing it.

Example Response to a Late Deadline Extension Request:

Hi [Student Name],

I understand that unexpected challenges can arise. Unfortunately, per the course policy, deadline extensions must be requested before the due date. However, I encourage you to submit what you have so far, and I'd be happy to provide feedback to help you for the next assignment. Let me know how I can support you moving forward.

Best,
[Your Name]

2.4 Mediating Student Conflicts and Interpersonal Issues

TAs may also need to mediate conflicts, such as disputes in group projects or tensions in class discussions.

Best Practices for Conflict Resolution:

- Stay Neutral – Avoid taking sides and facilitate a constructive dialogue.
- Encourage Direct Communication – Guide students to express their concerns respectfully to one another.
- Focus on Solutions – Help students identify actionable ways to move forward rather than

assigning blame.
- Refer to Faculty If Necessary – If conflicts escalate or disrupt class dynamics, faculty intervention may be needed.

Example Conflict Mediation Statement:
"I hear that there's frustration about task distribution in your group project. Let's go over the assignment expectations together and discuss how responsibilities can be adjusted so that everyone contributes fairly."

3. Maintaining Professionalism and Boundaries in Student Interactions

While TAs should be approachable and supportive, maintaining boundaries is essential to ensuring professionalism and avoiding favoritism or ethical dilemmas.

3.1 Establishing Clear Boundaries

- Stick to Academic Topics – If a student shares personal difficulties, listen empathetically but refer them to appropriate campus resources (e.g., counseling services).
- Avoid Overpromising – Do not agree to changes in grading, policies, or coursework without faculty approval.
- Maintain Confidentiality – Do not discuss student complaints with others unless necessary for resolution.

Example Boundary-Setting Response:
"I appreciate you sharing this with me. While I am not qualified to provide personal guidance, I encourage you to reach out to [campus resource] for additional support. If there's anything I can do academically, let me know how I can help."

4. Conclusion

Handling student concerns, complaints, and requests professionally, fairly, and empathetically is a core responsibility of a TA. By implementing clear communication strategies, maintaining boundaries, and applying institutional policies consistently, TAs can foster a supportive and equitable learning environment.

Ultimately, effective conflict resolution and student support enhance both academic integrity and the student experience, reinforcing the TA's role as a trusted mentor and academic facilitator.

Setting Boundaries and Managing Workload as a TA

Serving as a Teaching Assistant (TA) is a rewarding yet demanding role that requires balancing multiple responsibilities, managing time effectively, and setting clear professional boundaries. TAs are often responsible for grading assignments, leading discussion sections, assisting faculty, supporting students, and engaging in their own academic work. Without structured boundaries and workload management strategies, TAs may experience burnout, struggle with conflicting obligations, or feel overwhelmed by student demands.

By establishing clear expectations, prioritizing tasks, and maintaining professional limits, TAs can foster a sustainable and productive work environment, ensuring both teaching excellence and personal academic success. This section explores strategies for setting boundaries, managing workload effectively, and maintaining professional well-being while fulfilling TA duties.

1. Understanding the Importance of Boundaries as a TA

Boundaries are essential for maintaining a professional relationship with students, faculty, and peers while ensuring that TA responsibilities do not negatively impact personal academic progress or well-being. Without boundaries, TAs risk overcommitting, being taken advantage of, or feeling pressure to be constantly available.

1.1 Why Boundaries Matter for TAs

- Prevents Burnout – Protects against overwork, stress, and exhaustion.
- Ensures Fairness and Consistency – Reduces favoritism or ethical dilemmas in student interactions.
- Promotes Professionalism – Establishes clear roles, expectations, and limits in faculty and student relationships.
- Supports Time Management – Helps balance grading, teaching, research, and coursework efficiently.

TA Tip: Setting boundaries is not about being unhelpful—it's about ensuring that your support is sustainable and fair to all students.

2. Setting Professional Boundaries with Students

TAs must balance being approachable and supportive while maintaining a professional and structured relationship with students. This involves setting limits on availability, communication methods, and the scope of assistance provided.

2.1 Establishing Clear Communication Boundaries

- Define Office Hours and Availability

    - Set specific times for student meetings and avoid responding to emails outside those hours.

    - Post office hours in the syllabus, course website, or LMS (Canvas, Blackboard, Moodle).

Example Statement to Students:
"I am available for office hours on Tuesdays and Thursdays from 2:00 PM to 4:00 PM. Outside of these hours, please email me, and I will respond within 24 hours."

- **Use Professional Communication Channels**

    - Encourage students to use email or LMS messaging rather than personal messaging apps.

o   Avoid social media interactions with students to maintain professional distance.

Example Response to a Late-Night Student Email:

Hi [Student Name],

Thank you for reaching out. I wanted to acknowledge your email and let you know that I will respond during my working hours tomorrow. In the meantime, you may want to review [course resource] for clarification.

Best,
[Your Name]

2.2 Maintaining Fairness and Consistency in Student Interactions

- Apply Course Policies Uniformly

    o   Do not make exceptions for individual students unless explicitly approved by faculty.

    o   Ensure all students have equal access to resources and opportunities.

- Avoid Personal Attachments or Favoritism

    o   Keep student interactions strictly academic—do not develop close friendships with students during the course.

    o   If a student seeks personal advice or counseling, refer them to campus support services rather than becoming personally involved.

Example Response to a Student Requesting Special Treatment:

I understand that this deadline may be challenging. However, to maintain fairness for all students, I must follow the course policy, which does not allow for individual extensions. If you're struggling, I recommend reaching out to the professor to discuss your options.

2.3 Protecting Personal Time and Well-Being

- Avoid Overcommitting to Student Support

    o   Some students may expect immediate responses or extensive support beyond your responsibilities. Set clear expectations early.

- Limit Emotional Labor

    o   While being empathetic is important, do not take on students' personal struggles beyond your role as an academic support figure.

Example Boundary-Setting Response:

I appreciate you sharing your challenges with me. While I'm not trained to provide personal counseling, I encourage you to reach out to the student wellness center, which has great resources to support you.

3. Managing Workload and Time Effectively as a TA

Balancing TA responsibilities, coursework, and research requires efficient time management and workload prioritization. Without proper planning, grading deadlines can pile up, student emails can become overwhelming, and academic progress can suffer.

3.1 Prioritizing and Structuring Workload

- Use a Weekly Planning System – Schedule grading, office hours, research, and coursework in advance.
- Break Large Tasks into Smaller Steps – Set manageable daily goals rather than attempting to complete everything at once.
- Use Time-Blocking Techniques – Dedicate specific periods for different tasks (e.g., grading in the morning, research in the afternoon).
- Limit Multitasking – Focus on one task at a time to maintain efficiency and quality.

Example Weekly Time Management Plan:

- Monday: Research + Meeting with Faculty

- Tuesday: Grading Assignments + Office Hours

- Wednesday: Research + Personal Study

- Thursday: Teaching + Student Email Responses

- Friday: Research + Prep for Next Week

3.2 Managing Grading and Feedback Efficiently

- Use Grading Rubrics – Standardized rubrics help streamline grading, ensure fairness, and reduce time spent on subjective evaluation.

- Batch Similar Tasks Together – Grade all question 1 responses first, then move to question 2 to maintain consistency and speed.

- Set a Grading Time Limit – Avoid spending excessive time on individual assignments; aim for a set number of minutes per submission.

Example Grading Strategy:

- Step 1: Skim all submissions to get an overall sense of student performance.

- Step 2: Grade using the rubric, assigning marks systematically.

- Step 3: Provide brief, constructive feedback (e.g., highlight one strength and one area for improvement).

3.3 Communicating Workload Expectations with Faculty

- Clarify Responsibilities Early – Discuss workload expectations at the start of the semester to avoid unexpected burdens.

- Communicate When Overloaded – If responsibilities exceed agreed hours, address concerns professionally with faculty.

- Advocate for Reasonable Expectations – Some professors may unintentionally assign excessive grading or administrative tasks—TAs should feel comfortable requesting adjustments if needed.

Example Professional Email to Faculty About Workload:

Subject: Clarification on TA Responsibilities for [Course Name]

Dear Professor [Last Name],

I appreciate the opportunity to support [Course Name] this semester. As I manage my TA duties alongside my academic commitments, I wanted to clarify expectations regarding the grading volume and student inquiries. If possible, could we discuss workload distribution to ensure I can meet both TA and research responsibilities effectively?

Looking forward to your guidance.

Best regards,
[Your Name]

4. Conclusion

Setting boundaries and managing workload effectively as a TA is crucial for maintaining professional integrity, avoiding burnout, and balancing teaching responsibilities with personal academic progress. By establishing clear expectations with students, managing time efficiently, and advocating for fair workload distribution, TAs can create a sustainable and fulfilling teaching experience.

Ultimately, the ability to set limits while remaining a supportive and professional presence not only enhances the TA's well-being but also fosters a structured and equitable learning environment for students.

Ethics in Teaching and Avoiding Conflicts of Interest

Teaching Assistants (TAs) hold a unique position within the academic ecosystem, acting as mentors, facilitators, evaluators, and liaisons between students and faculty. With this role comes the ethical responsibility to uphold academic integrity, fairness, professionalism, and objectivity in all teaching-related interactions. Ethical teaching ensures that students are evaluated equitably, personal biases do not influence decisions, and professional relationships remain free from conflicts of interest.

As a TA, navigating ethical dilemmas can be complex—grading disputes, personal relationships with students, confidentiality issues, and power dynamics all present potential challenges. Understanding ethical principles and proactively avoiding conflicts of interest not only protects the integrity of the learning environment but also safeguards the TA's own professional reputation.

This section explores core ethical principles in teaching, common conflicts of interest, and strategies for maintaining professional and ethical boundaries as a TA.

1. The Foundations of Ethical Teaching

Ethical teaching is guided by four key principles:

- Fairness and Equity – Ensuring that all students receive equal opportunities and unbiased evaluations.
- Confidentiality – Protecting student privacy and maintaining discretion in academic matters.
- Integrity and Objectivity – Making impartial decisions that are free from personal, financial, or relational influences.
- Professionalism – Maintaining appropriate conduct in all interactions with students, faculty, and peers.

By adhering to these principles, TAs foster trust in the academic environment, uphold institutional values, and create an inclusive, ethical learning space.

2. Avoiding Conflicts of Interest in Teaching

A conflict of interest occurs when personal relationships, financial incentives, or external pressures compromise—or appear to compromise—a TA's ability to make fair and objective decisions. Even the perception of bias can damage credibility, erode trust, and undermine academic integrity.

2.1 Common Types of Conflicts of Interest for TAs

A. Personal Relationships with Students

- Teaching or grading a close friend, roommate, or family member.

- Engaging in romantic or social relationships with students under your supervision.

- Favoring certain students due to personal connections.

Ethical Approach:
- If assigned to grade or oversee someone you have a close relationship with, disclose this to faculty and request reassignment.
- Avoid socializing extensively with students during the semester to prevent perceptions of favoritism.
- Maintain professional boundaries—even outside the classroom, interactions should remain appropriate and ethical.

B. Bias in Grading and Evaluation

- Giving preferential treatment to students you like or penalizing students you find difficult.

- Allowing personal opinions, beliefs, or biases to influence grading.

- Changing grades to accommodate student pressure, persuasion, or special requests.

Ethical Approach:

- Use standardized rubrics and grading criteria to ensure objective assessments.

- Grade anonymously when possible to reduce unconscious bias.

- Keep detailed records of grading decisions in case of disputes.

- If students challenge a grade, follow department procedures rather than making discretionary changes.

C. Confidentiality Violations

- Sharing student grades, feedback, or academic concerns with unauthorized individuals.

- Discussing student performance with peers outside professional contexts.

- Publicly disclosing student issues in a way that compromises their privacy.

Ethical Approach:

- FERPA Compliance – Follow the Family Educational Rights and Privacy Act (FERPA) guidelines, which protect student records and personal data [83].

- Only discuss student performance with authorized faculty members.

- If a student confides in you about personal struggles, direct them to appropriate campus resources instead of discussing it with others.

D. Financial and Professional Conflicts

- Tutoring students for pay while also serving as their TA.

- Accepting gifts, favors, or financial incentives from students in exchange for special treatment.

- Using TA influence to promote personal business, political views, or external interests.

Ethical Approach:

- Avoid tutoring or mentoring students for money if they are enrolled in your class.

- Politely decline gifts or favors that could be perceived as influencing your grading or evaluation.

- Keep academic roles separate from personal financial interests.

2.2 Setting Boundaries to Prevent Ethical Conflicts

- Maintain Professional Distance:

- Be friendly but not overly familiar with students.
- If students request unofficial favors (e.g., extended deadlines, extra credit opportunities not available to others), refer to course policies.

- Document Key Interactions:

- Keep written records of grade changes, student complaints, and sensitive conversations to protect against ethical disputes.

- Seek Guidance When Uncertain:

- If facing a potential ethical conflict, consult with faculty, department heads, or institutional ethics guidelines for advice.

Example Statement for Setting Boundaries with Students:
"I appreciate your concern about the assignment grade. To maintain fairness for all students, I follow the grading criteria outlined in the rubric. If you still have questions, I encourage you to speak with the professor."

3. Handling Ethical Dilemmas and Difficult Situations

Despite best efforts, TAs may encounter situations where ethical decisions are not clear-cut. Here's how to navigate common dilemmas:

3.1 Scenario: A Student Asks for a Favor Outside of Policy

Situation: A student requests an extension on an assignment, citing personal stress but not providing documentation.

Response:
"I understand that coursework can be stressful, and I encourage you to reach out to student wellness resources if you need additional support. Unfortunately, I cannot grant individual extensions outside of the course policy, but I recommend discussing this with the professor."

3.2 Scenario: A Friend is Enrolled in Your Course

Situation: A close friend is in your section, and you are responsible for grading their assignments.

Response:
Notify faculty as soon as possible and request to have another TA grade the friend's work to avoid conflicts of interest.

3.3 Scenario: A Student Offers a Gift in Exchange for Special Treatment

Situation: A student brings a gift and thanks you in advance for "helping" with their grade.

Response:
"I appreciate the thought, but as a TA, I have to ensure fairness in grading. I can't accept gifts, but I'm happy to answer any questions you have about the material!"

3.4 Scenario: A Student Shares Personal Struggles with You

Situation: A student confides in you about mental health struggles, financial difficulties, or family emergencies affecting their performance.

Response:
- Listen empathetically, but avoid giving personal advice.
- Refer the student to counseling services, financial aid, or student support programs for professional assistance.

Example Response:
"I'm really sorry to hear that you're going through this. I encourage you to reach out to the counseling center—they have excellent resources that can help. If you'd like, I can also help you set up a meeting with an academic advisor to discuss your coursework options."

4. Conclusion

Upholding ethical teaching practices and avoiding conflicts of interest is essential for maintaining academic integrity, fairness, and professionalism as a TA. By setting clear boundaries, following institutional policies, and ensuring unbiased interactions, TAs can foster an inclusive and ethical learning environment.

When in doubt, TAs should always:
- Prioritize fairness and consistency.
- Consult faculty or ethics guidelines if unsure.
- Respect student confidentiality and maintain professionalism.

Ultimately, ethical teaching is not just about following rules—it's about creating a respectful, trustworthy, and equitable educational experience for all students.

Chapter 10: Continuous Improvement and Teaching Evaluations

Higher education is undergoing a period of rapid transformation, influenced by advancements in technology, shifts in student demographics, evolving pedagogical methods, and increasing emphasis on diversity, equity, and inclusion. As institutions adapt to these changes, the role of Teaching Assistants (TAs) is also evolving. No longer just graders or discussion leaders, TAs now play a critical role in shaping student engagement, facilitating hybrid and online learning, integrating artificial intelligence (AI) into education, and supporting mental health initiatives in academic settings.

This chapter examines how the role of TAs continues to expand, providing insights into emerging trends that will influence teaching and learning in the years to come. It explores how TAs can adapt to new instructional models, including blended learning, competency-based education, and flipped classrooms. Additionally, it discusses the growing importance of digital literacy, accessibility, and inclusive teaching practices to ensure that all students—regardless of background or ability—have equitable opportunities for success.

Figure 10.1. Teaching and Learning [113].

Moreover, this chapter highlights the intersection of technology and teaching, addressing how TAs can effectively incorporate AI tools, virtual reality (VR), and data-driven insights to enhance student learning. As education becomes more globalized, TAs are also increasingly involved in international collaborations, cross-cultural instruction, and the development of interdisciplinary learning approaches.

By the end of this chapter, TAs will be able to:

- Understand the evolving landscape of higher education and the TA's role within it.

- Adapt to emerging teaching methodologies, including hybrid and competency-based learning.

- Integrate AI, digital tools, and virtual learning platforms to enhance instruction.

- Promote accessibility, diversity, and inclusion in academic settings.

- Navigate changes in student expectations and mental health support in education.
- Stay ahead of educational trends and professional development opportunities for long-term career growth.

As education continues to change, TAs must remain adaptable, innovative, and proactive in their professional development. By embracing new teaching strategies, leveraging technology, and fostering inclusive learning environments, TAs will not only enhance student success but also position themselves as valuable contributors to the future of higher education.

Understanding Student Evaluations of Teaching Assistants

Student evaluations of Teaching Assistants (TAs) play a critical role in professional development, instructional refinement, and long-term career growth in academia. These evaluations provide direct feedback on a TA's teaching effectiveness, communication skills, approachability, and impact on student learning. Whether formal or informal, student evaluations serve as a valuable tool for self-reflection and continuous improvement—helping TAs refine their teaching methods, strengthen student engagement, and identify areas for development.

However, while student evaluations can offer constructive insights, they also come with challenges, biases, and limitations that must be interpreted thoughtfully. Understanding how to analyze and respond to student feedback effectively allows TAs to enhance their teaching strategies, address concerns, and develop a growth mindset that fosters excellence in both teaching and mentorship.

This section explores the purpose of student evaluations, common evaluation criteria, potential biases, and best practices for using feedback to improve teaching performance.

1. The Purpose of Student Evaluations for Teaching Assistants

Student evaluations are typically conducted through anonymous surveys, rating scales, or open-ended feedback forms, allowing students to assess their TA's effectiveness in various aspects of instruction. These evaluations serve multiple purposes, including:

- Assessing Teaching Effectiveness – Measuring how well the TA explains concepts, engages students, and supports learning.
- Providing Constructive Feedback – Offering insights into strengths and areas for improvement.
- Enhancing Course Delivery – Identifying instructional techniques that work well and those that need adjustment.
- Professional Development – Building a record of teaching performance that can be used for future academic or career opportunities.
- Institutional and Faculty Review – Informing faculty members and departments about TA performance for future appointments and teaching assignments.

2. Common Criteria in TA Evaluations

Student evaluations often assess several key dimensions of teaching effectiveness, typically categorized as follows:

2.1 Clarity and Communication Skills

- Was the TA clear and articulate in explanations?
- Did they break down complex concepts effectively?
- Were instructions for assignments and discussions easy to understand?

- Best Practice for Improvement: Use structured explanations, provide examples, and check for student understanding through questions or summaries.

2.2 Knowledge and Content Expertise

- Did the TA demonstrate strong subject knowledge?
- Were they able to answer student questions effectively?
- Did they connect course material to real-world applications?

- Best Practice for Improvement: Stay updated on course content, anticipate student questions, and admit when further research is needed rather than providing incorrect information.

2.3 Approachability and Support

- Did students feel comfortable asking the TA for help?
- Was the TA patient and respectful in interactions?
- Did the TA provide timely responses to student inquiries?

- Best Practice for Improvement: Foster an inclusive and non-judgmental atmosphere, encourage office hour attendance, and respond to emails or messages promptly.

2.4 Engagement and Teaching Strategies

- Did the TA actively engage students in discussions and learning activities?
- Were teaching methods interactive, dynamic, and inclusive?
- Did the TA adjust their teaching approach based on student needs?

- Best Practice for Improvement: Incorporate active learning techniques, ask students for real-time feedback, and adjust strategies to match different learning styles.

2.5 Grading Fairness and Feedback Quality

- Were grading criteria clear and consistently applied?
- Did students receive constructive feedback that helped them improve?
- Was the TA fair and impartial in grading?

- Best Practice for Improvement: Use grading rubrics, provide specific and actionable feedback, and maintain consistency across student assessments.

3. Challenges and Limitations of Student Evaluations

While student evaluations are valuable, they are not perfect measures of teaching effectiveness. Several challenges must be acknowledged:

3.1 Potential Bias in Student Evaluations

- Unconscious Bias – Research shows that gender, race, age, and accents can influence student ratings, sometimes unfairly [84].

- Personality vs. Pedagogy – Some students may favor likability over actual teaching effectiveness, rating more leniently if they like the TA personally.

- Grade Expectations – Higher grades can correlate with more favorable reviews, while tougher grading may lead to lower evaluations [85].

- How to Mitigate Bias: Focus on patterns in feedback rather than isolated negative comments. If possible, supplement student evaluations with peer observations, faculty feedback, or self-reflections.

3.2 The Challenge of Vague or Unhelpful Feedback

- Some evaluations may include overly general comments (e.g., "Great TA" or "Not helpful") without specific explanations.

- Some students may provide emotional reactions rather than constructive feedback.

- How to Mitigate: When possible, request mid-semester feedback to gain more actionable insights before final evaluations.

4. How to Interpret and Use Student Feedback Effectively

4.1 Identifying Trends Rather than Isolated Comments

- Look for recurring themes—if multiple students mention the same issue (e.g., unclear explanations), it signals an area for improvement.

- Separate subjective opinions (e.g., "The TA is too strict") from constructive critiques (e.g., "Grading criteria were unclear").

- Best Practice: Compile comments into categories (e.g., "Clarity," "Engagement," "Grading") to identify patterns and prioritize improvements.

4.2 Reflecting on Constructive Criticism

- Instead of reacting defensively to negative comments, view them as opportunities for growth.

- Ask:

    o   What changes can I realistically implement?

    o   Which suggestions align with my teaching philosophy?

    o   Are there faculty or peers I can consult for guidance?

- Best Practice: Develop an action plan for improvement (e.g., "Next semester, I will use more visual aids to improve clarity").

4.3 Seeking Additional Feedback Beyond Student Evaluations

- Mid-Semester Check-Ins – Conduct informal surveys or discussions to get early feedback.

- Peer Observations – Ask other TAs or faculty to observe and provide constructive feedback.

- Self-Reflection Journals – Maintain teaching reflections to track challenges and progress.

- Best Practice: Combine multiple sources of feedback for a holistic view of teaching effectiveness.

5. Using Student Evaluations for Career Growth

5.1 Leveraging Positive Evaluations for Future Teaching Opportunities

- Strong evaluations can enhance academic CVs, teaching portfolios, and recommendation letters.

- Highlight quantifiable achievements in applications (e.g., "94% of students rated my explanations as clear and effective").

- Best Practice: Save positive student feedback and teaching assessments for future job applications or teaching philosophy statements.

5.2 Addressing Weaknesses and Showing Growth

- Demonstrating that you acted on feedback and improved over time strengthens credibility as an instructor.

- Example Reflection Statement for Teaching Portfolios:
  "Early student evaluations indicated a need for clearer explanations. In response, I incorporated structured lecture outlines and interactive discussions, leading to improved feedback in subsequent semesters."

- Best Practice: Use specific examples of growth to show adaptability and a commitment to continuous teaching improvement.

6. Conclusion

Student evaluations provide valuable insights into a TA's effectiveness, offering opportunities for self-reflection, instructional refinement, and long-term growth in teaching. While feedback should be interpreted thoughtfully—recognizing potential biases and limitations—it serves as a powerful tool for enhancing teaching strategies, improving student engagement, and developing professional teaching skills.

By approaching evaluations with an open mind, focusing on constructive feedback, and implementing changes based on student needs, TAs can continuously evolve as educators, contributing to a more effective and inclusive learning environment.

Self-Assessment and Reflective Teaching Practices

Effective teaching is not a static skill—it is an evolving practice that benefits from continuous self-reflection and deliberate assessment. Teaching Assistants (TAs) play a vital role in shaping student learning experiences, and engaging in self-assessment and reflective teaching practices allows them to refine their instructional methods, enhance student engagement, and develop professional growth in academia.

Self-assessment is a systematic process of evaluating one's own teaching effectiveness by analyzing what works, identifying challenges, and making necessary improvements. Reflective teaching, on the other hand, goes beyond evaluating performance—it involves thoughtful introspection about teaching experiences, decisions, and their impact on student learning. By combining these practices, TAs can foster a growth mindset, adapt to student needs, and develop long-term teaching excellence.

This section explores the importance of self-assessment, key methods for reflective teaching, and strategies for incorporating feedback into continuous improvement.

1. The Importance of Self-Assessment and Reflective Teaching

TAs often receive feedback from students, faculty, and peers, but true professional development also requires self-directed analysis of teaching effectiveness. Self-assessment helps TAs:

- Identify Strengths and Areas for Improvement – Recognize effective teaching strategies while pinpointing aspects that need refinement.
- Enhance Student Engagement – Evaluate whether students are responding well to instructional methods and adapt accordingly.
- Develop Confidence and Self-Awareness – Gain insight into teaching style, classroom presence, and areas of expertise.
- Encourage Lifelong Learning – Promote a mindset of continuous pedagogical improvement and adaptability.
- Improve Communication and Classroom Management – Reflect on how well expectations, instructions, and feedback are conveyed to students.

Through regular self-reflection and assessment, TAs become more proactive, intentional, and student-centered educators.

2. Methods for Self-Assessment in Teaching

Self-assessment involves structured reflection on teaching practices, allowing TAs to track progress over time. Below are key strategies to facilitate meaningful self-evaluation:

2.1 Teaching Journals and Reflection Logs

- Maintain a teaching journal to record thoughts, experiences, and challenges after each class session.

- Include reflections on student engagement, effectiveness of explanations, and any unexpected classroom dynamics.

- Ask guiding questions such as:

    o *What worked well in today's session?*

    o *What challenges did students face, and how did I respond?*

    o *What could I do differently next time to improve learning outcomes?*

- Best Practice: Review past journal entries to identify patterns in teaching effectiveness and areas for growth.

2.2 Student Feedback Analysis

- Regularly analyze student evaluations, informal feedback, and classroom engagement levels.

- Compare student comments over time to track improvement or recurring concerns.

- Separate constructive feedback from subjective opinions to focus on actionable insights.

- Best Practice: Implement changes based on student feedback and observe how students respond to modifications.

2.3 Video Recording and Self-Observation

- Record teaching sessions or discussion sections (with permission) and review them critically.

- Observe body language, voice modulation, clarity of explanations, and student reactions.

- Identify moments of strong engagement versus disengagement and analyze contributing factors.

- Best Practice: Create a self-evaluation checklist to structure observations and track progress over time.

2.4 Peer Observations and Collaborative Feedback

- Invite a fellow TA, faculty member, or mentor to observe your teaching and provide constructive feedback.

- Exchange observations with other TAs to gain insights into different teaching approaches.

- Discuss classroom experiences, challenges, and techniques for improvement.

- Best Practice: Compare self-perception with peer feedback to uncover potential blind spots.

2.5 Self-Questionnaires and Teaching Inventories

- Use structured self-assessment tools to evaluate different aspects of teaching.

- Example self-assessment questions:

  - *Am I effectively engaging all students, including quieter ones?*

  - *Do I provide clear and actionable feedback on assignments?*

  - *How well do I manage classroom discussions and handle student inquiries?*

- Best Practice: Revisit responses periodically to measure growth and evolving teaching strategies.

3. Incorporating Reflective Teaching into Continuous Improvement

Self-reflection is only valuable if it leads to practical changes and instructional growth. TAs should develop strategic action plans based on self-assessment insights.

3.1 Setting Realistic and Measurable Teaching Goals

- Use the SMART framework (Specific, Measurable, Achievable, Relevant, Time-bound) to establish teaching improvement goals.

- Example goal:
  "By the end of the semester, I will incorporate at least three active learning strategies (group discussions, case studies, peer teaching) to increase student engagement."

- Best Practice: Regularly review progress and adjust teaching strategies accordingly.

3.2 Experimenting with New Teaching Methods

- Based on self-reflection, try alternative instructional strategies to enhance student understanding.

- Examples:

  - If students struggle with lecture-heavy sessions, incorporate interactive discussions or visual aids.

  - If student participation is low, implement think-pair-share or small-group activities.

    o   If grading feedback is unclear, develop detailed rubrics to enhance transparency.

- Best Practice: Observe student responses and refine approaches based on effectiveness.

3.3 Balancing Teaching with Personal Academic Growth

- Reflect on how teaching responsibilities affect your own coursework, research, and work-life balance.

- Ensure that teaching improvements do not come at the cost of personal academic progress.

- Seek mentorship from faculty or senior TAs on time management and teaching strategies.

- Best Practice: Schedule designated teaching reflection periods to maintain continuous yet balanced improvement.

4. Leveraging Self-Assessment for Career Growth

Reflective teaching and self-assessment are not just tools for immediate classroom improvement—they also contribute to long-term professional development.

4.1 Building a Teaching Portfolio

- Document successful lesson plans, student feedback, and self-reflections for future teaching positions.

- Include examples of teaching challenges and how they were addressed.

- Highlight evidence of growth and adaptation over time.

- Best Practice: A strong teaching portfolio strengthens academic job applications, grant proposals, and teaching award nominations.

4.2 Using Self-Assessment in Teaching Statements and Evaluations

- Demonstrate continuous teaching improvement in statements for faculty applications or professional reviews.

- Example Reflection Statement:
  "After reviewing student feedback, I identified a need for clearer grading explanations. I developed a detailed rubric for assignments, which improved transparency and student understanding in subsequent courses."

- Best Practice: Showcase specific examples of teaching refinement and student impact.

5. Conclusion

Self-assessment and reflective teaching practices are fundamental to continuous professional development as a TA. By engaging in thoughtful reflection, structured evaluation, and deliberate instructional adjustments, TAs can evolve into more effective, student-centered, and confident educators.

By adopting a growth mindset, setting clear teaching goals, and actively seeking feedback, TAs not only enhance their immediate classroom effectiveness but also lay the foundation for a lifelong commitment to teaching excellence.

Seeking Feedback from Faculty and Students

Feedback is a cornerstone of professional growth, particularly for Teaching Assistants (TAs) who are developing their instructional skills and refining their teaching approaches. While student evaluations provide direct insight into how students perceive their learning experience, faculty feedback offers mentorship, pedagogical guidance, and disciplinary expertise that can shape a TA's effectiveness in both teaching and academic leadership.

Actively seeking feedback from both students and faculty enables TAs to identify strengths, areas for improvement, and instructional strategies that enhance student learning outcomes. However, feedback is most valuable when it is sought intentionally, interpreted thoughtfully, and applied strategically to foster continuous improvement in teaching performance.

This section explores the importance of seeking feedback, effective strategies for gathering and interpreting it, and best practices for integrating feedback into meaningful instructional improvements.

1. The Importance of Seeking Feedback as a TA

Teaching is a dynamic and evolving process, and constructive feedback serves as an essential tool for refining instructional techniques. By actively seeking feedback, TAs can:

- Gain Insights into Teaching Effectiveness – Understand which teaching methods are engaging, clear, and effective.
- Identify Areas for Growth – Recognize gaps in communication, lesson structuring, or student engagement.
- Enhance Student Learning Experiences – Adjust instructional strategies based on student needs and faculty expectations.
- Build Professional Development – Demonstrate a commitment to self-improvement and pedagogical excellence.
- Strengthen Relationships with Faculty and Students – Foster an open, collaborative learning environment where dialogue and continuous improvement are valued.

By treating feedback as a learning opportunity rather than criticism, TAs can develop a resilient, adaptable, and reflective teaching mindset.

2. Seeking Feedback from Faculty: Mentorship and Professional Development

Faculty members serve as mentors and evaluators, providing disciplinary expertise, instructional insights, and career development guidance for TAs. Seeking faculty feedback is crucial for understanding teaching expectations, improving content delivery, and aligning instructional approaches with course objectives.

2.1 When and How to Seek Faculty Feedback

- Early in the Semester: Discuss teaching expectations, grading policies, and instructional responsibilities to ensure alignment.

- Mid-Semester Check-Ins: Request informal feedback on discussion facilitation, student engagement, and grading consistency.

- Post-Semester Reflection: Ask for a comprehensive review of teaching performance and recommendations for future improvement.

2.2 Effective Methods for Gathering Faculty Feedback

- Scheduled One-on-One Meetings – Request faculty feedback during office hours or scheduled check-ins to discuss teaching performance.
- Classroom Observations – Invite faculty to observe a discussion session or lecture and provide structured feedback.
- Review of Grading and Feedback Practices – Ask faculty to review a sample of graded assignments to ensure consistency and clarity.
- End-of-Semester Teaching Review – Request formal or informal feedback on instructional growth and future development areas.

Example Email Requesting Faculty Feedback:

Subject: Request for Teaching Feedback – [Course Name]

Dear Professor [Last Name],

I truly appreciate the opportunity to assist with [Course Name] this semester. As I continue refining my teaching skills, I would love to gather feedback on my performance as a TA.

If possible, I would appreciate a brief conversation or written feedback regarding my effectiveness in leading discussions, grading consistency, and overall student engagement. Your insights would be invaluable in helping me improve as an instructor.

Let me know if you are available for a brief meeting or if you prefer to share feedback via email. Thank you for your time and mentorship!

Best regards,
[Your Name]

- Best Practice: Faculty may have limited time, so be specific about what type of feedback you're looking for to encourage a more structured and actionable response.

3. Seeking Feedback from Students: Understanding the Learner Perspective

Students provide direct, first-hand insights into teaching effectiveness—how well they comprehend material, engage in discussions, and respond to instructional methods. However, students may be hesitant to offer candid feedback unless given a structured and comfortable opportunity to do so.

3.1 When to Seek Student Feedback

- Early in the Semester: Ask for feedback on course pacing, clarity, and engagement to make necessary adjustments.
- Mid-Semester Check-Ins: Identify challenges before final evaluations, ensuring time to implement improvements.
- End-of-Semester Evaluations: Analyze feedback for long-term teaching development in future TA roles.

3.2 Methods for Gathering Student Feedback

A. Informal Feedback through Office Hours and Discussions

- Ask open-ended questions:
    - *"What aspects of the discussion sections help you learn the most?"*
    - *"Are there any teaching strategies that could be improved?"*
- Observe student engagement and non-verbal cues to gauge understanding.

- Best Practice: Frame feedback as a way to enhance learning experiences, encouraging honest but constructive responses.

B. Anonymous Surveys and Mid-Semester Feedback Forms

- Use Google Forms, Qualtrics, or LMS-based surveys for anonymous feedback collection.
- Ask specific questions to guide students toward actionable feedback.
- Example survey questions:
    - *What teaching strategies help you understand the material best?*
    - *Are there any areas where my explanations could be clearer?*
    - *Do you feel comfortable asking questions in class? If not, what would help?*

- Best Practice: Mid-semester surveys allow for adjustments before final evaluations, improving student experiences in real-time.

C. Small Group Feedback Sessions

- Organize 5-10 minute discussions where students share what's working well and what could be improved.
- Have students write one thing they like about the class and one thing they would change.

- Best Practice: Create a low-pressure, non-judgmental space to encourage open responses.

4. Interpreting and Applying Feedback for Continuous Improvement

4.1 Identifying Patterns in Feedback

- Look for recurring themes—if multiple students mention a challenge (e.g., "Explanations could be clearer"), it signals an area for improvement.

- Distinguish between constructive feedback and isolated opinions—avoid overreacting to one negative comment.

- Best Practice: Categorize feedback into themes (e.g., Clarity, Engagement, Grading) for structured analysis.

4.2 Making Targeted Adjustments

- If students struggle with unclear explanations, incorporate more examples, visuals, or structured outlines.
- If student engagement is low, experiment with active learning techniques, discussions, or Q&A formats.
- If grading consistency is a concern, refine rubrics and provide more detailed feedback.

- Best Practice: Track progress by comparing feedback over multiple semesters to measure improvement.

4.3 Following Up on Feedback

- Acknowledge feedback by explaining which suggestions will be implemented.

- Example response to student feedback:

"I appreciate your feedback that some explanations could be clearer. Moving forward, I'll include more real-world examples and concept maps to reinforce key ideas."

- Best Practice: When students see their feedback valued, they engage more actively in learning.

5. Conclusion

Actively seeking feedback from faculty and students is a powerful tool for professional development and teaching refinement. By incorporating structured self-reflection, faculty mentorship, and student insights, TAs can enhance their instructional effectiveness and create a more impactful learning environment.

When feedback is sought intentionally, interpreted thoughtfully, and applied strategically, it transforms teaching from a static task into a continuous process of growth, adaptation, and excellence.

Staying Updated with Teaching Best Practices and Trends

Teaching is an ever-evolving discipline, shaped by new pedagogical research, advancements in educational technology, and shifts in student learning needs. As a Teaching Assistant (TA), staying informed about teaching best practices and emerging trends is essential for enhancing instructional effectiveness, improving student engagement, and developing long-term teaching skills.

Education is not static—learning theories evolve, new digital tools emerge, and student demographics shift—necessitating a commitment to continuous professional development. By actively seeking new knowledge and adopting innovative teaching strategies, TAs can create dynamic, inclusive, and effective learning environments.

This section explores why staying updated matters, key areas of teaching innovation, and practical strategies for continuous learning in pedagogy.

1. Why Staying Updated with Teaching Best Practices Matters

- Enhances Student Learning Outcomes – Incorporating evidence-based teaching methods improves student comprehension, retention, and engagement.
- Supports Adaptability – Being aware of new teaching strategies allows for flexibility in responding to different student needs and classroom challenges.
- Boosts Professional Development – Staying informed about trends in higher education builds expertise, strengthening academic and career opportunities.
- Improves Classroom Experience – Modern teaching approaches make learning more interactive, relevant, and inclusive.

TA Tip: Teaching excellence is a process, not a destination. Even experienced educators continuously refine their techniques based on new research and feedback.

2. Key Trends and Best Practices in Teaching

TAs can improve their teaching effectiveness by staying informed about three major areas of pedagogical innovation:

2.1 Active Learning and Student-Centered Pedagogy

- Traditional lecture-heavy approaches are increasingly replaced by interactive, student-driven learning experiences.
- Strategies include:
  - Flipped Classrooms – Students engage with material before class and apply concepts during in-class discussions.
  - Problem-Based Learning (PBL) – Encouraging real-world problem-solving to deepen student understanding.
  - Peer Instruction – Using collaborative discussions where students teach and challenge one another.

- Best Practice: Shift from passive lecturing to active student participation using structured engagement activities.

2.2 Inclusive and Equitable Teaching Strategies

- Recognizing diverse student needs and ensuring accessibility is central to modern pedagogy.

- Key principles:

    o Universal Design for Learning (UDL) – Providing multiple ways for students to access material and demonstrate learning [86].

    o Culturally Responsive Teaching – Integrating diverse perspectives into course content [87].

    o Trauma-Informed Teaching – Being aware of student mental health and well-being challenges while designing instruction [88].

- Best Practice: Use inclusive language, diverse examples, and accessible teaching materials to support all learners.

2.3 Integrating Educational Technology and AI Tools

- Technology enhances student engagement, personalization, and assessment efficiency.

- Emerging tools include:

    o Learning Management Systems (LMS) – Platforms like Canvas, Blackboard, and Moodle support digital coursework, grading, and student communication.

    o AI-Assisted Learning Tools – Chatbots, adaptive learning platforms, and AI-generated quizzes enhance personalized education.

    o Gamification and Interactive Simulations – Turning learning into an immersive, engaging experience.

- Best Practice: Explore digital tools that complement traditional teaching methods rather than replacing them entirely.

3. Strategies for Staying Updated on Teaching Innovations

3.1 Engaging in Professional Development Opportunities

- Attend Teaching Workshops and Seminars – Most universities offer teaching and learning centers that provide training sessions on instructional best practices.
- Participate in Faculty Development Programs – Some institutions allow TAs to attend faculty teaching conferences and pedagogy training.
- Seek a Teaching Certification – Many universities offer graduate teaching programs or certificates in higher education pedagogy to formalize teaching expertise.

Example: A TA interested in improving online instruction can enroll in a workshop on digital pedagogy and remote engagement strategies.

3.2 Following Educational Research and Literature

- Subscribe to Teaching Journals and Blogs – Stay informed about new pedagogical theories, case studies, and research findings.
- Read Books on Teaching Excellence – Examples include:

  - *How Learning Works: Seven Research-Based Principles for Smart Teaching* by Ambrose et al.

  - *Small Teaching: Everyday Lessons from the Science of Learning* by James M. Lang.
    - Follow Teaching and Learning Centers – University teaching centers often publish best practice guides and research summaries on innovative teaching methods.

Example: A TA struggling with low student engagement might research articles on active learning strategies to improve participation.

3.3 Networking with Teaching Communities

- Join Teaching Assistant Networks – Many institutions have TA mentorship programs, discussion groups, or listservs where TAs can share challenges and solutions.
- Engage in Online Forums and Educator Communities – Platforms like Chronicle of Higher Education, Inside Higher Ed, and Teaching in Higher Ed podcasts offer insights from experienced educators.
- Collaborate with Faculty and Peers – Observe faculty teaching styles, ask for recommendations on teaching strategies, and exchange ideas with fellow TAs.

- Best Practice: Establish a peer learning network with other TAs and instructors to exchange feedback, challenges, and innovative ideas.

3.4 Experimenting with New Teaching Techniques

- Pilot New Strategies in Small Steps – Instead of overhauling an entire teaching approach, introduce small changes and assess their impact.
- Solicit Student Feedback on Teaching Methods – If experimenting with flipped classrooms or peer learning activities, ask students how effective they found the method.
- Reflect on Teaching Adjustments – Maintain a teaching journal to track the effectiveness of new techniques and refine them accordingly.

Example: A TA integrating interactive polling tools (like Kahoot or Poll Everywhere) might track student engagement metrics to assess effectiveness.

4. Adapting Teaching Strategies for the Future

Higher education is in a constant state of transformation, influenced by technology, student demographics, and global events. As a result, TAs must remain adaptable and proactive in their teaching development.

- Monitor Shifts in Higher Education Trends – Keep an eye on emerging topics such as hybrid learning models, AI-assisted teaching, and evolving assessment strategies.
- Develop Digital and Pedagogical Literacy – Future educators must blend traditional teaching methods with technology-driven innovations.
- Embrace a Growth Mindset – The best instructors are lifelong learners who embrace change, experiment with new methods, and refine their approaches based on student feedback.

5. Conclusion

Staying updated with teaching best practices and emerging educational trends is essential for enhancing instructional effectiveness, improving student engagement, and advancing professional development as a TA.

By actively seeking professional development opportunities, engaging with educational research, networking with teaching communities, and experimenting with new teaching strategies, TAs can continuously evolve as educators while ensuring that students receive the highest quality learning experience.

Ultimately, a commitment to ongoing learning in pedagogy is not just about becoming a better TA—it is about shaping the future of education through dynamic, innovative, and student-centered teaching.

Chapter 11: Career Development for TAs

Figure 11.1. Teaching and Learning [113].

The role of a Teaching Assistant (TA) is more than just a temporary academic position—it is a transformative experience that builds essential skills in teaching, mentorship, communication, and leadership. As TAs navigate their responsibilities, they gain firsthand insight into the complexities of higher education, the challenges of student engagement, and the rewards of fostering academic success. Whether a TA plans to pursue a career in academia, industry, or another professional field, reflecting on this experience is crucial for personal and professional growth.

This chapter serves as a guide for TAs to assess their experiences, recognize their achievements, and strategically plan their next steps. It explores the importance of self-reflection in identifying strengths and areas for improvement, gathering feedback from students and faculty, and setting goals for continued learning. Additionally, this chapter discusses how TAs can translate their experiences into future career opportunities, whether through refining their teaching philosophy, building a professional portfolio, or leveraging transferable skills in different career paths.

Furthermore, this chapter highlights the value of lifelong learning and professional development. It provides guidance on staying connected with academic communities, engaging in continued education, and exploring advanced certifications or leadership roles in teaching and learning. Whether TAs transition into full-time educators, researchers, or professionals in other sectors, the skills gained in this role will remain a foundation for future success.

By the end of this chapter, TAs will be able to:
- Reflect on their TA experience to identify key learning moments and achievements.
- Develop a personalized teaching philosophy based on their experiences.
- Gather and utilize feedback to improve teaching effectiveness.
- Translate TA skills into career opportunities in academia and beyond.
- Build a professional portfolio to showcase teaching, research, and leadership experience.

- Engage in lifelong learning and professional development to continue growing as an educator and professional.

The journey of a TA does not end when the semester concludes. Instead, it serves as a launching pad for future opportunities and continued self-improvement. By taking time to reflect, refine their skills, and stay connected to academic and professional communities, TAs can ensure that their experience has a lasting impact on both their careers and the students they have supported.

How TA Experience Contributes to Academic and Career Growth

Serving as a Teaching Assistant (TA) is more than just an academic obligation or a means of financial support—it is a valuable professional development opportunity that builds essential skills for both academic and non-academic careers. Whether a TA aspires to pursue a faculty position, research-intensive role, industry job, or leadership role in education, the experience gained from assisting in teaching, grading, mentoring students, and managing classroom responsibilities translates into critical competencies applicable across diverse career paths.

The TA experience fosters pedagogical expertise, communication skills, leadership abilities, and problem-solving acumen, all of which are highly sought after in higher education, corporate environments, research institutions, and beyond. This section explores the impact of TA roles on career trajectories, the transferable skills developed, and strategies for leveraging TA experience in professional growth.

1. The Impact of TA Experience on Career Paths

Teaching Assistantships serve as a stepping stone to various academic and professional careers, offering hands-on training in teaching, research, mentorship, and communication. Depending on one's long-term goals, the experience gained as a TA can shape opportunities in the following ways:

1.1 For Those Pursuing Academia and Faculty Positions

- Teaching Preparation: TA roles provide practical classroom experience, preparing individuals for lecturer, professor, or educational leadership roles.
- Research and Scholarly Development: Many TAs also assist in research-based courses, honing data analysis, critical thinking, and academic writing skills.
- Conference and Publication Opportunities: Teaching-related research (e.g., pedagogical innovation, student learning methods) can contribute to conference presentations, journal articles, or grant proposals.

- Best Practice: Document teaching experiences in a teaching portfolio, including student evaluations, lesson plans, and reflections for future faculty applications.

1.2 For Those Transitioning to Industry Roles

- Communication and Presentation Skills: Teaching sharpens public speaking, technical communication, and the ability to explain complex topics clearly.

- Project and Time Management: Managing a classroom, grading assignments, and balancing coursework mirrors project management responsibilities in business and STEM fields.
- Leadership and Teamwork: TAs develop leadership skills through mentoring students, collaborating with faculty, and resolving classroom challenges.

- Best Practice: Highlight TA experience in job interviews and resumes by showcasing transferable skills such as training, communication, and problem-solving.

1.3 For Those Exploring Educational Administration and Policy

- Understanding Academic Operations: TAs gain insight into curriculum development, student assessment, and institutional policies, making them strong candidates for roles in educational leadership, advising, and policy-making.
- Experience in Student Support Services: Assisting students academically prepares TAs for careers in academic advising, student affairs, and diversity and inclusion initiatives.

- Best Practice: Seek additional opportunities, such as committee work or faculty mentorship programs, to build administrative experience.

2. Transferable Skills Developed Through TA Experience

A TA position cultivates a broad skill set that is applicable across various career paths. These competencies go beyond subject-matter expertise and include:

2.1 Communication and Public Speaking

- Teaching requires the ability to convey complex concepts in an understandable way, engage diverse audiences, and facilitate discussions.
- This translates to client communication, team presentations, and leadership in corporate and technical fields.

- Best Practice: Develop clear, concise communication techniques and practice explaining technical or abstract concepts to different audiences.

2.2 Leadership and Mentorship

- TAs take on leadership roles by guiding students, managing class dynamics, and resolving conflicts.
- These experiences are valuable for mentorship, coaching, and team management positions in both academic and professional settings.

- Best Practice: Highlight mentorship experiences in job applications by detailing how you provided academic support, advised students, or led study groups.

2.3 Problem-Solving and Adaptability

- Every classroom presents unique challenges—whether it's adjusting to different student learning styles, handling disruptions, or refining teaching approaches based on feedback.

- These skills are transferable to roles in consulting, program management, and leadership positions that require adaptability and quick decision-making.

- Best Practice: Reflect on specific instances where you adapted to challenges and use these examples in interviews to demonstrate problem-solving abilities.

2.4 Project and Time Management

- Balancing teaching responsibilities, grading, research, and coursework fosters strong organizational skills.
- Employers highly value the ability to prioritize tasks, meet deadlines, and efficiently manage workload.

- Best Practice: Use calendar tools, productivity apps, and structured schedules to enhance efficiency and demonstrate strong work ethic.

2.5 Assessment and Data Analysis

- Evaluating student performance through grading and assessment develops skills in analyzing patterns, measuring progress, and interpreting data.
- These skills apply to research roles, data analytics, and fields requiring performance evaluation.

- Best Practice: If interested in data-driven careers, leverage experience in grading rubrics, student performance metrics, and course evaluations as evidence of analytical abilities.

3. Leveraging TA Experience for Career Advancement

TAs should proactively document, reflect on, and translate their experience into marketable skills for future career opportunities.

3.1 Building a Teaching Portfolio for Academic Careers

- Include:

- Sample lesson plans and instructional materials

- Student feedback and evaluations

- Teaching philosophy statement

- Evidence of instructional innovation (e.g., active learning techniques, technology integration)

- Best Practice: Use the portfolio for faculty job applications, conference presentations, and research grant proposals.

3.2 Showcasing TA Experience on Resumes and Job Applications

- Tailor resume bullet points to highlight transferable skills, such as:

- *"Designed and delivered engaging lessons, improving student comprehension by 20% based on assessment scores."*

- *"Managed classroom discussions, demonstrating leadership, conflict resolution, and adaptability."*

- *"Provided detailed feedback on student assignments, developing strong analytical and communication skills."*

- Best Practice: Customize the resume and cover letter to match job descriptions, emphasizing teaching-related competencies in a non-academic context.

3.3 Expanding Career Networks and Seeking Mentorship

- Connect with faculty mentors, alumni, and professional organizations for career guidance.
- Join networks such as:

- Professional associations (e.g., American Educational Research Association, discipline-specific organizations)

- Online educator communities (LinkedIn groups, HigherEd forums, and teaching conferences)
  - Seek informational interviews with professionals who transitioned from TA roles to careers in academia, industry, or administration.

- Best Practice: Request letters of recommendation from faculty mentors that highlight both teaching and leadership potential.

4. Conclusion

A Teaching Assistantship is not just a temporary role—it is a launchpad for academic, professional, and leadership growth. The skills acquired—teaching, communication, leadership, problem-solving, and project management—position TAs for success in higher education, research, industry, and beyond.

By actively seeking mentorship, reflecting on teaching experiences, and strategically presenting TA skills on resumes and applications, individuals can leverage their assistantship as a powerful asset in their career trajectory.

Ultimately, the most successful TAs recognize that teaching is not just about instruction—it's about learning, growth, and the development of skills that transcend the classroom and shape future careers.

Building a Strong Teaching Portfolio for Future Faculty Positions

For Teaching Assistants (TAs) aspiring to pursue faculty positions, lecturer roles, or academic leadership positions, a well-structured teaching portfolio serves as an essential tool for showcasing teaching effectiveness, pedagogical philosophy, and instructional innovation. In the highly competitive world of academia, a comprehensive and reflective teaching portfolio not only demonstrates teaching competence but also distinguishes candidates in faculty hiring decisions, tenure evaluations, and grant applications [89].

A teaching portfolio is more than a collection of documents—it is a curated representation of an instructor's teaching philosophy, instructional methods, assessment strategies, and student engagement approaches [90]. It provides tangible evidence of teaching excellence and growth over time, offering insight into how an educator approaches learning, designs courses, and adapts to diverse student needs.

This section explores the key components of a strong teaching portfolio, best practices for structuring its contents, and strategies for leveraging it effectively in academic job applications.

1. The Purpose of a Teaching Portfolio

A teaching portfolio serves multiple functions in academic career advancement:

- Faculty Job Applications – Many universities require evidence of teaching experience and effectiveness as part of the hiring process for lecturer, assistant professor, and faculty roles.
- Promotion and Tenure Review – Tenure-track faculty must document teaching growth, innovations, and contributions to curriculum development.
- Professional Development – The portfolio allows instructors to reflect on their evolution as educators, identify strengths, and continuously improve their teaching methods.
- Grant and Fellowship Applications – Some educational grants require documentation of instructional contributions and pedagogical approaches.

- Best Practice: Begin building a portfolio early in your TA experience to gradually refine it over time rather than compiling it hastily when applying for jobs.

2. Key Components of a Strong Teaching Portfolio

A well-structured teaching portfolio should contain a diverse set of materials that reflect teaching philosophy, instructional strategies, assessment techniques, and student engagement approaches.

2.1 Teaching Philosophy Statement

A teaching philosophy statement is a foundational component that articulates an instructor's beliefs about teaching, learning, and student engagement [91]. This reflective essay should answer:

- What are your core beliefs about teaching and learning?
- How do you foster student engagement, critical thinking, and inclusivity?
- What instructional methods and assessment strategies do you prioritize?
- How have you adapted your teaching methods based on student feedback and self-reflection?

Example Excerpt from a Teaching Philosophy Statement:
"I believe that effective teaching is centered on student engagement, active learning, and critical thinking. My approach combines inquiry-based learning, real-world applications, and inclusive

teaching strategies to create an environment where all students feel valued and challenged. I strive to foster a classroom where students take ownership of their learning by integrating collaborative problem-solving and diverse perspectives."

- Best Practice: Keep the teaching philosophy statement concise (1-2 pages), reflective, and evidence-based.

2.2 Teaching Experience and Course Materials

This section provides concrete evidence of teaching involvement, including:

- Courses Taught or Assisted – List course titles, roles (TA, instructor, guest lecturer), and academic terms.
- Sample Lesson Plans and Lecture Notes – Include detailed outlines showcasing instructional structure and learning objectives.
- Slides, Handouts, and Digital Learning Tools – Provide examples of instructional materials used in class.

- Best Practice: Select two or three well-developed course materials that demonstrate teaching effectiveness and student engagement.

2.3 Student Evaluations and Feedback

Student feedback provides direct evidence of teaching effectiveness and impact [92]. This section may include:

- Summarized Course Evaluations – Highlight average ratings, positive trends, and key takeaways.
- Selected Student Comments – Showcase testimonials that reflect engagement, clarity, and teaching impact.
- Peer and Faculty Observations – If applicable, include faculty mentor feedback on instructional performance.

- Best Practice: Contextualize evaluation data—briefly summarize trends rather than presenting raw numerical scores without explanation.

2.4 Innovative Teaching Strategies and Pedagogical Development

Highlight evidence of instructional innovation, active learning techniques, and ongoing pedagogical growth.

- Use of Active Learning Methods – Describe how you integrate discussion-based learning, case studies, peer instruction, or flipped classrooms.
- Inclusive Teaching Practices – Showcase strategies that support diverse learners, including Universal Design for Learning (UDL) or culturally responsive teaching.
- Integration of Technology – If applicable, demonstrate how you use LMS platforms (Canvas, Blackboard), AI tools, or interactive simulations.

- Best Practice: Frame innovative teaching strategies with examples of student engagement and learning outcomes.

2.5 Evidence of Assessment and Grading Strategies

Assessment is a core teaching responsibility, and demonstrating a clear, fair, and structured approach to evaluation strengthens a portfolio [93]. Include:

- Sample Grading Rubrics – Show criteria for essays, projects, presentations, or exams.
- Examples of Constructive Feedback – Highlight how you provide detailed and meaningful feedback to students.
- Assessment Philosophy Statement – Explain how you balance summative (exams, final projects) and formative (quizzes, peer reviews) assessments.

- Best Practice: Choose examples that demonstrate consistency, fairness, and student-centered assessment methods.

2.6 Professional Development in Teaching

Show commitment to continuous improvement and learning in pedagogy. Include:

- Teaching Certifications or Workshops Attended – List teaching assistant training programs, pedagogy courses, or instructional design workshops.
- Conference Presentations on Teaching – Highlight any teaching-related presentations or discussions in educational conferences.
- Membership in Teaching Communities – Mention participation in teaching assistant mentorship programs or faculty development initiatives.

- Best Practice: If you lack formal teaching development experience, seek opportunities through university teaching centers, online courses, or workshops.

3. Structuring and Formatting a Teaching Portfolio

A teaching portfolio should be well-organized, professional, and easy to navigate.

- Organize Content Logically:

  - Teaching Philosophy

  - Teaching Experience and Course Materials

  - Student Evaluations

  - Instructional Innovations

  - Assessment and Grading Practices

  - Professional Development

- Choose a Digital or Print Format:

- Digital Portfolio (Website, PDF, or Google Drive Folder) – Easily accessible for faculty search committees.

- Print Portfolio – Professionally bound for in-person faculty interviews.

- Best Practice: Keep the portfolio clear, concise, and tailored for the specific faculty position or institution.

4. Leveraging the Teaching Portfolio in Faculty Job Applications

A well-prepared teaching portfolio can significantly strengthen faculty job applications when presented strategically.

- Customize for Specific Institutions – Align teaching philosophy and course materials with department priorities.
- Include in Application Materials – Some universities require teaching portfolios alongside CVs and cover letters.
- Use in Teaching Demonstrations – If invited for a teaching demonstration, reference portfolio materials to illustrate methodology.

- Best Practice: Treat the portfolio as a dynamic document, updating it regularly to reflect new teaching experiences and improvements.

5. Conclusion

A strong teaching portfolio is an essential tool for TAs aspiring to faculty positions, providing concrete evidence of teaching effectiveness, instructional philosophy, and continuous professional development. By carefully curating course materials, assessments, student feedback, and innovative teaching strategies, TAs can present themselves as reflective, adaptable, and student-centered educators.

Ultimately, a well-prepared portfolio not only enhances job market competitiveness but also fosters a lifelong commitment to teaching excellence and pedagogical innovation.

Networking Within Academia and Professional Development Opportunities

Networking is a fundamental aspect of academic and professional success [94]. For Teaching Assistants (TAs), building strong professional relationships within academia can lead to research collaborations, faculty mentorship, conference opportunities, and future career advancements. Beyond the university setting, networking also extends to industry connections, interdisciplinary collaborations, and leadership roles in professional organizations.

Effective networking is not just about meeting influential people—it's about establishing meaningful, reciprocal relationships that foster academic growth, career development, and long-term professional opportunities. A well-connected TA can access insider knowledge on faculty positions, research grants, pedagogical innovations, and cross-disciplinary career paths.

This section explores the importance of academic networking, strategies for building professional relationships, and leveraging networking opportunities for long-term career growth.

1. The Importance of Networking in Academia

In the highly competitive landscape of academia, networking provides access to mentorship, career guidance, and collaboration opportunities that might not be available through formal channels [95]. Networking helps TAs:

- Gain Faculty Mentorship – Establish meaningful relationships with professors and academic advisors who can offer career guidance, research collaboration opportunities, and recommendation letters.
- Enhance Research and Teaching Opportunities – Networking can lead to joint research projects, teaching assistantships, and future faculty positions.
- Stay Informed About Job Openings – Many academic positions, grants, and funding opportunities are shared through informal networks before public postings.
- Develop a Professional Identity – Engaging in professional discussions and academic communities builds credibility and visibility within a field.

- Best Practice: Networking is most effective when it is genuine, strategic, and based on shared academic interests.

2. Strategies for Networking Within Academia

2.1 Building Strong Faculty and Mentor Relationships

- Engage with Faculty Early:

  - Attend faculty office hours, departmental seminars, and academic workshops.

  - Show interest in faculty research and teaching philosophies—engage in meaningful discussions.

- **Seek a Faculty Mentor:**

  - Find a professor whose research aligns with your interests and ask for guidance on career planning, research, and teaching development.

  - Ask insightful questions about their career path and seek advice on academic publishing, grant writing, and conference presentations.

- Best Practice: A mentor relationship should be mutually beneficial—demonstrate initiative by offering research assistance, co-authoring papers, or contributing to faculty-led projects.

2.2 Networking with Fellow Graduate Students and TAs

- Collaborate on Research or Teaching Projects:

- Engage with peers in study groups, research collectives, and interdisciplinary collaborations.

- Co-author papers or present at student research symposia to build academic credentials.

- Join Graduate Student Associations and TA Networks:

- Many universities have graduate student organizations focused on academic and career development.

- Participate in TA mentoring programs where experienced TAs guide newer TAs on classroom management, grading, and student engagement.

- Best Practice: Stay connected with alumni who have transitioned into academia or industry roles—they can provide valuable job market insights.

2.3 Attending Academic Conferences and Workshops

- Present at Conferences:

- Conferences provide a platform to showcase research, engage with scholars, and receive constructive feedback.

- Major conferences in various disciplines offer networking sessions, panel discussions, and recruitment events.

- Participate in Teaching and Pedagogy Workshops:

- Many universities and academic organizations host teaching-focused workshops where TAs can learn new pedagogical strategies, network with faculty, and explore teaching career paths.

- Best Practice: Before attending a conference, research key speakers, panelists, and fellow attendees—having specific people to connect with makes networking more effective.

3. Leveraging Professional Development Opportunities

Beyond networking, professional development opportunities provide structured training, leadership experiences, and industry insights that can enhance career prospects.

3.1 Pursuing Teaching and Research Certifications

- Teaching Certifications:

- Many universities offer teaching certificate programs for graduate students that enhance pedagogical expertise and faculty job competitiveness.

- Examples include:

  - Certificate in University Teaching and Learning

o   Graduate Teaching Fellowships

- Research Fellowships and Grants:

- Apply for graduate research assistantships, dissertation fellowships, and external funding opportunities to build research credibility.

- Examples of funding sources:

o   NSF (National Science Foundation) Grants

o   Fulbright Research Scholarships

o   Institutional Research Awards

- Best Practice: Faculty mentors can provide guidance on writing strong applications for fellowships and teaching awards.

3.2 Engaging in Professional Associations and Academic Societies

- Join Discipline-Specific Organizations:

- Many fields have professional associations that provide career resources, academic journals, and networking events.

- Examples:

o   American Educational Research Association (AERA) – for education scholars

o   Association for Computing Machinery (ACM) – for computer science professionals

o   Modern Language Association (MLA) – for literature and humanities scholars

- Take on Leadership Roles:

- Volunteer for committee work, conference planning, or student leadership positions to gain organizational experience.

- Best Practice: List professional memberships on CVs and faculty job applications to demonstrate engagement with the academic community.

3.3 Utilizing Online Networking Platforms

- Create and Maintain a Strong LinkedIn Profile:

- Showcase teaching experience, research publications, and professional achievements.

- Join LinkedIn academic groups to connect with scholars, educators, and industry professionals.

- Engage with Academic Twitter (X) and ResearchGate:

- Follow leading scholars, institutions, and academic discussions on social media.

- ResearchGate allows TAs to share publications, follow academic discussions, and collaborate with researchers globally.

- Best Practice: Share research insights, teaching strategies, or academic reflections to engage with the broader academic community online.

4. Transitioning Networking Into Career Growth

Networking efforts should be strategic and long-term, leading to collaborations, career opportunities, and professional growth.

- Request Informational Interviews:

- If interested in a faculty role, research job, or industry position, request a brief informational interview with professionals in the field.

- Leverage Network for Job Referrals and Recommendations:

- When applying for faculty positions, faculty mentors and colleagues can provide strong recommendation letters.

- Referrals from professional contacts can increase job prospects in both academia and industry.

- Maintain and Nurture Relationships:

- Stay in touch with mentors, colleagues, and conference connections by sharing academic updates, congratulating them on achievements, and engaging in scholarly discussions.

- Best Practice: Follow up after networking events with a thoughtful email expressing appreciation for their time and interest in future discussions.

5. Conclusion

Networking within academia and engaging in professional development opportunities are essential steps for career advancement. By building strong relationships with faculty mentors, engaging with peers, participating in conferences, and leveraging online platforms, TAs can position themselves for success in academia and beyond.

The most effective networking is genuine, reciprocal, and built over time—rather than seeking immediate benefits, focus on fostering meaningful, long-term professional connections.

Ultimately, the ability to connect, collaborate, and continuously learn is what transforms a Teaching Assistant into a well-rounded scholar, educator, and future academic leader.

Preparing for Future Faculty or Research Positions

For Teaching Assistants (TAs) aspiring to pursue faculty roles or research-intensive careers, strategic preparation is essential. The transition from a graduate student or TA to a faculty or research position requires not only subject-matter expertise but also evidence of teaching effectiveness, scholarly contributions, and professional engagement. Whether aiming for tenure-track professorships, research fellowships, or postdoctoral positions, early career planning, skill development, and strategic networking can significantly enhance long-term academic success.

This section explores key steps for preparing for future faculty or research positions, including academic skill-building, professional development, research productivity, and application strategies.

1. Understanding the Path to Faculty and Research Careers

Careers in academia typically follow one of two primary tracks [96]:

1.1 Teaching-Focused Faculty Positions

- Lecturer, Assistant Professor, or Tenure-Track Faculty – Focus on teaching, curriculum development, and student mentorship while maintaining some level of research and service contributions.
- Community College Faculty – Primarily emphasize teaching and student engagement with limited research responsibilities.
- Teaching Fellowships and Postdoctoral Teaching Programs – Designed for recent PhDs who want to refine their teaching before securing a permanent faculty role.

- Best Practice: If pursuing a teaching-focused career, gain substantial classroom experience, teaching certifications, and pedagogical training during the TAship.

1.2 Research-Intensive Faculty and Industry Research Roles

- Research Professorships and Postdoctoral Fellowships – Primarily focus on research, grant writing, and publishing, with some teaching responsibilities.
- Industry Research Positions – Involves working in R&D departments, think tanks, or government research agencies where applied research is central.
- Hybrid Roles (Teaching & Research Combined) – Many tenure-track faculty positions require a balance of research, publishing, and teaching.

- Best Practice: If focusing on research careers, prioritize publishing, conference presentations, and securing research funding.

2. Strengthening Teaching and Instructional Competence

For faculty careers, demonstrating teaching effectiveness is crucial [97]. TAs should take intentional steps to build a strong instructional record.

2.1 Enhancing Teaching Experience

- Teach Independently – Seek opportunities to lead lectures, develop syllabi, and design assessments beyond standard TA responsibilities.
- Develop a Teaching Portfolio – Compile evidence of teaching philosophy, student evaluations,

and lesson plans for faculty job applications.
- Earn a Teaching Certification – Many institutions offer graduate-level pedagogy courses or certificates in college teaching.

- Best Practice: Collect student evaluations and faculty observations to demonstrate growth as an instructor over time.

2.2 Refining Pedagogical and Assessment Skills

- Experiment with Active Learning Strategies – Integrate flipped classrooms, problem-based learning, and technology-enhanced instruction into teaching practices.
- Develop Inclusive and Equitable Teaching Approaches – Gain experience with Universal Design for Learning (UDL) and culturally responsive teaching methods.
- Supervise Undergraduate Research or Mentorship Programs – Providing academic guidance to students enhances leadership and mentoring credentials.

- Best Practice: If possible, apply for TA mentoring roles, guest lecturer positions, or faculty co-teaching collaborations to diversify teaching experience.

3. Strengthening Research and Scholarly Contributions

For research-intensive careers, demonstrating a strong publication record, funding acquisition, and collaborative research projects is essential [98].

3.1 Building a Research Portfolio

- Publish in Peer-Reviewed Journals – Work with faculty mentors to submit research articles, literature reviews, or book chapters.
- Present at Academic Conferences – Share findings at discipline-specific conferences, symposia, and research colloquiums.
- Develop Independent Research Proposals – Start shaping original research ideas that can lead to future dissertation work, grant applications, or postdoctoral research.

- Best Practice: Maintain a research pipeline—juggling multiple projects at various stages (writing, submission, revision) to ensure continuous scholarly output.

3.2 Gaining Experience in Grant Writing and Research Funding

- Collaborate on Grant Proposals – Learn how to apply for research funding through faculty-led projects or graduate fellowships.
- Seek Internal and External Research Fellowships – Apply for funding from:

  - National Science Foundation (NSF) Grants

  - Fulbright Research Fellowships

- Institutional Research Assistantships
    - Gain Experience with Institutional Review Boards (IRB) – Understanding research ethics and proposal approvals is critical for independent research careers.

- Best Practice: Work with faculty mentors to review successful grant applications and develop a strong research funding strategy.

4. Networking and Professional Development

Building strong academic connections is critical for securing faculty and research positions.

4.1 Engaging with Faculty Mentors and Research Advisors

- Seek Research Collaborations – Engage in faculty-led projects to build publication records and research credibility.
- Request Career Mentorship – Discuss career pathways, job market strategies, and professional goals with faculty mentors.
- Attend Departmental Seminars and Academic Networking Events – Establish connections with scholars in your field.

- Best Practice: Maintain relationships with faculty mentors over time—they may serve as future collaborators, job references, or tenure reviewers.

4.2 Expanding Professional Networks

- Join Academic Associations – Membership in organizations like American Association of University Professors (AAUP), Modern Language Association (MLA), or American Physical Society (APS) provides networking opportunities.
- Engage in Interdisciplinary Collaborations – Broadening research partnerships outside of a primary discipline strengthens academic versatility.
- Participate in Online Academic Communities – Platforms like ResearchGate, LinkedIn, and Academic Twitter (X) help TAs engage in scholarly discussions, share research, and connect with academic professionals.

- Best Practice: Follow leading scholars, comment on academic discussions, and share research insights online to build a professional academic presence.

5. Preparing for Faculty and Research Job Applications

5.1 Crafting a Strong Academic Job Application

- Curriculum Vitae (CV): Include teaching experience, research publications, conference presentations, and service contributions.
- Teaching Statement: Describe pedagogical philosophy, instructional strategies, and classroom impact.
- Research Statement: Outline research agenda, past contributions, and future directions.

- Diversity Statement (if required): Demonstrate commitment to inclusive teaching and diverse learning environments.

- Best Practice: Tailor each application to the institution's teaching and research priorities—generic applications are less effective.

5.2 Preparing for Faculty Job Interviews and Research Presentations

- Teaching Demonstration: Prepare an interactive, well-structured sample lesson to showcase instructional abilities.
- Research Talk or Job Talk: Present research in a clear, engaging manner, demonstrating expertise and future research potential.
- Mock Interviews: Practice responding to common faculty job interview questions with mentors or peers.

- Best Practice: Be ready to discuss how research and teaching intersect, potential collaborations with faculty, and future scholarly contributions.

6. Conclusion

Preparing for faculty and research positions requires a long-term, strategic approach that includes gaining teaching experience, publishing research, securing funding, expanding professional networks, and crafting a compelling academic job application.

By actively engaging in teaching, research, professional development, and mentorship opportunities, TAs can position themselves as strong candidates for faculty roles, research fellowships, and industry research positions.

Ultimately, success in academia is not just about knowledge—it's about demonstrating impact, adaptability, and commitment to the advancement of both research and education. Through intentional preparation, strategic networking, and continuous skill development, TAs can navigate the transition from graduate study to a fulfilling academic or research career.

Chapter 12: Mentorship and Academic Guidance

A Teaching Assistant's (TA) role extends far beyond grading assignments, leading discussions, or assisting in labs—it is about leaving a lasting impact on students, shaping academic experiences, and contributing to the broader learning community. The influence of a TA is often felt long after students have completed a course, whether through the mentorship they provided, the learning strategies they introduced, or the confidence they instilled in struggling learners [99]. Building a legacy as a TA means embracing the role not just as a temporary position [100], but as an opportunity to create meaningful change in students' lives and in the academic environment.

This chapter explores how TAs can maximize their contributions, inspire students, and create a positive and lasting effect on their institutions. It delves into

Figure 12.1. Teaching and Learning [113].

mentorship and leadership within academia, highlighting ways TAs can support students beyond the classroom by fostering academic curiosity, encouraging resilience, and promoting inclusive learning spaces. Additionally, it discusses how TAs can document and showcase their contributions—whether through student impact, curriculum development, research collaborations, or instructional innovations.

A significant part of building a legacy involves paving the way for future TAs. This chapter will also provide strategies for mentoring incoming TAs, contributing to TA training programs, and advocating for improved support systems for teaching assistants. By sharing experiences, refining best practices, and leaving behind resources for others, TAs can ensure that their efforts continue to benefit students and faculty long after they have moved on to the next stage of their careers.

By the end of this chapter, TAs will be able to:
- Identify ways to create a meaningful and lasting impact on student learning.
- Serve as mentors and role models, fostering academic success and motivation.
- Develop instructional innovations that improve the student learning experience.

- Contribute to TA training programs and institutional teaching support initiatives.
- Document and share their teaching experiences for future professional opportunities.
- Advocate for ongoing improvements in TA roles, resources, and policies.

The most effective TAs are those who leave a mark not only on the students they teach but also on the educational structures they contribute to. Whether by mentoring, innovating, or advocating for change, TAs have the potential to shape the future of teaching and learning in higher education. This chapter provides the tools and inspiration needed to ensure that the work of a TA continues to make a difference long after the final grades are submitted.

Role of TAs in Mentoring Students

Teaching Assistants (TAs) play a multifaceted role in academia, extending beyond instruction and grading into mentorship and academic guidance. As mentors, TAs serve as a bridge between students and faculty, providing insights, support, and encouragement to help students navigate their academic journeys. Whether guiding students through complex coursework, advising on research projects, or offering strategies for academic success, effective mentorship fosters a supportive learning environment and enhances student engagement.

Mentoring is not simply about answering questions or clarifying course content—it is about cultivating intellectual curiosity, promoting academic growth, and empowering students to take ownership of their learning. By fostering strong mentor-mentee relationships, TAs help students build confidence, resilience, and critical thinking skills that extend beyond the classroom [101].

This section explores the responsibilities of TAs as mentors, effective mentorship strategies, and the long-term impact of mentoring on student success and professional development.

1. Understanding the Role of a TA as a Mentor

Mentorship within a TA role involves more than just providing academic support—it requires building rapport with students, guiding them through challenges, and offering advice on academic and career-related matters. Key aspects of mentorship include:

- Academic Guidance – Helping students grasp complex concepts, develop critical thinking skills, and improve study habits.
- Research Support – Advising students on research methodologies, data analysis, and scholarly writing.
- Professional Development – Offering career insights, networking opportunities, and graduate school advice.
- Encouragement and Motivation – Helping students build academic confidence, resilience, and problem-solving skills.
- Navigating University Resources – Directing students to library services, tutoring centers, mental health support, and career counseling.

TA Tip: Effective mentorship is not about providing all the answers—it is about guiding students to think independently and develop problem-solving abilities.

2. Key Responsibilities of a TA as a Mentor

2.1 Supporting Students' Academic Success

TAs serve as academic role models, helping students develop strategies for mastering coursework and achieving their learning goals [102].

- Clarifying Course Material – Providing supplemental explanations, real-world examples, and alternative perspectives on difficult topics.
- Developing Study Skills – Teaching students how to approach complex readings, take effective notes, and prepare for exams.
- Providing Constructive Feedback – Helping students improve their analytical writing, problem-solving, and presentation skills.

- Best Practice: Encourage students to develop metacognitive skills—help them reflect on how they learn best and adjust study strategies accordingly.

2.2 Fostering a Supportive and Inclusive Learning Environment

Effective mentorship involves creating a classroom culture where all students feel valued, respected, and encouraged to participate.

- Encouraging Student Engagement – Promote active participation in discussions, group projects, and collaborative learning activities.
- Recognizing Diverse Learning Styles – Tailor guidance to accommodate visual, auditory, and kinesthetic learners.
- Building an Inclusive Classroom – Acknowledge and address cultural, linguistic, and accessibility barriers to ensure equitable learning opportunities.

- Best Practice: Normalize help-seeking behavior—remind students that asking for guidance is a sign of academic strength, not weakness.

2.3 Mentoring Students in Research and Scholarly Activities

TAs often guide students through independent research projects, lab work, and scholarly writing. This mentorship fosters intellectual growth and prepares students for future academic endeavors.

- Advising on Research Methods – Help students formulate research questions, collect data, and apply analytical techniques.
- Providing Writing and Presentation Guidance – Offer feedback on literature reviews, research papers, and conference presentations.
- Encouraging Critical Thinking – Challenge students to analyze multiple perspectives, synthesize ideas, and defend arguments effectively.

- Best Practice: Connect students with faculty advisors, research opportunities, and academic conferences to expand their scholarly experience.

2.4 Providing Career and Graduate School Guidance

Many students look to TAs for advice on graduate programs, career pathways, and professional development opportunities.

- Sharing Insights on Graduate School Applications – Offer guidance on crafting statements of purpose, securing recommendation letters, and selecting research programs.
- Discussing Career Pathways – Help students explore potential careers in academia, industry, and beyond.
- Encouraging Professional Development – Recommend internships, research assistantships, and networking events.

- Best Practice: If students express interest in a specific career or academic path, help them identify mentors, workshops, and professional organizations in their field.

3. Effective Mentorship Strategies for TAs

3.1 Establishing Trust and Approachability

- Be Accessible – Set clear expectations for office hours, email communication, and response times.
- Show Empathy and Patience – Recognize that students come from diverse backgrounds and may face unique challenges.
- Create a Judgment-Free Space – Foster an environment where students feel comfortable asking questions and expressing concerns.

- Best Practice: Use active listening techniques—validate student concerns, ask clarifying questions, and offer thoughtful guidance.

3.2 Encouraging Independent Learning and Self-Advocacy

Mentorship should empower students to develop autonomy in their academic and professional journeys.

- Ask Open-Ended Questions – Instead of giving direct answers, ask:

  - *"How would you approach solving this problem?"*

  - *"What strategies have worked for you in the past?"*
    - Guide, Don't Dictate – Provide resources and options rather than making decisions for students.
    - Encourage Reflection – Help students assess their strengths, weaknesses, and academic goals.

- Best Practice: Teach students how to advocate for themselves in academic settings, including seeking faculty mentorship and research opportunities.

3.3 Providing Constructive and Actionable Feedback

Feedback should be specific, balanced, and focused on growth.

- Use the "Praise-Critique-Suggest" Model:

  - Praise – Acknowledge strengths.

  - Critique – Identify areas for improvement.

  - Suggest – Offer actionable strategies for progress.

- Balance Encouragement with Realistic Expectations:

  - Avoid over-praising or sugarcoating critical feedback.

  - Help students set realistic academic and professional goals.

- Best Practice: Feedback should be timely, clear, and tailored to individual student needs.

4. The Long-Term Impact of Effective Mentorship

- Academic Growth and Confidence – Students who receive strong mentorship are more likely to excel academically and persist in their studies [103].
- Stronger Faculty-Student Connections – Effective TA mentors help bridge the gap between students and faculty.
- Leadership Development for TAs – Mentoring hones communication, problem-solving, and leadership skills that benefit TAs in future careers.
- Creation of a Mentorship Cycle – Students who receive positive mentoring experiences are more likely to become mentors themselves in the future [104].

- Best Practice: The most impactful mentorship extends beyond the semester—stay open to continued guidance and support as students progress through their academic journey.

5. Conclusion

TAs serve as mentors, role models, and guides, helping students navigate academic challenges, research endeavors, and career aspirations. Through thoughtful mentorship strategies—building trust, fostering critical thinking, and encouraging professional development—TAs contribute significantly to student success and growth.

Effective mentorship is not about providing all the answers; it is about empowering students with the skills, confidence, and resources they need to thrive. By embracing this role, TAs enhance their own leadership abilities, strengthen academic communities, and create lasting impacts on students' educational journeys.

Identifying Struggling Students and Offering Academic Guidance

Teaching Assistants (TAs) play a critical role in recognizing and supporting struggling students, serving as early intervention points when students experience academic challenges [105]. Whether due to gaps in foundational knowledge, difficulty grasping course concepts, time management struggles, personal issues, or a lack of engagement, students may face obstacles that hinder their academic progress.

Identifying struggling students requires keen observation, active listening, and a proactive approach to academic mentorship. Offering effective guidance, in turn, demands a balance of empathy, structured support, and the ability to connect students with the right resources to foster resilience and self-improvement.

This section explores how TAs can recognize signs of academic struggle, strategies for providing meaningful guidance, and best practices for connecting students with institutional support systems.

1. Recognizing Signs of Academic Struggle

Many students may not openly express that they are struggling, making it essential for TAs to identify early warning signs and intervene before academic setbacks become insurmountable.

1.1 Academic Performance Indicators

- Consistently Low Grades or Declining Performance – A sudden or consistent drop in scores on quizzes, exams, assignments, or participation may indicate conceptual difficulties or external challenges.
- Incomplete or Poor-Quality Assignments – Late, rushed, or incomplete work may signal confusion about expectations, time management issues, or disengagement.
- Frequent Requests for Extensions or Rewrites – Students who frequently ask for deadline extensions may struggle with organization, workload balance, or comprehension of course material.

- Best Practice: Monitor grading trends and note students who struggle persistently rather than those who experience occasional difficulties.

1.2 Behavioral and Engagement Indicators

- Lack of Participation in Class Discussions – Students who avoid engaging in lectures, discussions, or group work may feel intimidated or lost.
- Frequent Absences or Tardiness – Repeated class absences may indicate lack of motivation, personal struggles, or disengagement.
- Signs of Frustration or Anxiety – Students who appear withdrawn, stressed, or excessively anxious about coursework may need additional academic or emotional support.

- Best Practice: Notice changes in student demeanor, participation, and attendance patterns, as these often correlate with academic difficulties.

1.3 Communication Indicators

- Unclear or Overly Vague Questions – Struggling students may ask broad, unclear, or overly general questions because they don't know where to start.

- Avoidance of Office Hours or Help Sessions – Some students may not seek help due to embarrassment, lack of confidence, or not knowing they are struggling until it's too late.

- Emails Expressing Overwhelm or Confusion – Students who reach out with repeated concerns about coursework difficulty, anxiety about grades, or frustration with concepts may need tailored academic guidance.

- Best Practice: Encourage a low-pressure, judgment-free space where students feel comfortable discussing challenges without stigma.

2. Strategies for Supporting Struggling Students

Once struggling students are identified, the goal is to offer academic guidance that empowers them to improve rather than creating dependence on external help.

2.1 Initiating Conversations with Struggling Students

Approaching struggling students requires sensitivity and professionalism to ensure they feel supported rather than judged.

- Use a Non-Confrontational Approach:

  - Instead of: *"You're not doing well in class. What's the problem?"*

  - Say: *"I've noticed that you've been facing some challenges with the coursework. How can I help?"*

- Ask Open-Ended Questions:
Encourage students to reflect on their challenges:

  - *"What part of the material do you find most challenging?"*

  - *"How do you typically study or prepare for assignments?"*

  - *"Are there any external factors affecting your academic performance?"*

- Best Practice: Frame discussions as a collaborative effort—TAs and students should work together to find solutions.

2.2 Offering Targeted Academic Support

Tailored guidance ensures that struggling students receive specific, actionable strategies rather than generic advice.

- Clarify Course Expectations: Some students struggle due to misinterpretations of assignment guidelines, grading rubrics, or study expectations. Ensure that they:

  - Understand syllabus requirements.

- Are familiar with grading rubrics.

- Know how to approach different question types (e.g., essays, problem sets, projects).

- Teach Effective Study Strategies:
Many struggling students lack efficient study habits—offer evidence-based learning techniques:

- Active Recall & Spaced Repetition: Encourages reviewing material in intervals rather than cramming.

- Concept Mapping: Helps students visualize connections between concepts.

- Chunking Information: Breaking large amounts of material into smaller, manageable sections.

- Encourage Use of Office Hours and Study Groups:
Some students benefit from one-on-one review sessions or peer-based learning environments.

- Best Practice: Encourage self-reliance by guiding students toward learning strategies rather than simply providing answers.

2.3 Connecting Students with Additional Resources

In some cases, students require institutional support beyond TA assistance.

- Refer Students to Academic Support Services:

- Writing Centers: Assistance with academic writing, structuring arguments, and grammar.

- Tutoring Centers: Subject-specific peer tutoring sessions.

- Supplemental Instruction (SI) Programs: University-run workshops for difficult courses.

- Encourage Mental Health and Wellness Support:
Students struggling with coursework due to stress, anxiety, or personal difficulties may benefit from counseling services. Universities typically offer:

- Mental health counseling centers.

- Time management and productivity workshops.

- Disability and accessibility services.

- Best Practice: Frame resource recommendations positively, emphasizing that successful students seek help proactively.

3. Encouraging Long-Term Academic Resilience

While offering immediate support is crucial, TAs should also help students build academic resilience for sustained improvement.

3.1 Promoting a Growth Mindset

Many struggling students feel defeated by poor performance rather than viewing it as an opportunity for learning.

- Reframe Mistakes as Learning Opportunities:

  - Instead of: *"You didn't do well on this assignment."*

  - Say: *"This is a chance to learn from mistakes and improve for the next one."*

- Encourage Self-Reflection: Ask students to analyze:

  - *"What study methods worked for you in the past?"*

  - *"What changes can you make moving forward?"*

- Best Practice: Normalize academic struggles—remind students that even top scholars faced setbacks but improved through persistence.

3.2 Teaching Self-Advocacy Skills

Students should learn to identify their own challenges and seek appropriate help proactively.

- Encourage Students to Ask for Help Early:

  - Many students wait until the end of the semester to seek support—encourage earlier interventions [106].
    - Teach Communication Skills for Seeking Assistance:

  - Guide students on how to effectively ask professors, TAs, or tutors for help.
    - Promote Time Management and Organization Skills:

  - Suggest study planners, digital calendars, and prioritization techniques to help students balance coursework effectively.

- Best Practice: Help students develop independence rather than creating reliance on external help for academic success.

4. Conclusion

Identifying and supporting struggling students is one of the most impactful roles a TA can play. By recognizing early warning signs, initiating supportive conversations, offering structured academic guidance, and connecting students with appropriate resources, TAs empower students to overcome challenges and develop the skills needed for long-term success.

Ultimately, the goal is not just to help students pass a course—it is to cultivate resilience, self-awareness, and the ability to navigate academic challenges with confidence. By fostering a proactive and supportive learning environment, TAs contribute to student success, retention, and a culture of continuous academic improvement.

Navigating Campus Student Services (Tutoring, Career Services, Counseling)

Teaching Assistants (TAs) play a vital role in not only facilitating classroom learning but also guiding students toward academic and personal support systems that can enhance their overall success. Universities offer a wide range of student services designed to support students in areas such as academic improvement, career development, and mental well-being. However, many students are either unaware of these resources or hesitant to seek help.

TAs serve as a bridge between students and campus services, ensuring that those in need of academic assistance, career planning guidance, or personal support can access the right resources. By understanding the functions of key campus services and proactively directing students to them, TAs help foster a holistic learning environment that supports not just intellectual growth but also emotional and professional well-being.

This section explores the various student services available on most campuses, the role of TAs in connecting students to these resources, and best practices for promoting their use effectively.

1. Understanding Key Campus Student Services

Universities provide a range of services to address different aspects of student development and success. These services generally fall into three primary categories:

- Academic Support Services – Tutoring, writing centers, study skills workshops, and disability services.
- Career and Professional Development Services – Resume building, internship placement, career counseling, and job fairs.
- Wellness and Mental Health Services – Counseling, student wellness programs, and accessibility support.

1.1 Academic Support Services

Students struggling with coursework, writing, or study habits can benefit from academic support services that provide structured guidance and skill development.

- Tutoring Centers: Many universities offer subject-specific tutoring (e.g., math, science, business) where students can get one-on-one or group support from trained tutors.
- Writing Centers: Provide students with assistance on essays, research papers, and thesis development, helping improve clarity, structure, and argumentation.
- Supplemental Instruction (SI) and Study Skills Workshops: Some institutions offer peer-led review sessions for challenging courses or workshops on time management, note-taking, and exam strategies.
- Disability and Accessibility Services: Assist students with learning disabilities, physical impairments, or other academic accommodations such as extended exam times or assistive technology.

- Best Practice: If a student is struggling academically, suggest tutoring or study workshops early in the semester before issues become overwhelming.

1.2 Career and Professional Development Services

Students often need guidance in career planning, resume building, and securing internships or job placements. Career services help students translate academic skills into professional success by offering:

- Resume and Cover Letter Workshops: Provide structured guidance on professional writing, formatting, and tailoring applications for specific fields.
- Mock Interviews and Job Coaching: Helps students build confidence and interview skills through practice sessions with career advisors.
- Internship and Job Search Support: Career centers often maintain databases of job and internship opportunities and help students develop networking strategies.
- Graduate and Professional School Advising: Assist students in navigating graduate school applications, personal statements, and recommendation letter requests.

- Best Practice: If students express uncertainty about career paths or job readiness, encourage them to visit career services early rather than waiting until graduation approaches.

1.3 Wellness and Mental Health Services

Beyond academic and career success, students need emotional and psychological support to manage stress, anxiety, and personal challenges. Universities provide services to help students navigate mental health, stress management, and crisis intervention.

- Counseling and Psychological Services: Offer confidential support for anxiety, depression, stress, and academic pressures through licensed professionals.
- Student Wellness Programs: Many institutions offer stress management workshops, mindfulness programs, and support groups tailored to student needs.
- Crisis Intervention and Peer Support: Some universities have hotlines, peer counseling programs, and wellness centers that provide immediate assistance to students in distress.
- Financial Aid and Student Assistance Programs: Many institutions offer emergency financial support, food pantries, and housing assistance for students facing financial hardships.

- Best Practice: If a student seems overwhelmed, stressed, or emotionally distressed, gently encourage them to seek support through campus wellness services.

2. The TA's Role in Connecting Students to Campus Resources

TAs often serve as first responders when students face academic or personal challenges. While TAs are not expected to act as academic advisors, career counselors, or therapists, they can play a critical role in guiding students toward appropriate campus services.

2.1 Recognizing When a Student Needs Additional Support

Students may not always explicitly state their challenges, but TAs should be attentive to cues that indicate they could benefit from campus services.

- Signs of Academic Struggles: Consistently poor performance, missing assignments, frequent absences, or lack of engagement may indicate a need for tutoring or study support.

- Signs of Career Uncertainty: If students express anxiety about post-graduation plans, struggles with job applications, or confusion about career options, they might benefit from career services.

- Signs of Emotional Distress: Unusual withdrawal, expressions of frustration or anxiety, mentions of extreme stress, or significant changes in behavior may indicate a need for counseling or wellness support.

- Best Practice: Approach students with empathy and discretion, suggesting resources in a way that normalizes seeking help rather than stigmatizing it.

2.2 How to Recommend Campus Services Effectively

The way TAs frame recommendations can influence whether students feel comfortable seeking support.

- Normalize Help-Seeking Behavior:

  - Instead of: *"You seem to be struggling; you should probably see a tutor."*

  - Say: *"Many students find tutoring helpful for reinforcing course concepts. I can help you find a session that fits your schedule."*

- Provide Specific Information:

  - Instead of: *"You should talk to career services."*

  - Say: *"Career services has a great resource for internship searches—I can send you the link to their database."*

- Offer Encouragement and Follow-Up:

  - Instead of: *"You should check out counseling services."*

  - Say: *"The university offers confidential counseling services. If you'd like, I can help you find out how to schedule a session."*

- Best Practice: Keep a list of campus resources handy to provide students with specific recommendations, contact information, and office locations.

3. Encouraging Proactive Engagement with Student Services

Many students hesitate to seek help until academic issues escalate, making early intervention crucial.

- Mention Services Early in the Semester:

  - Discuss tutoring, career services, and counseling resources during introductory classes or office hours so students know where to seek help.

- Highlight Success Stories:

  - Share examples of students who benefited from tutoring, career coaching, or wellness services to reduce stigma around seeking help.

- Incorporate Campus Resources in Course Materials:

  - Add links to writing centers, study skills workshops, and career planning guides in the course syllabus or Learning Management System (LMS).

- Best Practice: Regularly remind students that these resources exist—students may not remember they are available unless they hear about them multiple times.

4. Conclusion

Navigating campus student services is an essential skill for academic success, professional growth, and personal well-being. As TAs, guiding students toward the right resources at the right time can make a significant impact on their learning experience, career trajectory, and overall mental health.

By recognizing when students need support, normalizing help-seeking behavior, and effectively directing them to tutoring, career counseling, or mental health resources, TAs contribute to a more supportive, inclusive, and thriving academic community. Ultimately, helping students connect with available services empowers them to take ownership of their education, develop resilience, and build the skills needed for lifelong success.

Encouraging Professional Development and Career Readiness

As a Teaching Assistant (TA), your influence extends beyond the classroom—you serve as a mentor, advisor, and role model for students navigating both academic and professional aspirations. One of the most impactful ways TAs can support students is by encouraging professional development and career readiness, helping them cultivate the skills, experiences, and confidence necessary for success beyond the university setting.

Career preparation is not just about finding a job after graduation; it is about fostering lifelong learning, adaptability, and professional growth. Many students—especially undergraduates—are uncertain about career paths, how to apply their academic knowledge in real-world settings, or what steps to take toward professional success [107]. By guiding students toward internship opportunities, career development resources, and skill-building activities, TAs help bridge the gap between academic learning and professional application.

This section explores the importance of professional development, strategies for guiding students toward career readiness, and best practices for instilling a proactive approach to career growth.

1. The Importance of Professional Development for Students

Many students focus heavily on academic performance but often neglect career preparation until their final year. Encouraging students to develop professional skills early helps them gain a competitive edge in the job market and ensures a smoother transition into their careers.

1.1 Why Professional Development Matters

- Enhances Career Competitiveness – Employers seek candidates with both academic knowledge and practical skills such as teamwork, problem-solving, and adaptability.
- Builds Confidence and Career Awareness – Students who engage in internships, networking, and professional development activities feel more prepared for career decisions [108].
- Encourages Skill Development – Beyond technical expertise, students need soft skills such as leadership, communication, and critical thinking.
- Facilitates Academic and Industry Connections – Engaging in mentorship programs, professional associations, and career events helps students build valuable professional networks.

- Best Practice: Encourage students to start developing career skills early—waiting until graduation to think about professional development can limit opportunities.

2. Strategies for Encouraging Career Readiness

TAs can actively support students in building professional skills, exploring career paths, and taking advantage of career resources offered by the university.

2.1 Introducing Students to Career Services and Development Resources

Many students underutilize career services because they are unaware of the valuable tools and programs available to them. TAs can help by:

- Referring Students to Career Centers: Encourage students to visit the university's career office for:

- Resume and cover letter assistance

- Mock interviews and networking events

- Internship and job search resources

- Highlighting Professional Workshops and Webinars: Many universities host career-focused workshops on personal branding, professional writing, and industry trends.

- Best Practice: Include career service information in the course syllabus, Learning Management System (LMS), or class announcements so students consistently see it as a resource.

2.2 Encouraging Internship and Research Opportunities

Internships and research experiences allow students to apply classroom knowledge in real-world settings, making them more marketable to employers and graduate programs.

- Promote Research Assistantships: Encourage students interested in academia or specialized fields to participate in faculty-led research projects to develop critical analytical and research skills.
- Discuss the Value of Internships: Explain how internships provide real-world experience,

professional networking, and potential job offers post-graduation.

- Share Opportunities Through Departmental and Professional Networks: Many universities have internship databases, faculty research opportunities, and alumni networks that students can access.

- Best Practice: If a student expresses interest in research or an industry role, guide them toward specific opportunities rather than vague suggestions.

2.3 Encouraging Networking and Mentorship Connections

Building professional connections is key to career success, yet many students struggle with networking or lack confidence in reaching out to professionals.

- Promote the Value of Faculty and Industry Mentorship: Encourage students to:

- Attend office hours and build relationships with professors who can provide career guidance and letters of recommendation.

- Connect with alumni through LinkedIn or university mentorship programs to gain insights into career paths.

- Introduce Students to Professional Organizations: Many fields have academic and industry associations that offer career development events, scholarships, and networking opportunities.

- Examples include:

  - American Psychological Association (APA) – Psychology

  - Association for Computing Machinery (ACM) – Computer Science

  - Institute of Electrical and Electronics Engineers (IEEE) – Engineering

- Encourage Conference Participation: Many students are unaware that they can attend academic or industry conferences even as undergraduates. Presenting research or simply networking at such events provides significant career exposure.

- Best Practice: Teach students how to approach networking—many feel intimidated but benefit from practicing informational interviews or LinkedIn outreach strategies.

2.4 Helping Students Develop Transferable Skills

Many students struggle to connect academic coursework to real-world applications. TAs can help by emphasizing transferable skills that are valuable across multiple career paths.

- Highlight Soft Skills Development: Emphasize that coursework teaches critical thinking, teamwork, problem-solving, and communication skills, all of which are crucial in professional settings.

- Encourage Leadership Experience: Suggest extracurricular activities, student organizations, or peer mentoring roles that build leadership experience.

- Guide Students in Self-Assessment: Encourage students to reflect on:

- *"What are my strengths and interests?"*

- *"What type of work environment suits me best?"*

- *"What skills do I need to develop further?"*

- Best Practice: Connect coursework to real-world scenarios—for example, explain how group projects mirror workplace collaboration and research papers enhance analytical writing skills.

2.5 Supporting Graduate School and Advanced Study Planning

For students interested in academia or specialized fields, early preparation for graduate school applications is crucial. TAs can help by:

- Providing Guidance on Graduate Programs: Encourage students to explore different types of graduate degrees, required qualifications, and funding options.
- Discussing Standardized Tests: Offer insights on exams such as GRE, GMAT, LSAT, or MCAT and their role in admissions.
- Assisting with Personal Statements and Applications: Share tips on crafting strong application essays and securing letters of recommendation.

- Best Practice: If a student is considering graduate school, suggest they start preparing at least a year in advance to allow time for test-taking, applications, and faculty recommendations.

3. Encouraging a Proactive Approach to Career Readiness

The most successful students take ownership of their professional development by continuously seeking growth opportunities. TAs can foster this mindset by:

- Encouraging Early Career Exploration: Remind students that it's never too early to think about career goals, internships, or graduate school.
- Teaching Professionalism and Workplace Etiquette: Guide students on email etiquette, workplace communication, and professional behavior.
- Instilling a Growth Mindset: Emphasize that career paths are not always linear—adaptability, persistence, and lifelong learning are key to success.

- Best Practice: Share your own experiences or those of successful alumni to illustrate different career trajectories and the importance of professional development.

4. Conclusion

Encouraging professional development and career readiness is an essential role of a TA. By introducing students to career resources, internships, research opportunities, and networking strategies, TAs help them take meaningful steps toward building successful futures.

The transition from academia to the professional world can be daunting, but with the right guidance, tools, and encouragement, students can develop the skills, confidence, and knowledge to thrive. By fostering a culture of career preparedness and continuous learning, TAs not only support students' immediate academic success but also contribute to their long-term professional achievements.

Chapter 13: Academic Integrity and Ethical Responsibilities

The role of a Teaching Assistant (TA) is a pivotal stage in the professional journey of many aspiring educators, researchers, and industry professionals. However, at some point, every TA must transition to the next phase of their career—whether that means pursuing a faculty position, continuing graduate studies, entering the corporate world, or leveraging their skills in a different professional field. Understanding how to effectively navigate this transition is essential for long-term success.

This chapter provides guidance on making a smooth and strategic move beyond the TA role. It explores the various career pathways available to former TAs, from academia and research to industry, government, and nonprofit sectors. Additionally, it offers practical advice on leveraging the skills gained as a TA—such as leadership, communication, and instructional expertise—when applying for jobs or academic positions.

Figure 13.1. Teaching and Learning [113].

A critical component of this transition is documenting and showcasing teaching experience effectively. This chapter outlines how TAs can build a professional portfolio, craft compelling CVs and résumés, and use networking opportunities to expand career prospects. It also provides insights into navigating the job market, preparing for interviews, and seeking mentorship to support career growth.

By the end of this chapter, TAs will be able to:
- Identify potential career pathways beyond the TA role, both within and outside academia.
- Translate teaching and mentorship experience into valuable career skills.
- Develop a strong teaching portfolio, CV, and résumé for job applications.
- Network effectively with faculty, peers, and industry professionals.

- Prepare for job interviews and professional advancement opportunities.
- Continue personal and professional development for long-term career success.

Leaving the TA role does not mean leaving behind the valuable skills and experiences gained through teaching and mentoring. Instead, it marks the beginning of a new professional chapter where these experiences serve as assets in a variety of career settings. By planning ahead, refining professional materials, and strategically positioning themselves in their chosen fields, TAs can ensure a successful transition to their next opportunity.

Understanding Academic Honesty in Higher Education

Academic honesty is the foundation of intellectual integrity and scholarly pursuit in higher education. It ensures that students engage in ethical learning, original thinking, and responsible scholarship. Universities uphold strict policies to prevent plagiarism, cheating, fabrication, and other forms of academic misconduct, as these violations undermine the credibility of academic institutions and devalue the learning process.

Teaching Assistants (TAs) play a crucial role in fostering a culture of academic integrity by educating students on ethical academic practices, detecting potential violations, and promoting responsible research and writing. Beyond enforcing rules, TAs should strive to proactively teach students about the importance of academic honesty and equip them with strategies to maintain integrity in their academic work.

This section explores the principles of academic honesty, common forms of academic misconduct, and strategies TAs can use to promote integrity in higher education.

1. The Importance of Academic Honesty in Higher Education

Academic honesty is more than just following institutional policies—it is a commitment to ethical scholarship, intellectual growth, and professional credibility. In the university setting, students are expected to develop their own ideas, conduct authentic research, and give proper credit to the intellectual contributions of others.

1.1 Why Academic Integrity Matters

- Preserves the Value of Degrees – If academic dishonesty is widespread, the credibility of degrees and certifications diminishes, affecting graduates' employability and institutional reputation.
- Encourages Independent Thinking – Ethical scholarship fosters originality, critical analysis, and problem-solving skills that are essential for career and research success.
- Builds Trust in Academic and Professional Communities – Ethical research and citation practices ensure knowledge is built upon legitimate sources, strengthening scholarly dialogue.
- Develops Strong Work Ethic – Learning to engage with sources responsibly, manage time effectively, and uphold integrity in coursework translates into lifelong professional skills.

- Best Practice: TAs should emphasize that academic honesty is not just about avoiding punishment but about developing intellectual responsibility and ethical scholarship.

2. Common Forms of Academic Misconduct

Understanding the different forms of academic dishonesty helps TAs identify potential violations and educate students on what constitutes unethical behavior.

2.1 Plagiarism (The Most Common Violation)

Plagiarism occurs when students use someone else's work, ideas, or words without proper attribution [109]. It can be intentional or unintentional but is always considered a violation of academic integrity.

Types of Plagiarism:
- Direct Copying: Submitting work that includes verbatim text from another source without citation.
- Paraphrasing Without Attribution: Rewriting someone else's ideas in one's own words without citing the original author.
- Self-Plagiarism: Reusing one's own work from previous courses or assignments without permission.
- Contract Cheating: Hiring someone else to complete an assignment, using essay-writing services, or submitting AI-generated content as original work.

- Best Practice: Teach students how to properly cite sources and use plagiarism detection tools to check their work before submission.

2.2 Cheating on Exams and Assignments

Cheating involves gaining an unfair advantage through dishonest means during examinations or coursework.

- Unauthorized Collaboration: Working with others on individual assignments without permission.
- Using Unauthorized Materials: Consulting notes, devices, or online resources during closed-book exams.
- Impersonation: Having someone take an exam or submit work on behalf of another student.

- Best Practice: Promote academic fairness by explaining clear exam policies and reinforcing guidelines on permitted collaboration.

2.3 Fabrication and Falsification

Fabrication involves inventing data, sources, or research findings, while falsification refers to manipulating or distorting data or results to support a desired outcome.

- Examples Include:

  • Creating fake citations or sources to support an argument.

  • Altering research data to make results seem more convincing.

- Submitting false attendance or participation records.

- Best Practice: If TAs oversee research projects, they should educate students about ethical research practices and data integrity standards.

2.4 Unauthorized AI Use and Generative Content

With the rise of AI-powered writing tools, universities have developed guidelines on appropriate and ethical AI use in academic work [110].

- Ethical AI Use: Some universities permit AI assistance for brainstorming, outlining, or refining ideas but require students to disclose their use of AI tools.
- Unethical AI Use: Submitting AI-generated text as one's own without revision or critical engagement is considered academic dishonesty.

- Best Practice: TAs should be aware of institutional policies on AI use and educate students on how to use AI ethically while maintaining academic integrity.

3. Promoting Academic Honesty: The TA's Role

TAs are often the first point of contact when students have questions about ethical scholarship. By taking a proactive, educational approach, TAs can reduce instances of academic dishonesty and foster responsible academic behavior.

3.1 Educating Students About Proper Citation and Research Practices

- Teach Citation Methods: Provide guidance on MLA, APA, Chicago, or discipline-specific citation styles.
- Encourage the Use of Citation Tools: Introduce students to Zotero, EndNote, or citation generators to help them format references properly.
- Discuss Proper Paraphrasing: Show examples of acceptable vs. unacceptable paraphrasing to prevent accidental plagiarism.

- Best Practice: Offer students plagiarism-checking tools (e.g., Turnitin, Grammarly) to review their work before submission.

3.2 Encouraging Academic Integrity Through Classroom Policies

- Clearly Define Collaboration Rules: Specify what forms of group work, peer editing, or discussion participation are allowed.
- Set Transparent Expectations: Include an academic integrity statement in course materials and syllabi.
- Provide Ethical Exam Guidelines: Clarify acceptable materials, testing conditions, and expectations before exams.

- Best Practice: Reinforce that integrity is not just about following rules but about maintaining self-respect and credibility.

3.3 Recognizing and Addressing Academic Dishonesty

If a TA suspects academic dishonesty, they should:

- Gather Evidence: Document inconsistencies in work or use plagiarism detection software.
- Consult Faculty Supervisors: Discuss concerns with the professor before taking action.
- Have a Private Conversation: If appropriate, meet with the student to discuss concerns in a non-accusatory manner.
- Follow Institutional Procedures: Every university has a formal process for reporting academic misconduct—TAs should familiarize themselves with these protocols.

- Best Practice: When addressing dishonesty, frame discussions as learning opportunities rather than punitive encounters.

4. Conclusion

Academic honesty is the cornerstone of intellectual growth, scholarly credibility, and ethical professionalism. As educators, TAs must actively promote integrity by educating students on proper research practices, setting clear expectations, and addressing dishonesty with fairness and consistency.

Rather than viewing academic integrity solely as a disciplinary issue, TAs should frame it as an essential component of academic and professional development. By fostering a culture where students understand the value of originality, critical inquiry, and ethical scholarship, TAs contribute to a stronger, more responsible academic community.

Teaching Students About Proper Citation and Attribution

Proper citation and attribution are fundamental elements of academic writing and research, ensuring that ideas and contributions are accurately credited while maintaining the integrity of scholarly work. In higher education, students are expected to engage in original thought while responsibly integrating external sources to support their arguments. However, many students—particularly those new to academic research—struggle with when, how, and why to cite sources correctly.

Teaching Assistants (TAs) play a critical role in guiding students through the complexities of citation and attribution, helping them understand the importance of ethical scholarship, avoid unintentional plagiarism, and develop strong research practices. Beyond enforcing citation rules, TAs should focus on building students' confidence in incorporating sources effectively, equipping them with the skills to engage in scholarly discourse with academic integrity.

This section explores the importance of citation and attribution, common challenges students face, different citation styles, and effective strategies for teaching proper citation practices.

1. Why Citation and Attribution Matter in Academic Writing

Academic work is built on an ongoing conversation of ideas, where scholars engage with previous research, critique arguments, and contribute new insights. Citation and attribution serve as the foundation of this scholarly exchange by ensuring that:

- Intellectual Contributions Are Acknowledged – Proper citation gives credit to the original authors and researchers whose work informs new studies.
- Plagiarism Is Avoided – Failing to cite sources appropriately can lead to unintentional plagiarism, which is a violation of academic integrity.
- Readers Can Verify and Explore Sources – Accurate citations allow readers to trace ideas back to their original sources for further study.
- Scholars Build Credibility and Authority – Using and citing reputable sources enhances the legitimacy of a student's argument and situates their work within a broader academic framework.

- Best Practice: Emphasize that citation is not just about avoiding plagiarism—it is about engaging in ethical scholarship and contributing to the academic community.

2. Common Challenges Students Face with Citation

Many students struggle with citation not because they intend to plagiarize, but because they are unfamiliar with citation rules, unsure of when to cite, or overwhelmed by different formatting requirements. Common challenges include:

- Uncertainty About When to Cite – Students may not know whether to cite paraphrased ideas, common knowledge, or information found in multiple sources.
- Confusion About Citation Styles – Different disciplines use varied citation formats (APA, MLA, Chicago, IEEE, etc.), leading to inconsistency and formatting errors.
- Poor Integration of Sources – Some students either overquote, underquote, or awkwardly insert citations without proper contextualization.
- Misuse of Citation Tools – While citation generators (e.g., Zotero, EndNote, or Citation Machine) can be helpful, students often rely on them without verifying accuracy, leading to errors.

- Best Practice: Address these challenges proactively by teaching citation as an essential writing skill, not just a technical requirement.

3. Different Citation Styles and Their Applications

Students must learn how to apply the correct citation style based on their academic discipline. The most commonly used citation styles include:

3.1 APA (American Psychological Association)

- Used in social sciences, psychology, education, and business.
- Focuses on author-date format (e.g., *Smith, 2020*).
- Example: *(Brown, 2021, p. 35)*

3.2 MLA (Modern Language Association)

- Used in humanities, literature, and cultural studies.
- Emphasizes author-page format (e.g., *Smith 35*).
- Example: *(Brown 35)*

3.3 Chicago/Turabian

- Used in history, political science, and some humanities fields.
- Supports two formats:

  - Notes and bibliography (footnotes or endnotes).
  - Author-date system (similar to APA).
    - Example (Footnote): *Brown, Title of Book, 35.*

3.4 IEEE (Institute of Electrical and Electronics Engineers)

- Used in engineering, computer science, and technology disciplines.
- Uses numerical in-text citations corresponding to a reference list.
- Example: *[1]*

- Best Practice: Provide clear examples and discipline-specific guidance to help students select the correct citation style for their field.

4. Teaching Effective Citation Practices

As a TA, your goal is to move beyond simply enforcing citation rules and instead help students integrate citations seamlessly into their writing. The following strategies can be used to improve student citation skills:

4.1 Teaching When and How to Cite

- **Explain What Requires Citation:**

  - Direct quotes and paraphrased ideas.
  - Statistical data, figures, and research findings.
  - Unique theories, concepts, or methodologies developed by others.

- **Discuss What Does Not Need Citation:**

  - Common knowledge (*e.g., "The Earth orbits the Sun"*).
  - Widely known historical facts (*e.g., "The Declaration of Independence was signed in 1776"*).

- Best Practice: Use real-life examples of correct and incorrect citation to illustrate proper attribution techniques.

4.2 Teaching Proper Paraphrasing and Quotation Use

- Show the Difference Between Paraphrasing and Direct Quoting:

  - *Original Source:* "Climate change has led to a measurable increase in global temperatures over the past century" (*Smith, 2020*).

  - Proper Paraphrase: *Smith (2020) argues that rising global temperatures are a direct result of climate change.*

  - Improper Paraphrase (Plagiarism): *Climate change has increased global temperatures over the last hundred years (Smith, 2020).*

- Teach Students to Blend Citations Naturally:

  - Instead of: *"Global temperatures are rising. (Smith, 2020)"*

  - Encourage: *"Smith (2020) explains that global temperatures have been steadily increasing due to climate change."*

- Best Practice: Have students practice paraphrasing and summarizing sources in class to reinforce proper attribution techniques.

4.3 Using Citation Tools Responsibly

While citation management tools can be helpful, students should be taught to verify automatically generated citations for accuracy.

- Introduce Students to:

  - Zotero (for managing research sources).

  - EndNote (for generating citations).

  - Turnitin or Grammarly Plagiarism Checkers (for verifying originality).

- Best Practice: Remind students that citation generators are not foolproof—they should double-check formatting and accuracy before submission.

5. Encouraging a Culture of Ethical Scholarship

TAs should promote a proactive approach to academic integrity by reinforcing why citation matters beyond avoiding penalties.

- Discuss Academic Honesty Policies: Ensure students understand the university's plagiarism policies and consequences of academic misconduct.
- Frame Citation as a Skill for Professional Success: Proper attribution is not only important in academia but also in professional writing, journalism, research, and legal documentation.
- Encourage Transparency in Source Use: Students should feel comfortable asking for citation help rather than resorting to poor practices out of uncertainty.

- Best Practice: Foster an open dialogue about ethical scholarship, encouraging students to view citation as a way to build credibility rather than an obligation.

6. Conclusion

Teaching students about proper citation and attribution is essential for developing ethical academic habits and fostering responsible research practices. As a TA, your role is to not only enforce proper citation but also educate students on its significance, help them navigate citation styles, and equip them with tools to integrate sources effectively.

By promoting a culture of academic integrity, reinforcing strong citation habits, and encouraging students to take ownership of their scholarship, TAs help prepare students for lifelong engagement in ethical and professional research practices.

Using Plagiarism Detection Tools Effectively

Plagiarism detection tools have become an essential part of academic integrity enforcement in higher education. These tools help identify instances of unoriginal work, improper citation, and potential academic misconduct, but they should not be viewed merely as punitive measures. Instead, they should be used as educational aids that help students develop better research, citation, and writing practices.

As a Teaching Assistant (TA), your role extends beyond identifying plagiarism—you should also teach students how to use plagiarism detection tools as learning resources, interpret similarity reports accurately, and refine their academic writing. By guiding students through responsible use of these tools, TAs can foster a culture of academic integrity, encourage original thought, and help students avoid unintentional plagiarism.

This section explores the purpose of plagiarism detection tools, best practices for interpreting results, strategies for integrating these tools into student learning, and ethical considerations for their use.

1. The Role of Plagiarism Detection Tools in Higher Education

Plagiarism detection tools are designed to analyze written work and compare it against a vast database of sources, including:

- Academic Journals & Published Papers – Helps detect if content is lifted from scholarly sources without proper attribution.
- Student Submissions (Past & Present) – Identifies cases of self-plagiarism or unauthorized paper recycling.
- Web-Based Sources – Flags material copied from websites, blogs, Wikipedia, or other online content.

While these tools are often associated with academic misconduct detection, they also serve an educational function by helping students:

- Identify Citation Errors – Allows students to see where proper attribution is missing or incorrect.
- Improve Paraphrasing Skills – Helps students recognize when they are too closely mimicking the original text.
- Develop Awareness of Academic Integrity – Encourages students to engage in ethical writing practices from the start.

- Best Practice: Frame plagiarism detection tools as learning aids rather than punitive measures, reinforcing that their purpose is to support ethical scholarship.

2. Common Plagiarism Detection Tools and Their Features

Different plagiarism detection software tools are used in academic institutions, each with unique capabilities. The most widely used include:

2.1 Turnitin

- One of the most commonly used plagiarism detection tools in universities.
- Compares student work against an extensive database of academic articles, student papers, and web content.
- Provides a similarity report highlighting matching text with percentage scores.
- Allows for peer review and AI-driven feedback on writing quality.

- Best Practice: Instruct students to review their Turnitin reports before final submission, giving them a chance to correct citation errors.

2.2 Grammarly Plagiarism Checker

- Primarily used for grammar, clarity, and plagiarism detection.
- Scans open web content and some academic sources.
- Offers real-time writing improvement suggestions alongside plagiarism checks.

- Best Practice: Encourage students to use Grammarly for early-stage writing review but cross-check with institutional tools like Turnitin for final submission.

2.3 Unicheck, Copyscape, and Plagscan

- Unicheck – Frequently used in Learning Management Systems (LMS) like Canvas and Moodle.
- Copyscape – Primarily scans web-based sources and online content.
- Plagscan – Compares documents to both academic and general web sources.

- Best Practice: Familiarize yourself with your institution's chosen plagiarism tool to provide accurate guidance on report interpretation.

3. Understanding and Interpreting Similarity Reports

Plagiarism detection tools generate similarity reports, which indicate the percentage of text that matches external sources. However, a high similarity percentage does not automatically indicate plagiarism, and a low percentage does not guarantee originality [111].

3.1 What a Similarity Score Means

- 0-10% Similarity – Likely to be original work with proper citations.
- 10-25% Similarity – May include common phrases, quotations, or properly cited material.
- 25-50% Similarity – Requires closer inspection to determine if excessive quoting or poor paraphrasing is present.
- 50%+ Similarity – Potentially problematic, indicating extensive unoriginal content or improper citation [111].

- Best Practice: Teach students that not all flagged content is plagiarism—it could include direct quotes, bibliographies, or common academic phrases.

3.2 Distinguishing Acceptable vs. Unacceptable Matches

- Properly Cited Quotes – If quotation marks and citations are present, the match is not plagiarism.
- Reference Lists & Bibliographies – Often flagged in similarity reports, but not considered plagiarism.
- Common Phrases & Terminology – Standard discipline-specific phrases (e.g., *"Photosynthesis is the process by which plants convert light into energy"*) may trigger false positives.
- Patchwriting (Problematic Paraphrasing) – When students slightly alter words but keep sentence structure too close to the original, it may require revision.

- Best Practice: Encourage students to focus on rewriting ideas in their own words rather than merely substituting synonyms.

4. Using Plagiarism Detection Tools as Teaching Aids

Rather than only using plagiarism detection software for grading and misconduct cases, TAs can integrate these tools into the learning process to help students strengthen their academic writing skills.

4.1 Encouraging Students to Pre-Check Their Work

- Allow students to submit drafts to plagiarism checkers before final submission.
- Encourage them to analyze flagged sections and refine paraphrasing or citations accordingly.

- Best Practice: Set up optional pre-submission checks to help students identify unintentional citation mistakes before they become academic violations.

4.2 Teaching Students How to Address High Similarity Scores

- If a similarity report flags too many direct matches:

- Instruct students to reduce reliance on direct quotations and instead focus on paraphrasing ideas in their own words.
  - If citations are missing:

- Encourage students to review citation guidelines (APA, MLA, Chicago) and properly credit sources.
  - If self-plagiarism is detected:

- Explain the ethical issues with reusing one's previous work without disclosure.

- Best Practice: Offer workshops or office hours focused on interpreting plagiarism reports, so students gain confidence in their writing process.

4.3 Framing Academic Integrity as a Growth Process

Rather than viewing plagiarism detection tools only as enforcement mechanisms, emphasize their role in:

- Improving Academic Writing – Encourage students to see citation as an essential research skill, not a punishment.
- Developing Scholarly Confidence – Help students become comfortable integrating credible sources while maintaining originality.
- Encouraging Ethical Research Practices – Reinforce that proper citation and original work enhance their credibility as scholars.

- Best Practice: Use plagiarism detection as an opportunity for learning, not just for penalization.

5. Conclusion

Plagiarism detection tools are valuable assets in upholding academic integrity, improving writing skills, and preventing unintentional plagiarism. However, these tools should be used proactively to educate students rather than solely as disciplinary measures.

As a TA, your role is to guide students in understanding similarity reports, using citation tools effectively, and developing stronger research habits. By fostering a learning-centered approach to plagiarism detection, you help students navigate the complexities of academic writing with integrity, confidence, and accountability.

Addressing and Reporting Cases of Academic Misconduct

Academic integrity is the foundation of higher education, ensuring that students engage in ethical scholarship, demonstrate original thought, and uphold the principles of honesty in research and coursework. However, instances of academic misconduct—such as plagiarism, cheating, falsification of data, and unauthorized collaboration—can undermine the credibility of the academic system and diminish the value of degrees.

Teaching Assistants (TAs) play a critical role in upholding academic integrity by identifying, addressing, and reporting cases of academic misconduct. This responsibility requires a balanced approach—one that is firm in maintaining ethical standards while also educating students on responsible academic practices. TAs must be familiar with institutional policies, procedural protocols, and ethical considerations when handling suspected violations.

This section explores the types of academic misconduct, the steps TAs should take when identifying potential violations, best practices for addressing misconduct with students, and the formal reporting procedures required by academic institutions.

1. Understanding Academic Misconduct

Academic misconduct encompasses a range of violations that compromise the integrity of academic work and research. It is crucial for TAs to be able to identify different forms of misconduct and differentiate between intentional violations and unintentional errors stemming from lack of knowledge or misunderstanding of academic expectations.

1.1 Common Forms of Academic Misconduct

- Plagiarism – Using someone else's work, ideas, or wording without proper attribution.
- Cheating – Using unauthorized materials or methods to gain an unfair advantage on assignments or exams.
- Falsification and Fabrication – Inventing or altering data, sources, or research findings.
- Unauthorized Collaboration – Working with others on assignments designated as independent work.
- Impersonation and Proxy Work – Having someone else take an exam or complete coursework on behalf of a student.
- Self-Plagiarism – Reusing one's own previous work without proper citation or permission from instructors.

- Best Practice: Ensure students understand what constitutes academic misconduct by providing clear definitions and examples in class discussions or syllabus materials.

2. Steps for Addressing Suspected Academic Misconduct

When a TA identifies potential academic misconduct, it is important to follow a structured and objective approach to ensure fairness and uphold due process.

2.1 Initial Assessment and Evidence Collection

- Review the Work Carefully – If a TA suspects misconduct (e.g., plagiarism or unauthorized collaboration), they should carefully analyze the submission before making assumptions.
- Document the Evidence – If plagiarism is suspected, highlight matching sections and provide citations of original sources from plagiarism detection tools (e.g., Turnitin).
- Check for Previous Violations – Some institutions track repeat offenses, so it is helpful to check if the student has prior misconduct cases.

- Best Practice: Avoid immediately confronting a student based on assumptions—verify all details first.

2.2 Determining the Severity of the Violation

Not all cases of academic misconduct are intentional acts of dishonesty. Some students may violate policies due to:

- Lack of understanding of citation rules (e.g., incorrect paraphrasing).
- Misinterpretation of collaboration guidelines (e.g., working together on an assignment they thought allowed discussion).
- Time management struggles leading to poor decisions (e.g., last-minute plagiarism out of desperation).

- Best Practice: If the issue appears to be a genuine misunderstanding, a teaching moment (e.g., discussing citation rules) may be more effective than formal disciplinary action.

2.3 Addressing the Student Privately

Before formally reporting a case, it is often appropriate to speak with the student to clarify concerns and allow them to provide context.

- Schedule a Private Meeting – Never accuse a student publicly; discuss concerns in a confidential setting.
- Adopt a Neutral, Non-Accusatory Tone – Avoid making immediate judgments; instead, present the findings objectively:

  - *"I noticed that sections of your assignment closely match an external source without citation. Can you help me understand how you approached your research process?"*
    - Give the Student a Chance to Respond – Sometimes, students may acknowledge errors, provide explanations, or admit to unintentional mistakes.
    - Explain Institutional Policies – Ensure students understand the severity of academic integrity violations and future consequences.

- Best Practice: If the student appears genuinely unaware of academic integrity standards, providing educational guidance (e.g., a refresher on citation practices) may be more appropriate than disciplinary action.

3. Reporting Academic Misconduct

If a TA determines that a violation is significant or intentional, the next step is to follow the institution's formal reporting procedures.

3.1 Understanding Institutional Policies

Each university has specific guidelines for handling academic misconduct [112]. TAs should be familiar with:

- The reporting process – Some institutions require TAs to submit a report directly to faculty

supervisors, while others mandate filing cases with an academic integrity office [112].
- The consequences for students – Penalties range from a failing grade on an assignment to academic probation or expulsion for severe or repeat violations [112].

- Best Practice: Review the academic integrity policy of your institution to ensure compliance with procedural requirements.

3.2 Submitting a Misconduct Report

When filing an official report, TAs should provide clear documentation to support their claims.

- Include the Student's Work – Attach the original assignment and indicate problematic areas.
- Provide Evidence of Misconduct – This may include plagiarism reports, copies of the original sources, or exam records.
- Describe the Nature of the Violation – Clearly explain why the case constitutes misconduct and whether the student has prior violations.
- Follow Institutional Protocols – Submit the report through the designated academic integrity office or faculty member.

- Best Practice: Maintain confidentiality when handling academic misconduct cases—discussions should be restricted to faculty, administrators, and authorized personnel.

4. Supporting Academic Integrity Through Proactive Teaching

While reporting misconduct is necessary, TAs can also take proactive measures to prevent academic dishonesty by promoting a culture of integrity.

4.1 Clarifying Expectations Early

- Discuss academic integrity at the start of the semester – Ensure students are aware of plagiarism policies and citation requirements.
- Provide Clear Collaboration Guidelines – Specify when students can and cannot work together.

- Best Practice: Include an academic integrity statement in course syllabi and discuss it periodically.

4.2 Teaching Responsible Research Practices

- Offer citation workshops – Help students learn proper attribution and paraphrasing techniques.
- Encourage use of plagiarism detection tools for self-checking – Students can review similarity reports to refine their citations before submission.

- Best Practice: Shift the focus from punishing misconduct to educating students on ethical academic practices.

4.3 Designing Assignments That Reduce Academic Misconduct

TAs can help prevent academic dishonesty by structuring assignments in a way that encourages originality.

- Use Open-Ended Prompts – Personalized topics make it harder for students to copy existing content.
- Incorporate Draft Submissions – Reviewing drafts before final submission helps detect early signs of plagiarism and allows students to improve.
- Use Varied Assessment Methods – Incorporating oral presentations, reflection papers, and project-based assessments reduces opportunities for cheating.

- Best Practice: A well-designed assignment structure can minimize opportunities for academic dishonesty.

5. Conclusion

Addressing and reporting academic misconduct is a key responsibility of Teaching Assistants, requiring a balance of enforcement and education. By identifying potential violations, engaging in constructive discussions with students, and following institutional protocols for reporting misconduct, TAs help maintain the integrity of the academic system.

Ultimately, academic integrity is not just about rules and penalties—it is about fostering a culture of ethical scholarship, critical thinking, and responsibility. By proactively teaching students about ethical research, proper citation, and institutional policies, TAs can reduce misconduct and empower students to engage in honest, meaningful academic work.

References

1]   (2025). *Teaching for, as, and with an undergraduate interdisciplinary curriculum in Hong Kong: dynamic positionings of teaching assistants*. Asia Pacific Education Review 26(3), pp. 345-357. https://doi.org/10.1007/s12564-025-10063-0

2]   (December 31, 2024). *Inclusive Education and the Role of Teaching Assistants*. Nature Research Intelligence. https://www.nature.com/research-intelligence/nri-topic-summaries/inclusive-education-and-the-role-of-teaching-assistants-micro-36711

3]   (n.d.). Teaching (TA) Information. Princeton University Graduate School. https://gradschool.princeton.edu/academics/courses-research-teaching/teachin

4]   (n.d.). *Teaching assistants roles and responsibilities*. University of Waterloo. https://uwaterloo.ca/statistics-and-actuarial-science/graduate-studies/resources-students/teaching-assistants-program/roles-and-responsibilities

5]   English, D. o. (n.d.). *Teaching Assistant Responsibilities and Expectations*. University of Pennsylvania. https://www.english.upenn.edu/node/25970

6]   (March 23, 2020). *Tech TAs helped faculty navigate remote teaching technology during pandemic*. Penn State University. https://www.psu.edu/news/academics/story/tech-tas-helped-faculty-navigate-remote-teaching-technology-during-pandemic

7]   Wilson, D. (2020). The Role of Teaching Assistants and Faculty in Student Engagement. ASEE Conferences. https://doi.org/10.18260/1-2--35365

8]   (2023). *Training learning assistants to employ inclusive pedagogy and teaching tools in the classroom*. https://doi.org/10.1186/s12909-023-04234-0

9]   Ghimire, A. & Singh, C. (2025). *Using Unguided Peer Collaboration to Facilitate Early Educators' Pedagogical Development: An Example from Physics TA Training*. arXiv:2510.14046. https://doi.org/10.48550/arXiv.2510.14046

10]   (n.d.). *Learning Assistant Model*. Wikipedia. https://en.wikipedia.org/wiki/Learning_Assistant_Model

11]   (n.d.). *Grading and Effective Feedback – Graduate Assistant and Teaching Assistant Handbook*. eCampusOntario. https://ecampusontario.pressbooks.pub/uwindsorgata/chapter/effective-assessment-and-evaluation/

[12] (n.d.). *Graduate Teaching Assistant Mentoring Program*. University of Wisconsin-Milwaukee. https://uwm.edu/english/composition/composition-mentoring-program/

[13] (2025). *Inclusive Education and the Role of Teaching Assistants*. Nature Research Intelligence. https://doi.org/10.1038/s41599-025-01000-0

[14] (2026). *Teaching Assistant Job Description*. University of Washington, Department of Gender, Women, and Sexuality Studies. https://gwss.washington.edu/sites/gwss/files/documents/official_ta_job_description_from_labor_rel ations.pdf

[15] (n.d.). *FERPA for Faculty and Teaching Assistants*. Registrar's Office. https://registrar.caltech.edu/records/ferpa/ferpa-faculty

[16] (n.d.). *Code of Conduct*. TASC Education. https://www.tasceducation.org/code-of-conduct

[17] Saunders, L., Wong, M. A. & Appedu, S. (2025). *Graduate Students as Adult Learners: Andragogy and Instructional Design*. Proceedings of the ALISE Annual Conference. https://doi.org/10.21900/j.alise.2025.1963

[18] Muhajirah. (2020). *Basic of Learning Theory (Behaviorism, Cognitivism, Constructivism, and Humanism)*. International Journal of Academic Education 1, pp. 23-37. https://doi.org/10.46966/ijae.v1i1.23

[19] (2023). *Behaviorism Learning Theory Explained*. Learn.org. https://learn.org/articles/behaviorism_learning_theory.html

[20] (n.d.). *Cognitivism - Learning - Library Services at Cardiff Metropolitan University*. Cardiff Metropolitan University. https://library.cardiffmet.ac.uk/learning/learning_theories/cognitivism

[21] (2025). *Constructivism (philosophy of education)*. Wikipedia. https://en.wikipedia.org/wiki/Constructivism_%28philosophy_of_education%29

[22] (2025). *Constructivism (philosophy of education)*. Wikipedia. https://en.wikipedia.org/wiki/Constructivism_%28philosophy_of_education%29

[23] (2025). Humanistic Learning Theory. Growth Engineering. https://www.growthengineering.co.uk/humanistic-learning-theory/

[24] (2023). *Adult Learning Theory and the Principles of Andragogy*. University of Phoenix. https://www.phoenix.edu/articles/education/adult-learning-theory-and-the-principles-of-andragogy.html

25] (n.d.). *Adult Learning Theory | University of Phoenix*. University of Phoenix. https://www.phoenix.edu/articles/education/adult-learning-theory-the-principles-of-andragogy.html

26] (n.d.). *Adult Learning Theory*. University of Phoenix. https://www.phoenix.edu/articles/education/adult-learning-theory-and-the-principles-of-andragogy.html

27] (2026). *Adult Learning Theory: How Adults Learn Differently*. Park University. https://www.park.edu/blog/adult-learning-theory-how-adults-learn-differently/

28] (n.d.). *Adult Learning Theory*. Virginia Commonwealth University School of Nursing. https://nursing.vcu.edu/preceptors/resources/adult-learning-theory/

29] Paz, H. R. (2026). *Longitudinal Trends in Pre University Preparation. A Cohort Evaluation Using Introductory Mathematics and Physics Courses (1980-2019)*. arXiv preprint arXiv:2601.04360. https://doi.org/10.48550/arXiv.2601.04360

30] Huang, Q., Sockalingam, N., Willems, T. & Poon, K. W. (2025). *Designing Knowledge Tools: How Students Transition from Using to Creating Generative AI in STEAM classroom*. arXiv preprint. https://doi.org/10.48550/arXiv.2510.19405

31] Woolley, A. L. (2002). *Differences Between Undergraduate and Graduate Students in Self-concept and Depression*. Dissertations. https://doi.org/10.32597/dissertations/1560

32] (2020). *The Importance of Diversity in the Classroom*. WGU Academy. https://www.wgu.edu/blog/improving-diversity-classroom2005.html

33] (n.d.). *Multisensory learning techniques for inclusion*. educate.sohayota.gov.bd. https://educate.sohayota.gov.bd/special-needs-and-inclusive-teaching/multisensory-learning-techniques-for-inclusion/

34] (n.d.). *Cultural Awareness and Unconscious Bias - Graduate Assistant Handbook*. University of Wisconsin-Milwaukee. https://uwm.edu/graduate-assistants/handbook/best-practices-for-graduate-assistant/cultural-awareness-and-unconscious-bias/

35] Benítez-Agudelo, J. C., Restrepo, D., Navarro-Jimenez, E. & Clemente-Suárez, V. J. (2025). *Longitudinal effects of stress in an academic context on psychological well-being, physiological markers, health behaviors, and academic performance in university students*. BMC Psychology 13. https://doi.org/10.1186/s40359-025-03041-z

36] Marzano, R. J., Marzano, D. J. & Pickering, T. J. (2003). *Classroom Management That Works: Research-Based Strategies for Every Teacher*. Association for Supervision and Curriculum Development. https://www.ascd.org/books/classroom-management-that-works

[37] (n.d.). *Discussion/Lab Sections*. Yale University Registrar's Office. https://registrar.yale.edu/registration/discussionlab-sections

[38] (2023). *A Systematic Literature Review on Anxiety Among Undergraduate Students: Causes and Coping Strategies*. PubMed. https://doi.org/10.1007/s12144-023-03056-0

[39] (2025). *Imposter Phenomenon - StatPearls - NCBI Bookshelf*. StatPearls Publishing. https://www.ncbi.nlm.nih.gov/books/NBK585058/

[40] Muneer, R. & Farid, H. (2022). *The Impact of Classroom Management on Students*. Siazga Research Journal 2(3), pp. 28-35. https://doi.org/10.58341/srj.v2i3.28

[41] (n.d.). *Active Learning Strategies*. Carnegie Mellon University Eberly Center. https://www.cmu.edu/teaching/resources/instructionalstrategies/activelearningstrategies/index.html

[42] (n.d.). *Active Learning: Evidence-based Teaching: Teaching Resources: Center for Innovative Teaching & Learning: Indiana University Bloomington*. Center for Innovative Teaching & Learning. https://citl.indiana.edu/teaching-resources/evidence-based/active-learning.html

[43] (2020). *Hybrid Learning*. University of Glasgow - MyGlasgow - Learning & Teaching - Blended teaching - Definitions. https://www.gla.ac.uk/myglasgow/learningandteaching/blendedteaching/definitions/

[44] Pennsylvania, D. o. (n.d.). *Teaching Assistant Responsibilities and Expectations*. University of Pennsylvania. https://www.english.upenn.edu/node/25970

[45] Messier, N. (2022). *Equitable Assessments & Grading Practices*. University of Illinois Chicago. https://teaching.uic.edu/cate-teaching-guides/assessment-grading-practices/equitable-assessments-grading-practices/

[46] (2020). *Fair student assessment: A phenomenographic study on teachers' conceptions*. Studies in Educational Evaluation 65. https://doi.org/10.1016/j.stueduc.2020.100860

[47] University, C. f. (2025). *Tips for efficient and effective grading*. Concordia University. https://www.concordia.ca/ctl/resources/assessment-grading/tips-for-efficient-and-streamlined-grading.html

[48] Learning, M. C. (n.d.). *Evaluating Student Work*. Princeton University. https://mcgraw.princeton.edu/node/543

[49] (n.d.). *Feedback - Office of Curriculum, Assessment and Teaching Transformation - University at Buffalo*. University at Buffalo. https://www.buffalo.edu/catt/teach/develop/teach/feedback.html

50]   (2025). *Assessment and Feedback in Higher Education*. Nature Research Intelligence.
https://www.nature.com/research-intelligence/nri-topic-summaries/assessment-and-feedback-in-
higher-education-micro-7587

51]   (2025). *Highly informative feedback using learning analytics: how feedback literacy moderates
student perceptions of feedback*. International Journal of Educational Technology in Higher
Education 22. https://doi.org/10.1186/s41239-025-00539-9

52]   (2025). *Plagiarism*. Wikipedia. https://en.wikipedia.org/wiki/Plagiarism

53]   (2023). *Self-Plagiarism and Redundant Publications: A True Scientific Misconduct*. Mathematics
11(9). https://doi.org/10.3390/math1109102

54]   (2026). *Patchwriting – English Language Institute*. University of Hawaii.
https://www.hawaii.edu/eli/patchwriting/

55]   (2025). *Plagiarism*. arXiv preprint. https://doi.org/10.48550/arXiv.2506.08634

56]   (n.d.). *Preventing Plagiarism*. University of Manitoba. https://umanitoba.ca/centre-advancement-
teaching-learning/integrity/preventing-plagiarism

57]   (2025). *Turnitin*. Turnitin. https://www.turnitin.com

58]   (n.d.). *Avoiding Plagiarism*. University of Wisconsin–Madison Libraries.
https://www.library.wisc.edu/instruction-support/resources-to-support-instructors/plagiarism/

59]   (2024). *The Role of e-Learning Platforms in a Sustainable Higher Education: A Cross-Continental
Analysis of Impact and Utility*. Sustainability 17(7). https://doi.org/10.3390/su17073032

60]   Garcia, J. G., Gangan, M. G., Tolentino, M. N., Ligas, M., Moraga, S. D. & Pasilan, A. A. (2021).
*Canvas Adoption Assessment and Acceptance of the Learning Management System on a Web-Based
Platform*. arXiv:2101.12344. https://doi.org/10.48550/arXiv.2101.12344

61]   Zhang, Y., Wang, Y., Fan, G., Song, Y. & Hu, Y. (2023). *Multimodal teaching analytics: the
application of SCORM courseware technology integrating 360-degree panoramic VR in historical
courses*. Scientific Reports 13. https://doi.org/10.1038/s41598-023-46229-2

62]   Fadieieva, L. O. (2025). *Differential effects of Moodle course design on student subpopulations:
advancing personalized learning in higher education*. Smart Learning Environments 12.
https://doi.org/10.1186/s40561-025-00400-6

63]   Moldez, C., Crisanto, M. A., Cerdeña, M. G., Maranan, D. S. & Figueroa, R. (2024). *Innovation in
Education: Developing and Assessing Gamification in the University of the Philippines Open*

University Massive Open Online Courses. arXiv preprint. https://doi.org/10.48550/arXiv.2409.03309

[64]   (2025). *Automated Grading of Open-Ended Questions in Higher Education Using GenAI Models*. International Journal of Artificial Intelligence in Education 35. https://doi.org/10.1007/s40593-025-00517-2

[65]   Sajja, R., Sermet, Y., Cikmaz, M., Cwiertny, D. & Demir, I. (2023). *Artificial Intelligence-Enabled Intelligent Assistant for Personalized and Adaptive Learning in Higher Education*. arXiv preprint. https://doi.org/10.48550/arXiv.2309.10892

[66]   Barenji, R. V., Salimi, N. & Khoshgoftar, S. (2026). *An LLM-Powered Assessment Retrieval-Augmented Generation (RAG) For Higher Education*. arXiv preprint. https://doi.org/10.48550/arXiv.2601.06141

[67]   Hao, Z., Cao, J., Li, R., Yu, J., Liu, Z. & Zhang, Y. (2025). *Mapping Student-AI Interaction Dynamics in Multi-Agent Learning Environments: Supporting Personalised Learning and Reducing Performance Gaps*. arXiv preprint. https://doi.org/10.48550/arXiv.2506.02993

[68]   Kumar, A., DiJohnson, T., Edwards, R. & Walker, L. (2021). *The application of adaptive minimum match k-nearest neighbors to identify at-risk students in health professions education*. arXiv preprint. https://doi.org/10.48550/arXiv.2108.07709

[69]   Radway, S., Quintanilla, K., Ludden, C. & Votipka, D. (2025). *An Investigation of US Universities' Implementation of FERPA: Student Directory Policies and Student Privacy Preferences*. Proceedings of the 2025 CHI Conference on Human Factors in Computing Systems, pp. 1-13. https://doi.org/10.1145/3459443.3459444

[70]   R, L. A. (2025). *Perceptually-Minimal Color Optimization for Web Accessibility: A Multi-Phase Constrained Approach*. arXiv preprint. https://doi.org/10.48550/arXiv.2512.05067

[71]   (2024). *WebAIM: Screen Reader User Survey #10 Results*. WebAIM. https://webaim.org/blog/screen-reader-user-survey-10-results/

[72]   Greenberger, S., Holbeck, R., Steele, J. & Dyer, T. (2016). *Plagiarism Due to Misunderstanding: Online Instructor Perceptions*. Journal of the Scholarship of Teaching and Learning 16, pp. 72-84. https://doi.org/10.14434/josotl.v16i6.20062

[73]   Berry, H. (December 5, 2023). *New Study on Students' Plagiarism Views*. TypeCite. https://www.typecite.com/learn/writing-help/new-study-on-students-plagiarism-views/

[74] (2023). *The Importance of Research Experience for Graduate School Applicants*. MoldStud. https://moldstud.com/articles/p-the-importance-of-research-experience-for-graduate-school-applicants

[75] Program, D. C. (n.d.). *Academic Integrity | Writing Program*. Dartmouth College. https://writing.dartmouth.edu/support/sources-and-citations/academic-integrity

[76] (2023). *COVID-19: Academic, Financial, and Mental Health Challenges Faced by International Students in the United States Due to the Pandemic*. PubMed Central. https://doi.org/10.1007/s11096-023-03556-0

[77] (2024). *The Impacts of Imposter Syndrome in Higher Education*. International Online Journal of Education and Teaching 11, pp. 189-202. https://iojet.org/index.php/IOJET/article/view/2109/1019

[78] (2025). *Supporting First-Generation Students on Campus*. https://www.eandi.org/wp-content/uploads/Article-9-Supporting-First-Generation-Students-on-Campus.pdf

[79] (n.d.). *Introduction to Universal Design for Learning (UDL) 3.0 in Higher Education*. University of Alberta Centre for Teaching and Learning. https://www.ualberta.ca/en/centre-for-teaching-and-learning/resources/access-community-belonging/access-and-accessibility/intro-to-udl-in-higher-ed.html

[80] (n.d.). *Introduction to Universal Design for Learning (UDL) 3.0 in Higher Education*. University of Alberta Centre for Teaching and Learning. https://www.ualberta.ca/en/centre-for-teaching-and-learning/resources/access-community-belonging/access-and-accessibility/intro-to-udl-in-higher-ed.html

[81] Benítez-Agudelo, J. C., Restrepo, D., Navarro-Jimenez, E. & Clemente-Suárez, V. J. (2025). *Longitudinal effects of stress in an academic context on psychological well-being, physiological markers, health behaviors, and academic performance in university students*. BMC Psychology 13. https://doi.org/10.1186/s40359-025-03041-z

[82] (n.d.). *Mental Health Services – Northeastern Health and Wellness*. Northeastern Health and Wellness. https://healthandwellness.northeastern.edu/findnortheastern/

[83] (1996). *Protecting the Privacy of Student Education Records*. National Center for Education Statistics. https://nces.ed.gov/pubs/web/96859.asp

[84] (February 12, 2024). *Gender can shape how TAs are evaluated, study finds*. Cornell Chronicle. https://news.cornell.edu/stories/2024/02/gender-can-shape-how-tas-are-evaluated-study-finds

[85] (1997). *Grading leniency is a removable contaminant of student ratings*. Journal of Educational Psychology 89(4), pp. 629-634. https://doi.org/10.1037/0022-0663.89.4.629

[86] (n.d.). *Universal Design for Learning (UDL)*. Center for the Advancement of Teaching Excellence. https://teaching.uic.edu/resources/teaching-guides/inclusive-equity-minded-teaching-practices/universal-design-for-learning-udl/

[87] Kuwari, K. (2024). *Culturally Responsive Teaching: Strategies for Promoting Inclusivity and Diversity in the Classroom*. Academy of Educational Leadership Journal 28(1), pp. 1-3. https://www.abacademies.org/articles/culturally-responsive-teaching-strategies-for-promoting-inclusivity-and-diversity-in-the-classroom.pdf

[88] (2023). *Trauma-Informed Pedagogy: Instructional Strategies to Support Student Success*. PubMed 12(3), pp. 45-67. https://doi.org/10.1016/j.jmwh.2023.04.001

[89] (n.d.). *Teaching Portfolios*. DePaul University Teaching Commons. https://resources.depaul.edu/teaching-commons/teaching-guides/reflective-practice/Pages/teaching-portfolios.aspx

[90] (2023). *Teaching Portfolio Guide*. Northern Arizona University. https://in.nau.edu/wp-content/uploads/sites/161/2023/10/Teaching-Portfolio-Guide.pdf

[91] (n.d.). *Teaching Philosophy Statement*. Graduate School. https://gradschool.cornell.edu/career-and-professional-development/pathways-to-success/prepare-for-your-career/take-action/teaching-philosophy-statement/

[92] Mart, C. T. (2018). *Student Evaluations of Teaching Effectiveness in Higher Education*. International Journal of Academic Research in Business and Social Sciences. https://doi.org/10.6007/IJARBSS/v7-i10/3358

[93] (n.d.). *Teaching Portfolios – OTEAR*. Rutgers University. https://otear.rutgers.edu/teaching/teaching-portfolios/

[94] Wani, P. (2024). *Connecting for Success: The Role of Networking in Medical Education*. Cureus 16(11). https://doi.org/10.7759/cureus.74643

[95] (2014). *Networking in academia: Generating and enhancing relationships with your acquaintances and colleagues will create a diverse network of sponsors eager to help you succeed*. EMBO reports 15(11), pp. 1230-1233. https://doi.org/10.15252/embr.201439626

[96] (n.d.). *Getting Ahead in Neonatology Academics*. American Academy of Pediatrics. https://www.aap.org/en/get-involved/aap-sections/sonpm/tecan/career-development--leadership/exploring-and-evaluating-practices-of-neonatal-perinatal-medicine/practice-environments/getting-ahead-in-academics/

97]   (2024). *Statement on Teaching Evaluation*. American Association of University Professors.
https://www.aaup.org/report/statement-teaching-evaluation

98]   (2021). *Is funding related to higher research impact? Exploring its relationship and the mediating role of collaboration in several disciplines*. Journal of Informetrics 15(1).
https://doi.org/10.1016/j.joi.2020.101102

99]   (n.d.). *Working with Teaching Assistants*. McGraw Center for Teaching and Learning.
https://mcgraw.princeton.edu/faculty/teaching-princeton/faculty-resource-library/working-teaching-assistants

100]   Elliott, Rhoades, Jackson & Mandernach. (2018). *Impact of Mentorship on Graduate Students*.
Journal of College Student Development 59(1), pp. 1-15. https://doi.org/10.1353/csd.2018.0001

101]   AlShebli, B., Makovi, K. & Rahwan, T. (2019). *The Impact of Informal Mentorship in Academic Collaborations*. arXiv preprint arXiv:1908.03813. https://doi.org/10.48550/arXiv.1908.03813

102]   (n.d.). *Teaching Assistant Responsibilities and Expectations*. University of Pennsylvania Department of English. https://www.english.upenn.edu/node/25970

103]   (2015). *The effects of high-quality student mentoring*. Economics Letters 136, pp. 227-232.
https://doi.org/10.1016/j.econlet.2015.09.043

104]   Boeder, J., Fruiht, V., Erikson, K., Hwang, S., Blanco, G. & Chan, T. (2021). *Reflecting on an Academic Career: Associations Between Past Mentoring Investments and Career Benefits*.
Mentoring & Tutoring: Partnership in Learning 29(5).
https://doi.org/10.1080/13611267.2021.1986797

105]   (2024). *Graduate Teaching Assistants' Perception of Student Difficulties and Use in Teaching*.
International Journal of Research in Undergraduate Mathematics Education.
https://doi.org/10.1007/s40753-024-00239-1

106]   Gao, A. & Sakhnini, V. (2025). *Reducing Procrastination on Programming Assignments via Optional Early Feedback*. arXiv preprint arXiv:2510.16052.
https://doi.org/10.48550/arXiv.2510.16052

107]   Shaffer, L. S. & Zalewski, J. M. (2025). *Career Advising in a VUCA Environment*. NACADA Journal 44(2). https://doi.org/10.12930/NACADA-24-99

108]   Shethiya, Y. C., Gaur, A. K. & Sharma, L. M. (2025). *EVALUATING THE IMPACT OF INTERNSHIPS ON CAREER PREPAREDNESS AND EMPLOYABILITY SKILLS*. Journal of East-West Thought 15(1), pp. 1-15. https://doi.org/10.7492/jt29s353

[109] Yavich, R. & Davidovitch, N. (2024). *Plagiarism among Higher Education Students*. Education Sciences 14(8). https://doi.org/10.3390/educsci14080908

[110] (2025). AI Writing Tools. University of Illinois Chicago Center for the Advancement of Teaching Excellence. https://teaching.uic.edu/ai-writing-tools/

[111] (2025). *Turnitin Similarity | Comprehensive plagiarism detection*. Turnitin. https://www.turnitin.com/products/similarity/

[112] (n.d.). *Graduate TA Academic Policy*. University of Minnesota. https://cse.umn.edu/cs/graduate-ta-academic-policy

[113] "Dall-E," OpenAI, [Online]. Available: https://chatgpt.com/g/g-2fkFE8rbu-dall-e. [Accessed 24 12 2024].

About the Author

Dr. David A. Schippers, Sc.D., CISSP, is a scholar-practitioner, systems thinker, and faculty architect whose work sits at the intersection of teaching, mentorship, and institutional design. With a doctorate in cybersecurity and decades of leadership across higher education and industry, he is known for translating complexity into scalable, human-centered academic systems.

As a Chief Academic Officer, technology and cybersecurity director, and long-time faculty leader, Dr. Schippers has designed and led programs that strengthen instructional quality from the ground up. His work focuses on a simple but often neglected truth: faculty effectiveness is not accidental—it is engineered through alignment, support, and ethical clarity.

The Teaching Assistant Key reflects his belief that Teaching Assistants are not peripheral labor, but a critical instructional keystone. When TAs are properly prepared, mentored, and aligned with faculty expectations, they become force multipliers for student engagement, instructional consistency, and academic integrity. When they are not, the entire learning system fractures under avoidable strain.

Dr. Schippers' writing blends practical frameworks with systems-level insight, offering faculty and academic leaders clear structures for communication, assessment, mentorship, and instructional support. He emphasizes professionalism, inclusivity, and ethical responsibility—without romanticizing burnout or tolerating ambiguity disguised as rigor.

Across his work, he challenges inherited academic assumptions while equipping educators with concrete tools to lead well. He believes teaching excellence is not an individual trait but an institutional obligation—and that mentoring, when done intentionally, is one of the most powerful levers for educational transformation.

Dr. Schippers continues his mission to develop faculty, teaching assistants, and academic leaders who are ready to move beyond improvisation and toward intentional, aligned, and humane instruction.

This book is not theoretical.
It is structural.
And it is written for those responsible for making learning actually work.

Continue the Conversation with Dr. David A. Schippers

If *The Teaching Assistant Key* resonated with you, your journey does not end here.

Dr. David A. Schippers writes at the intersection of leadership, higher education, cybersecurity, and artificial intelligence, challenging conventional thinking while equipping professionals with practical frameworks for real-world impact. His books confront complexity directly, offering clarity where institutions, systems, and leaders often fall short.

Explore other titles by Dr. Schippers:

Burn the Script: Kill the Leadership Theater, Lead for Real
A direct challenge to performative leadership culture. Built from decades of executive and academic experience, this book equips leaders to make difficult decisions, build trust under pressure, and lead with clarity rather than slogans.

The Force of Technology
A comprehensive examination of innovation, cybersecurity, and risk management in a rapidly evolving digital landscape. Designed for leaders and professionals navigating technological disruption with strategic discipline.

The Scholar's Key: Hidden Knowledge for Doctoral Achievement
A structured, principled roadmap for doctoral candidates seeking clarity, momentum, and resilience in advanced academic work.

Across disciplines and industries, Dr. Schippers' work shares a common thread: formation over performance, integrity over appearance, and leadership grounded in responsibility.

Whether you serve in higher education, industry, government, or executive leadership, his books provide frameworks that endure beyond trends and tactics.

To discover more titles, speaking engagements, and academic resources, search for **Dr. David A. Schippers** wherever books are sold.

Lead intentionally. Build wisely. Strengthen what holds everything together.